CONOR McPHERSON

Conor McPherson was born in Dublin in 1971. Plays include *Rum and Vodka* (Fly by Night Theatre Co., Dublin); *The Good Thief* (Dublin Theatre Festival; Stewart Parker Award); *This Lime Tree Bower* (Fly by Night Theatre Co. and Bush Theatre, London; Meyer-Whitworth Award); *St Nicholas* (Bush Theatre and Primary Stages, New York); *The Weir* (Royal Court, London, Duke of York's, West End and Walter Kerr Theatre, New York; Laurence Olivier, Evening Standard, Critics' Circle, George Devine Awards); *Dublin Carol* (Royal Court and Atlantic Theater, New York); *Port Authority* (Ambassadors Theatre, West End, Gate Theatre, Dublin and Atlantic Theater, New York); *Shining City* (Royal Court, Gate Theatre, Dublin and Manhattan Theatre Club, New York; Tony Award nomination for Best Play); *The Seafarer* (National Theatre, London, Abbey Theatre, Dublin and Booth Theater, New York; Laurence Olivier, Evening Standard, Tony Award nominations for Best Play); *The Veil* (National Theatre) and *The Night Alive* (Donmar Warehouse). Theatre adaptations include Daphne du Maurier's *The Birds* (Gate Theatre, Dublin and Guthrie Theater, Minneapolis) and August Strindberg's *The Dance of Death* (Donmar at Trafalgar Studios).

Work for the cinema includes *I Went Down*, *Saltwater*, Samuel Beckett's *Endgame*, *The Actors*, and *The Eclipse*. He also adapted John Banville's *Elegy for April* for the BBC.

Awards for his screenwriting include three Best Screenplay Awards from the Irish Film and Television Academy; Spanish Cinema Writers Circle Best Screenplay Award; the CICAE Award for Best Film Berlin Film festival; Jury Prize San Sebastian Film Festival; and the Méliès d'Argent Award for Best European Film.

Other Titles in this Series

Conor McPherson

PLAYS: THREE

Shining City
The Seafarer
The Birds
The Veil
The Dance of Death

with a Foreword by the Author

NICK HERN BOOKS
London
www.nickhernbooks.co.uk

A Nick Hern Book

McPherson Plays: Three first published in Great Britain as a paperback original in 2013 by Nick Hern Books Limited, The Glasshouse, 49a Goldhawk Road, London W12 8QP

Shining City, *The Seafarer* and *The Veil* first published by Nick Hern Books in 2004, 2006 and 2011 respectively. *The Veil* has been slightly revised for this edition.

Conor McPherson has asserted his right to be identified as the author of these works

Cover image: Conor McPherson
Cover design: Ned Hoste, 2H

Typeset by Nick Hern Books, London
Printed and bound CPI Group (UK) Ltd

ISBN   978 1 84842 209 4

Contents

Foreword

The best plays come in a flash. An image, a feeling, and that's it.
You know these ideas because they are the undeniable ones that
won't let go. They pull you in and compel you to start scribbling
notes. If you are a playwright and you have one of these on the go,
you know you have a responsibility. To what? Something that
doesn't exist? But the good ideas feel like they do exist. They're
just beyond view, and you're trying to capture them with glimpses
that may or may not be accurate.

So many things can go wrong along the way between the vision and
its presentation on stage – missed beats in the writing (or too many
beats), the wrong cast, wrong director, wrong theatre or just the
wrong time. Any and all of these may consign your hard work to the
'Who Cares?' file. And you know you are playing Russian roulette –
it all comes down to those couple of hours on opening night. But
you keep the faith and you pull the trigger. What else can you do?

You start scribbling. Worry, issues of control, and even, ironically, a
sense of longing to be free of the process, all propel you to write
your first draft. Subsequent drafts can never quite fix all the
problems, yet neither can they prompt the same exhilaration. Many
playwrights I've talked with agree that the best moments are often
those tentative notes when the ghosts first present themselves in your
mind. They are so insubstantial, yet bear their complete mysterious
history within. This is when playwriting is at its most private and,
paradoxically, when the play is at its most beautiful. The more real
you make it, the less magic it retains. You are aware of this but what
can you do? You keep going. Always writing at the very edge of
your limitations. And your limitations are not necessarily a bad
thing. Your limitations are in fact what give you your unique voice.
But it's hard to view your limitations in a warm light when you've
just read over your work and it makes you embarrassed.

The truth is nobody really knows how to write a good play. You just
do your best to avoid writing a bad one. The rest falls to fate. Joe
Penhall once said to me, 'Who knows if the magic is there and – even
if it is – will the bastards see it?', which I think sums up the car crash
of hope, despair and paranoia that accompanies artistic creation.

And the enemy of art is not the pram in the hallway, it is self-consciousness. When you are young you know nothing, least of all yourself. You write plays quickly, perhaps in a matter of days. As you grow older – and if you've managed to survive some decades of playwriting – you may gain a little wisdom. But you lose your recklessness. Why? Because, like the ageing stuntman, you know exactly what's at stake each time you do it. Further, you are no longer new. Everyone knows what you can do and they have certain expectations. So you go the long way round, trying to surprise everyone. But going the long way round kills spontaneity.

And what's wrong with that? Well, Neil Young's late producer, David Briggs, said that the best way to record music is the simplest way. You get the mic as close to the sound as you possibly can and just record it as it is. 'The more you think, the more you stink' was his mantra. Neil Young's albums are full of first takes – often the very first time the band have ever played the song – because that's where the magic is. Neil Young calls it, 'the spook'. In other words, you've got to be careful not to perfect what you are doing to the extent it has no soul left. Perfect is not best. Okay, so he's talking about rock 'n' roll, but there's something in that for playwriting too.

And this book contains a decade of playwriting. And if there's anything I can see that's worth passing on, it's this: it's as important to *forget* what you've learned as it is to learn.

Shining City came in a flash. The last image of the play came first. I wrote the play in a few weeks. There are scenes in the play, perhaps the best ones, which never altered from the first scribbled draft. *The Seafarer* came in a more bizarre, slow-motion flash. I had written an entirely different play with entirely different characters – except for this one character at the heart of the play, Sharky. But there was something wrong with it. Somehow a deadness had crept in somewhere. And then suddenly I saw the living room in *The Seafarer* and the blind Richard Harkin sitting there. And I knew that Richard was the brother of Sharky, who was still stuck in the bad play. So Sharky walked from the bad play straight into *The Seafarer* to look after his brother. It was a hard play to write, however, because it presented many technical difficulties (the second-act card games, for instance), but I felt I had something. And I always lit a candle while I was writing it (the only time I've ever done that). And it stayed alive.

The short story *The Birds* by Daphne du Maurier was presented to me by the inimitable producer David Pugh. I had no flash of inspiration, just a desire to write it and to explore the female psyche (i.e. it has self-consciousness written all over it!). People have said it's their favourite play of mine, but I suspect there are many others who felt I should stick to my more well-trodden ground. For myself, I like it because it really feels like someone else wrote it, and that's a rare enough relief for any playwright watching their work on stage. I want to thank Joe Dowling at the Guthrie Theatre in Minneapolis and Henry Wishcamper, who directed the American premiere. Their belief in the play has undoubtedly ensured its continued life in the United States, where it's regularly being produced. Whatever I was working out in that play continues to draw directors and actors – and that's everything.

David Hare was once asked what advice he'd give to young playwrights, and he said: to enjoy the moment if your first play or two finds an audience. People are interested and you're confident – because you have lots of ideas you haven't tried yet. But, he cautioned, you must remember that sustaining that for thirty or forty years, fighting through the sheer incomprehension that may greet your efforts to develop your craft, is no picnic.

Bearing this in mind, I recognise that, in some quarters, a certain incomprehension greeted *The Veil*. In some ways it reflects a sense of disgust and panic at how my country had managed to almost destroy itself over the previous ten years. And personally I was also in thrall to the world of eighteenth- and nineteenth-century German transcendental philosophy, not to mention a fascination with James Joyce's concept of time in *Finnegans Wake*. Talk about a heady brew! I think we presented a beautiful show (incredible design by Rae Smith and lighting by Neil Austin), and every performance was top notch, but when all the moments were strung along together, maybe some people – certainly more than usual anyway! – emerged wondering what all the ideas had to do with each other. And yet something tells me this play will be back in my life at some point, and that I may even begin to see it as one of my favourites some day because, strangely, it's the tricky ones you end up most proud of.

And then, out of nowhere, August Strindberg walked into my life, kicked me up the arse, and reminded me what it's all about. Josie Rourke, who had just taken over at the Donmar Warehouse, asked me to consider adapting *The Dance of Death* for their young directors' programme. And Strindberg just took me right back to the beginning: i.e. it doesn't matter what's happening on stage as long as it has energy and emotion. Ideas flow from the energy, not the other way round. And we ended up with a cracking little production, directed by Titas Halder, starring Kevin McNally, Indira Varma and Daniel Lapaine, that really blew people away.

And I decided that my next play would have no 'ideas' (if that's possible), only feelings. And it came in a flash one day while I was pushing my daughter on the swing in the park. And when I went home I started scribbling.

But that's a story for another day.

Conor McPherson
Dublin, January 2013

SHINING CITY

For my wife
Fionnuala

Shining City was first performed at the Royal Court Theatre, London, on 4 June 2004, with the following cast:

NEASA	Kathy Kiera Clarke
IAN	Michael McElhatton
LAURENCE	Tom Jordan Murphy
JOHN	Stanley Townsend

Director	Conor McPherson
Designer	Rae Smith
Lighting Designer	Mark Henderson
Sound Designer	Ian Dickinson

The play received its American premiere at the Biltmore Theater, New York, in a production by the Manhattan Theater Club, in May 2006, with the following cast:

IAN	Brían F. O'Byrne
JOHN	Oliver Platt
NEASA	Martha Plimpton
LAURENCE	Peter Scanavino

Director	Robert Falls
Designer	Santo Loquasto
Costume Designer	Kaye Voyce
Lighting Designer	Christopher Akerlind
Sound Designer	Obadiah Eaves

Setting

The play is set in Ian's office in Dublin, around Phibsboro maybe, or
Berkeley Road, an old part of the city which, while it retains a sense of
history, is not a salubrious area. It has a Victorian feel, lots of redbrick
terraced houses dominated by the Mater hospital, Mountjoy Prison, and
the church spires of Phibsboro Church and the church at Berkeley
Road. It doesn't feel like a suburb, if anything it feels like a less
commercial part of the city centre, which is only a short walk away.

Ian's office is perhaps in an older, larger building than most in the
area, up on the second floor. From his elevated position, at the back of
the building, one or two church spires loom outside.

There is a big sash window at the back. There are some shelves with
books on them. A stereo and some CDs. There are more books on the
floor, as though they have been unpacked but have yet to be put away.
Ian has a desk, stage left-ish, with a chair behind it. There is also a
chair in front of the desk which Ian uses for sitting with clients.
Clients sit on a little two-seater sofa near the middle of the room, a
little more stage right. There's a coffee table near the sofa with a box
of tissues and a jug of water.

At the back, stage right, is a door to a little toilet. Stage right is a
cabinet of some kind, a filing cabinet maybe, or a bookcase.

The door is stage right, and when it is open we can see out to the
banister and the top of the stairs. Beside the door is a handset for an
intercom to the main door to the street on the ground floor.

The play has five scenes and about two months elapse between each
scene.

The time is the present.

Characters

IAN, *forties*
JOHN, *fifties*
NEASA, *thirties*
LAURENCE, *twenties*

Dialogue in square brackets [ ] is unspoken.

Scene One

*As the lights come up there is no one onstage. It is daytime. We hear
distant church bells. Music is playing softly on the stereo. We hear the
toilet flush, and* IAN, *a man in his forties, comes out of the bathroom.
He takes a tissue from the box and goes to the window, blowing his
nose. He is a man who has struggled with many personal fears in his
life and has had some victories, some defeats. The resulting struggle
has made him very sharp. He is essentially a gentle man, but
sometimes his desire to get to the lifeboats, to feel safe, drives him in
ways that even he himself doesn't fully understand. A loud ugly
buzzer goes off.* IAN *turns off the stereo and goes to the intercom,
picking up the handset.*

IAN. Hello? (*Pushing a button on the intercom.*) Okay, come in.

   Pause.

   Are you in? Okay. (*Pushing the button.*) Push the door. Are you
   in?

   Pause.

   Hello? No? Okay, okay, hold on.

   *He hangs up the handset and goes out, leaving the door open. He
   goes down the stairs.*

   (*Off.*) Now.

JOHN (*off*). Sorry.

IAN (*off*). No, I'm sorry. Come on up. Yeah. It was fixed. I don't
   know if all this rain… We're all the way up, I'm afraid.

JOHN (*off*). Straight on?

IAN (*off*). Eh, the next one. Yeah. And that's it there. The door is
   open.

   JOHN *comes in. He is in his fifties and dressed quite respectably.
   He has an air of confusion when we first see him, not just because
   of his recent experiences but also because he has yet to accept that
   the world is not as orderly and predictable as he thought. He has*

*always found problems to arise from what he regards as other
people's ignorance. He almost regards himself as a benchmark for
normality. He carries an anorak. He seems very tired.* IAN *follows
him in and indicates for him to have a seat on the sofa.*

Now, right.

JOHN (*sits*). Thanks.

IAN (*sits*). I'm sorry about that.

JOHN. No, sure I wasn't sure I had the right... I was in a bit of a flap,
God, the parking around here is horrendous, isn't it?

IAN. I know.

JOHN. I left myself a bit of time but I was almost like a kerbcrawler
out there looking for a spot.

IAN. I know. I tell you I'm only here, I've only been here two weeks,
and I'm not sure... between ourselves... that I'm going to...
(*Nods.*) because there's... many disadvantages...

JOHN. Ah, no, I parked up in the hospital in the end, which is what I
should have done in the first place. I'll know the next time. It's my
own fault.

IAN. No, I know, I should have probably... But like I say, I'm still
sort of only getting myself sorted out here but I should have...

JOHN. Ah sure no, it's grand, sure I'm here now.

IAN. Yes! Well, good.

JOHN. Yeah, well, that's the main thing... Can I eh... (*Indicates
water.*)

IAN (*indicates affirmatively*). Please.

JOHN *pours himself some water and drinks a few mouthfuls.* IAN
reaches around behind him and takes a letter from his desk.

So... (*Glancing at letter.*) John... (*Pause.*) How are you?

JOHN. Not too bad. A bit... Eh... heh... eh... I've never... ehm...
been to see... someone before...

IAN. Alright. Well, that's okay.

JOHN. Em... (*Doesn't seem to know where to begin.*)

IAN. I got a, I have a letter...

JOHN. Right.

IAN. From Dr Casey…

JOHN. That's right. Yeah, he was… there was some guy he wanted me to see and… we couldn't get an appointment, for four months or something!

IAN. Okay.

JOHN. Yeah, so…

IAN. And you haven't been sleeping so well. Is that right?

JOHN. Well, yeah…

Pause.

IAN. Which can be very debilitating, I know.

JOHN. Yeah… and ehm… (*Holds his hand up to the bridge of his nose as though he is about to sneeze and there is silence. He is silently crying.*) Can I…? (*Indicates tissues.*)

IAN. Of course. Please.

JOHN (*composes himself*). Sorry.

IAN (*reassuringly*). That's fine. That's fine.

JOHN. You have the tissues ready and everything.

They smile.

I'm, em. I'm recently bereaved. I don't know if Dr Casey…

IAN (*affirmative*). Mm-hm.

JOHN. My wife passed away a few months ago. And em…

Pause.

She… she, she died in em, horrible circumstances, really, you know?

IAN. Okay.

JOHN. She was in a taxi. And a… stolen car crashed into them. And she was… trapped, in, the car. It was a, a horrific crash, and she… didn't, she couldn't survive. And I was on my… I was too late getting to the hospital. And the eh… reality of… the reality of it. It's been absolutely… It really, now… It's… (*Nods.*) You know…

Pause.

IAN. I can, em… I can only imagine what…

JOHN. We have no children. And eh… (*Pause.*) And I've eh… been on my own an awful lot, you know? Like, I've really been on my own an awful lot of the time, really, you know?

IAN. Okay.

JOHN. And I don't… I mean I don't even know where she was that night, you know? Or where she was coming from. Do you know what I mean, you know? Like we weren't even… communicating. At the time, do you understand me?

IAN. Okay.

JOHN. And no one else was injured. And I've no… idea… wh… (*Long pause.*) But, em, I've… em… I've seen her. (*Short pause.*) I've em…

IAN. Sorry. You've seen her?

JOHN. I've seen her in the house. She's been in the house.

IAN. You've…

JOHN. Yeah.

IAN. This is…

JOHN. Yeah.

IAN. Since…

JOHN. Yeah, since…

IAN. Since she…

JOHN. Yeah since she…

IAN. Sorry, go on…

JOHN. Yeah, no, she em… about eh, about two months ago. I… met up with my brother, I have a brother, Jim, and we met one evening, for a pint in Clontarf Castle. We're just, are we just going into this? You just…

IAN. Well, no, just whatever you want, you just tell me… in your own, we don't have to, you can… You're telling me so, I'd like to…

JOHN. No I just, I wasn't sure if, but, you know, we… my brother, you know, we don't, we haven't… eh… I don't see him. You know, to a certain degree, we've been out of contact. He only lives in

Clontarf. But for... you know... he... but since the... funeral...
He, you know, we've had contact again. And it's fine, you know.
But for a long time... he's been very supportive, but you know we
don't get on, basically, you know? And I don't... there's no need
for me... to infringe on his privacy and his family. And you know,
so we've drifted again. But em, the... the last time that I saw him,
this night that I'm talking about a couple of months ago. I mean, I
could feel... that... it was a sympathy vote, like... we'd... very
little to... to say to each other. And I mean, he's very quiet anyway,
you know? And I... didn't feel... right, myself that evening,
anyway and... And I mean, there was no... problem, as such. But
I... just wanted to leave, you know? And I kind of just got a bit
annoyed and I kind of... fucking... just went home, you know?

He checks with IAN, *to see if this is all alright to continue with.*
IAN *nods gently.*

And eh...

And I didn't really... when I got home, there was nothing
untoward when I got in the door. Only that I remember
now, because I heard it again, there was the sound, the tune of
an ice-cream van. The music, you know? But there couldn't have
been because they don't go round at night. But, I heard it when I
got in the door. And I... didn't think about it or... But eh... I was,
I was just going into the living room and I put the lights on, and...
when I turned around I could see that she was standing there
behind the door looking at me.

Pause.

IAN. Your wife?

JOHN. Yeah. She... I could only see half of her, behind the door,
looking out at me. Eh... but I could see that... her hair was soaking
wet, and all plastered to her face. And I, I fucking jumped, you
know? And I fucking just stood there, I froze, it was terrifying. And
I mean she was as real as... you know if you've ever seen a dead
body? How strange it is, but... it's... real! That feeling...

IAN. And what happened then?

JOHN. I just, I don't know how long we were standing there looking
at each other. I mean it might have been only a few seconds. But it
was like if you're a kid and you get a fright, it's only for a second,
you know, if you have a bad dream or you think you see

something, but then, you wake up or there's nothing there or whatever, but this just didn't stop, I mean she was just there, and it was real. The feeling is like... I mean, I mean it's unbelievable, you know? It's... it's... I can't describe it.

IAN. And did she... did you...

JOHN. Well, finally, I don't know how, but I just got my legs going and I just had no choice and I just went straight out the door, straight by her, I mean the door was open, she was behind it, and I just went straight out and right out of the house. (*Pause.*) And then, of course, I was just standing in the garden with no coat on, with really no fucking idea what I was doing, you know? So I just got in the car. (*Pause.*) And I kind of just sat there. Where I live is just a quiet cul-de-sac. There wasn't anyone around even that I could... even the neighbours, I've never, you know, those people... I just sat there, looking at the house, just so... frightened, you know? And... there was just nothing I could do. So I just drove away. (*Short pause.*) Just down to this B&B. Bec... because I... I just didn't want to be on my own like. (*Short pause.*) The woman there, I'd say she knew there was something weird going on alright. I had no luggage and it was so late. She probably thought I'd had a row, you know?

IAN. You didn't go to your brother?

JOHN. No. (*Pause.*) He's... we'd, we'd had a... I mean I'd walked out on him, earlier, you know?... No.

IAN. Did you tell anyone? Is there anyone that you... who you...

JOHN. No, I... I... I just... I just went back the next day, you know? I... I just, I suppose, I made myself, I refused to... the next morning it was like, 'What the fuck am I doing?' You know? I mean you just don't know what to do. I rang them in work and said I wouldn't be in, because I sort of knew if I didn't go back... I mean when it gets bright you just... For some reason I was, I was just able to go back.

IAN. But you didn't talk to anybody about what had happened?

JOHN. No. I suppose I should have but...

Silence.

IAN. And did you see... her again? Or...

JOHN. Yeah, no, well the next time I didn't... see anything, I was in the bath, and...

IAN. When, how long was this, after…

JOHN. Two… days later, you know, not long…

IAN. Okay.

JOHN. I figured, you know, I, I rationalised it, that maybe… I hadn't… seen her or… Like there was nothing there! And I thought maybe it… that… just the fucking grief I suppose… you know…

IAN. Of course.

JOHN. You might say it's mad, but what choice did I have?

IAN. No.

JOHN. I mean, I have to get on with my life!

IAN. I know.

JOHN. So yeah, there I was, having a bath. It was fairly late. And I was just trying to relax. I had the radio on. I was listening to Vincent Browne. And the door was closed. I had… I had locked it. It's stupid 'cause there was… I was there on my own, but, I don't know. It's just a habit or it made me feel a bit better, you know, more safe. And I was lying there and I thought I, I thought I heard something, you know? Like… someone in the house. Just not even a noise, just a feeling. You can just feel, you know, don't you? When someone is there. But I, I just turned off the radio, just to see if… and then I heard her, she was knocking on the door and going… (*Bangs his fist urgently on the wooden arm of the sofa.*) 'John! John!'

IAN. Oh my God.

JOHN. Yeah! So I, I leapt up out of the bath, and I slipped, and I took an awful… I went right over and really bruised my hip and my shoulder, and by the time I had sorted myself out, I got a grip and I… eventually, opened the door, but of course, and I know you're going to think I was dreaming or whatever, there was nothing there. But it was absolutely terrifying. And at the same time I was completely frantic, do you understand me?

IAN. Well, of course you were. What, what did you…

JOHN. Back down to the B&B! What could I do?! (*Pause.*) I'm still there!

IAN. You're still…

JOHN. I'm living there! What can I do?

IAN. I know.

JOHN. I mean I have to sell the house! That's where I'm at, you know? I'm not working. I'm completely on my own. I mean the woman in the B&B doesn't know what to make of me. I mean she's very nice and everything, but what can I say to her? I told her I'm getting work done. And her husband is a builder, and he was asking me all these questions one morning. And I know nothing about it, you know? I think they think I'm a nutcase!

Silence.

IAN. Okay. (*Pause.*) Well…

JOHN. Do you believe me?

IAN (*taking up a writing pad*). Well, let's, let me get some details, is that alright?

JOHN *nods.*

How old are you, John?

JOHN. Fifty-four.

IAN. And what do you do?

JOHN. I'm a… I'm a rep for a catering suppliers… on an independent basis…

IAN. And have you…

JOHN (*interrupting* IAN). Wait. Do you believe me?

IAN.…had any… sorry?

JOHN. Do you believe what I'm saying to you? That this is happening to me?

Pause.

IAN. I believe you… that… I believe something is… I believe you, in that I don't think you're making it up.

JOHN. I'm not making it up.

IAN. Yes but… I believe you're telling me you saw something, but if you're asking me if I believe in ghosts, I…

JOHN. Yeah but can you help me with this? Because… (*His voice suddenly cracks.*) I really don't know what the fuck I'm going to do here… (*Puts his hand to his mouth.*)

Pause.

IAN. I know. I know. Don't worry. You're not on your own now, okay? We'll sort it out.

Pause.

Don't worry. (*Short pause.*) Don't worry.

Lights down.

Scene Two

It is night. IAN and NEASA are in the office. Perhaps she sits on the clients' couch. Maybe at the beginning it looks like a therapy session. She is in her thirties and is more working class than IAN. She is rooted in a harder, less forgiving reality. She has always had a stubbornness which has kept her focused, but has also sometimes blinded her so that while she is a strong person, often it is others who have used her strength.

NEASA. Are you fucking joking me, Ian?

IAN. No, I'm…

NEASA. No, no no no no no no…

IAN. Look, I know, but…

NEASA. No no no – (*As though it's so obvious.*) you come home now.

IAN. Neasa, I'm… I'm just not going to do that.

He goes to the desk and takes a cigarette from a pack.

NEASA. No. Because people have fights, Ian, and everybody hates it – but you know you have to do it sometimes, you know? That's… Please don't smoke, Ian, 'cause it'll make me want to smoke.

IAN. Okay! What's that smell?

NEASA. It's new... stuff for the... thing... on my leg.

Beat.

IAN. And this is not because we had a fight! What do you think I
   am?! I know that people have fights – this is not because... It's not
   because I'm 'hurt' or something – it's, it's because...

NEASA. Oh, it's not because you're hurt, no? It's not because you're
   sulking and you've been letting me stew in my own juice for four
   days, no?

IAN. No I haven't actually – I've been trying to just fucking think
   about what I need to figure out what I need to do, you know?

NEASA. But you couldn't phone me, to tell me that, no? You just
   let... me just...

IAN (*shouts*). Any time I thought about phoning you I knew that it
   would just turn into this! We said, both of us said that we should
   give it a bit of time to... but oh no...

NEASA (*shouts*). I didn't know you were going to leave me on my
   own for a whole week, and I didn't even know where you were!

IAN. It's not a week, it's a couple of days, Jesus!

NEASA. It's not just a couple of days when you're on your own with
   a baby – it's completely fucking exhausting not knowing where
   you are – and I can't fucking do it!

   What am I supposed to say to your brother? He hasn't even asked
   me where you are! No one knows what to say – of course – she's
   delighted – she hates me – they think I've ruined your life. She's
   delighted with herself that I'm sitting up there on my own – she's
   so fucking smug now!

IAN (*annoyed, embarrassed, dismissive*). It doesn't matter what they
   think.

NEASA. That's easy for you to say! I have nowhere to fucking go!
   It's their house! What right do I have to stay there if you're not
   there?

IAN. It's none of their business!

NEASA. What do you mean it's none of their business? You don't
   know what it's like! I'm sitting up there on my own in the
   boxroom with the baby, they don't even come near me. And I

can't go downstairs! You should have seen the face on her when I asked her to mind Aisling tonight! (*Shouts.*) You don't know what it's like!

IAN. Look! This is all… getting sorted out! I nearly have a thousand euros in the bank – if you just let me get on with my work, if you just let me do it my way, you'll have your own place, there'll be no more of this and we can get on with it, but if you're going to… [harass me]. I can't… [work].

NEASA. What do you mean, my own place?

IAN. Can you not see that this is happening!? I don't… want… I can't… I can't… I can't… I don't… I don't want this relationship any more!

NEASA. What the fuck are you talking about? What the *fuck* are you talking about?

IAN. God! Can you not hear me?! Can you not listen to what I'm saying?

NEASA. I don't know if I can! Because have you completely lost touch with reality? Have you completely fucking lost touch with fucking reality?

IAN. This is reality!!

NEASA. What are you talking about? What about the baby?!

IAN. But this is not about the baby!

NEASA. What are you talk… How can it not be about the baby?!

IAN (*shouts*). Because it's not about that! Because it's about that *I* can't continue with *you*! With you and me!

NEASA. But what do you mean? What have I done? What have I done?

IAN. It's not what you've *done* or what I've *done*. It's… It's…

NEASA. What… What, Ian…

IAN. IT'S BECAUSE I CAN'T DO IT!

Pause.

NEASA. I knew this. I knew this was going to happen. I knew it. I knew it.

IAN. Look, if you'd just listen to me for once, and hear something that goes in, we're going to get you out of my brother's house. It's all going to be sorted out and I'm earning some money now and everything.

NEASA. Yeah, now that it's all… Now you're on your feet. My father fucking said this to me, you know? He fucking said it to me. A priest…?

IAN. I'm not a…!!

NEASA. An ex-priest? Forget it – he said anyone who goes next or near the priests is a fucking headcase to begin with. But I wouldn't listen to him!

IAN. Oh yeah, and your dad is a real one to know.

NEASA. Yeah, he's a drunk. But he's a human being, you know? He has feelings – he knows things, you know?

IAN. Yeah, well, is your father going to find you somewhere to live?

NEASA. Oh yeah, like you really found us somewhere to live, Ian. Squashed into your brother's house with that fucking bitch always fucking looking at me like I'm going to rob something, like she has anything…

IAN. Wait, now, don't fucking… What did you think was going to fucking happen?! I said it to you, I have to start all over again and it's gonna be tough! (*Sarcastic.*) Of course you didn't know that – you didn't know any of that!

NEASA. Yeah but I didn't think that at the end of it all you were… (*Despair, bewilderment.*) Are you breaking it off with me!? (*Pause.*) I was just thinking about it. Do you remember the week you left the order – about… a day later, you were so worried about money, I'd say like a *day* later – I *immediately* started working all the extra shifts I could get. I kept having to lick up to that sleazy bollocks Darren, just to keep working in that fucking *kip* of a pub…

IAN. Look, I know, I know that.

NEASA. Just so you wouldn't have to worry about anything! No one could understand how I put up with the things that he said to me in front of people. But I did it so you could have the money for your course!

IAN. I know. I know. And… look… I'm… going to do everything that I can. And, I promise, I'm going to look after you, you know?

NEASA (*shouts*). But I don't want for you to 'look after' me! I never wanted for anyone to have to look after me! I even said – when I got pregnant – I even said then we should leave it and we should wait until we have some more money – I said, 'This is too soon.' YOU SAID, 'NO', YOU SAID, 'NO, NOT TO DO THAT!' Because you thought it was 'wrong'! Now look! (*Short pause.*) What am I going to do? How can I go back there on my own again tonight? What am I going to say to your brother?

IAN. Don't say anything to him. I'll talk to him.

She stands there. She is ruined. Pause.

NEASA. What am I going to do?

IAN. Can you not go back around to your granny, even for a few...?

NEASA. My dad is back there!

IAN *throws his eyes to heaven as if this is an endless saga...*

IAN. Look, I know. I know that this... seems... like... but... this is the worst point, you know? And I've... I know I've made some huge mistakes, and I'm the first person who'll say that, you know? But I've got to put it right, and I'm going to put it right. But we can't continue like this and...

NEASA. Ian, I don't think I can do this on my own. I didn't think that this was going to happen.

IAN. I know but... you're not on your own. I'm with you in this, you know?

NEASA. But what are you saying to me?

IAN (*calmly, reasonably, almost sweetly*). Look. Aisling is our daughter. And I'm her father and you're her mother. And I fully... you know? I want to be her father and... be, you know... but you and I... are breaking up. And that's all, you know? That's all that's happening here. That's all it is.

NEASA. How can you say that? How can you say that that's all it is? Can you see what this is doing to me?

IAN. I know. But we can't... I... can't...

NEASA. Do you not love me any more?

IAN. I... I'll always... I mean, you have been... you were the only... when... when it was all so hard for me... And I had to make that big decision – and it was a *huge* thing for me – (*As though he has accomplished something completely unthinkable.*) to turn my back on the church?! – that was a *huge* thing for me. You were there for me, and I couldn't have come through it without you. I just couldn't have done it, I just couldn't have, you know? But... the fucking huge mistake I made was thinking that that was the end of the journey for me – and it wasn't.

Pause.

NEASA. Have you met somebody else?

IAN. No, no I haven't. I promise you. It's not that... (*Pause.*) I can't stay with you, with us, I can't do it. But I'm going to make sure that you want for nothing.

NEASA. But I just don't understand any of this. I just can't believe that it's happening even, you know?

She takes a bottle of wine from her bag.

I bought this this afternoon because I thought we were going to make up, and then you were going to come home with me.

She is shaking with fear and dread.

IAN. I'm sorry. I'm sorry. I'm sorry.

Silence.

NEASA. Is this... Is this because of me and Mark Whelan?

IAN. What?

Pause.

NEASA. Is it because...

IAN. Because what? (*Pause.*) Because what? (*Pause.*) What do you, what are you...?

NEASA. Look, it doesn't matter, okay? Forget I asked.

IAN. No, wait, hold on. What do you mean is this because of you and Mark Whelan? What about you and Mark Whelan?

NEASA. Please, Ian, just... Please...

IAN. What do you mean it doesn't matter? What doesn't matter?

NEASA. Nothing, just... because I wanted just to ask you... if that was why.

IAN. But why are you asking me that? Did you…

NEASA. Ian, please, I'm asking you not to ask me about this now, please!

IAN. Not to ask you about what though?

Pause.

Not to ask you about what?

Pause.

I'm not… [surprised.] Because, do you remember, I asked you about him before.

NEASA. And I told you.

IAN. You said there was nothing going on!

NEASA. There wasn't… then, when…

IAN. So what? Have you something you want to tell me?

NEASA. It doesn't make any difference, Ian, please, believe me. I just wanted to know if it was because…

IAN. Yeah, but, like I mean, what?

NEASA. Please, Ian. Please, I'm asking you, okay?

IAN. Yeah, but… I mean… wait a minute… What about you and Mark Whelan, you know? (*Pause.*) Have you had sex with him?

Pause. She doesn't know what to say – all she knows is that it feels like her world is ending.

That's a 'yes' then, I suppose then, yeah?

Pause.

NEASA. Can you not see what this is doing to me, Ian? Can you not see what this is doing to me? You're doing it anyway, Ian, you're leaving me anyway. Please don't leave me, please don't do it.

IAN *knows that he shouldn't continue with this, but he can't help it. He feels angry, frightened, powerless, but also adrenalised.*

IAN. Yeah, but you know what? This is fucking… You're throwing the baby in my face… and you're screwing around!

NEASA. I'm not!

IAN. But it's like I'm the one who, you know, that I...

NEASA. It was before the baby, Ian, I wasn't screwing around!

IAN. When before the baby? Just before?

NEASA. No, she's our baby, Ian, no!

IAN. Is she? I mean, wh... because I don't *know*... anything, here.

Pause.

Because I was shocked when you got pregnant, we both were. I thought we both were.

NEASA. No, no no no, she's your baby, she's your baby, she's yours and mine – this is crazy! Just, you have to believe me. Don't even...

IAN. Look, wait, hold on, hold on. This is... What are we talking about here?

Pause.

NEASA. Nothing. Really. Nothing. There was just... no one to talk to and...

IAN (*interrupting*). When?

NEASA. Just in, all around that time. When you came out and you were freaked out all the time, and you were starting your course. And I was working all the time. I just couldn't... keep going back up to your brother's house on my break, with her always there, Ian, it was horrible.

IAN. You know they've been so good to us really when you think about it, you know that?

NEASA. I know but, I was just always on my own!

IAN. But you weren't! When?

NEASA. I just... I didn't have anyone even that I could just have a normal talk to.

Pause.

I just feel like it's all my fault now, you know? And I was... I was worried all the time about everything, even then, you know? Mark just, would always ask me if I was alright, and how I was getting on...

IAN. Oh, I never asked you how you were? I'm just a fucking animal, yeah?

NEASA. I just believed him, when he asked.

Pause.

IAN (*dismissive*). Yeah, well.

NEASA. I didn't know what was going on. It was just like things were supposed to get better and they just kept getting worse and worse. I couldn't go back up there on my break. She always was saying something about the smell of smoke off me. I was working in a pub! You know? What did she want me to do? And... I started going around to Mark's flat – I told you, I told you I was doing that.

IAN. Yeah but...

NEASA. Yeah, well, I didn't... I didn't know that... anything... was... going to happen. I didn't think that there was even anything like that with him... But one day he was... he didn't say anything to me... We just got in the door and I just knew that... what he was... I didn't know what to do. I just, I only kind of realised when we got in the door that... he was... It was just really, I didn't... it was just really quick and it was, I didn't even want to do it. We both felt terrible after it. I'm sorry, Ian. I'm sorry. It was only once. It was only one time. It wasn't anything, really. And I've never gone there after.

I'm sorry, Ian.

I don't love him, Ian. I never loved him. I only ever wanted to be with you. Really. Really.

And I don't know what happened.

Say something. Say something to me, will you?

Long pause.

IAN. I'm sorry.

Silence.

NEASA *starts to get her stuff together. She leaves the bottle of wine.*

NEASA. I better go. 'Cause I'm gonna miss the last bus.

IAN. Look. I'll... I'll call you tomorrow, and...

NEASA (*almost silently*). Yeah.

She goes to the door.

IAN. Neasa.

She pauses.

Look, I'm…

Pause.

NEASA. It's not your fault.

She leaves. He stands there.

Lights down.

Scene Three

Lights up on the office. It is the afternoon, six or eight weeks later. The door is open and there is no one in the office. There is a bit more furniture around the place, maybe a plant or two. JOHN *comes in and stands there. He looks a bit better than he did in Scene One, and there is something more focused about him, he means business.* IAN *follows him in.*

IAN (*slightly exasperated*). Well, I don't know…

JOHN. I'm sorry, God, I can never…

IAN. No! You know I've asked them every single week, and they say they have a caretaker who keeps missing me. I think it's a total spoof.

JOHN. Don't give them the rent.

IAN. You think?

JOHN. They'll be round in a flash. That's the language they speak, you know. Money talks in this town. It rules really, you know?

IAN. God, tell me about it! Keeps me fit anyway, going up and down the stairs.

JOHN. Yeah! Well…

JOHN *really has his bearings in the office now. He throws his jacket over a chair and sits, unbidden, on the sofa, pouring himself a glass of water.* IAN *sits.*

IAN. So... how are you?

JOHN. Yeah, well I'm... this helps, you know...

IAN. Good, good...

JOHN. I, you know, I focus around it. It's been a good week em... They're, you know still very good about everything at work, there's no pressure to go in... em... the time is... good... it's...

Pause.

IAN. Are you sleeping or...

JOHN. Well, the same really. You know, I do... get a few hours. But, it's like there's something in me's determined to keep me up all night, you know? I never go off till around five, six, even. Then, of course, nine o'clock, the woman knocks on the door so I won't 'miss breakfast'. God forbid! You know?

They smile.

So... of course I'm in bits but, I get up, go down. I'm always the last. She usually has a few staying there, but, they're on business or whatever, they're... they're gone out, you know? So, I sit there, watching the traffic outside, and... I have an egg, cup of coffee... Get myself going then... you know...

IAN. You're still getting your walk in...

JOHN. Rain or shine. I get out, go down the coast. Down as far as the Bull Wall. The B&B is more the Fairview end so, you know, it's a good walk... Get the paper, throw any stuff into the laundry there. There's a little café next door, there near the Dollymount House. So, you know... that's... been the little routine, but I've em... I've bitten the bullet and done what you suggested. Couple of mornings I got in the car, dropped into the house, you know?

IAN. Okay. So, how is that?

JOHN. It's okay, you know, it's okay. (*Pause.*) So quiet, obviously... but I... did, I do what you say, and I focus on eh, a small, objective. I stay... [centered on it.] There were a couple of bills there, or whatever, there on the mat. Okay. Down to the post office, paid that... Em...

Pause.

IAN. And how does it feel in the house? When you're there.

JOHN. In the house, itself? Like I say. I'm aware, I'm wary… but in a funny way I… I can't… I can… hardly accept what I saw… you know… But, I know that I did, and so, obviously…

IAN. You're a little…

JOHN. I'm a little uneasy.

IAN (*nods*). Okay.

JOHN. But that's… that's also to do with… Like, when Mari was alive, you know, we had… stopped communicating. But now… she's gone, I really feel like there was a lot of communication. Even though, it wasn't… verbal… I suppose. I mean, she was there. And I was there. And in that, there's obviously, the presence of… you know, a living person, I'm not saying this very well. But I think, you know, I believe that… we had a huge importance in each other's lives. You know?

IAN. I don't doubt it for a second.

JOHN (*very affirmative*). Yeah. (*Beat.*) Yeah. I know.

Pause.

You know, when you're young. And you're told about… what to expect I suppose. It is kind of happy ever after. But it's… you know, it's weird to accept what happiness really is, you know, or what it is… nothing is ever like anyone expects, is it, you know? Like, it's not a fairy tale… I mean, it has to be just kind of ordinary, you know? A bit boring even, otherwise it's probably not real, you know?

IAN. …Yeah…?

JOHN. No, it's, it's just that… we probably had it, you know? I mean when I think of it, really, we… we had it all, you know? But it's, it's hard to… accept… that this is it. You… you go… searching, not *searching*, I wasn't going anywhere searching for anything, but, I think I was always slightly… waiting… you know?

This is something I probably wouldn't even have admitted before, you know? But maybe I felt that when we were married, and all settled in and eh… maybe even before we found out that we couldn't, that Mari couldn't, have children, I think that maybe even before that… I felt that I had kind of settled for second best, you know? I mean I mean I look at it now, and man, these are old feelings. Just fucking there all the time, for… all the way along.

Silence.

That's terrible, isn't it?

IAN. You felt what you felt…

JOHN (*slight self-disgust*). Yeah but, what… who the fuck did I think I was? You know?

Pause.

You see, we'd, I think, we'd been slightly left behind, a little bit, you know? All our… all our friends, they, you know, they had families. And, that… that… bound them together, you know? And, you see, I think that that… that we were… we were slightly left behind a little bit maybe. And that we felt that there was something kind of wrong with us, not anything serious or really wrong, but that there was a whole… you know, a whole experience, a whole way, maybe, of… of relating to everything, that wasn't… it wasn't available to us. (*Suddenly.*) It was a pain in the fucking hole to tell you the truth!

You know. I don't know if you have children, and I don't mean anything, because this is nothing about those people, but you know, I found, we found, that, okay, of course we were invited to places, you know, to parties and everything. But that's what there was to talk about, you know? 'Oh my sons are ten and eleven.' 'Oh my son is eleven!' You know?

And of course! Look, that's what people talk about. Of course they do. It's perfectly normal to want to talk about the things that are happening in your life. But, you know, that was what we were always sort of on the edge of. You know, those conversations. You know, you'd be trying to, waiting for the subject to change and then of course, some stupid fucker would turn around and go, 'Do you have any kids, yourself, John?' And I'd be, and I know that this happened to Mari too, I'd be like, 'Eh, no, no actually, I don't.' Which'd be then… 'Oh! Right! Okay!' You know?

I mean, I don't know if it felt like a big thing at the time, in a funny way, but it must have been, because I always felt… that it… wasn't… addressed because in a way, maybe I felt that the whole thing should be different – not just that we should adopt some kid or something – but that I should change the whole… the whole fucking thing, you know? Start again, somewhere else. Which then, of course, just feels mad and you want to let yourself believe that all these things aren't that important but... it was there and... what can I say? There was all this shit going on and I... our life just carried on and we grew up basically and our child-bearing years were over and we got on with it, and that's, but then, out the fucking blue, about three years ago...

Pause.

I met someone, you know?

Pause.

I mean... I didn't meet her, we'd already met her, we both had met her, up at a... party up there in Howth up there, you know? House of a guy I was doing some business with.

(*Suddenly.*) This is fucking mad fucking shit, now, you know?

IAN. I know. I know. It's okay...

JOHN. Yeah, well, like I say it was someone we'd both seen around a little bit for years. She's wealthy, you know? The husband is loaded, you know? And I suppose just the ordinary feelings of that... surface... glamour... I mean you'd see this woman, there was no doubt about it, she was, you know, the most beautiful woman in the room or whatever, or even wherever you'd go she'd be one of the top five best-looking women there, you know? I mean, that's what we're talking about here, you know? And obviously that's... that's very attractive, you know?

But about three years ago we were invited up to this guy, O'Leary, big hotel guy, up to his mansion up there on Howth Head. And both of us were excited about it and looking forward to it, you know, Mari liked, dressing up. She had a good figure and she could, she could definitely hold her own, and this would have been a big deal and we were in good form going up there beforehand. And it was, you know, there were people up there parking the cars for you and all this, you know what I mean? Up these steps like, and butlers standing there with champagne and hot ports and all this, serious stuff now, you know?

And in we go, into this place, serious mansion now, you know? And as usual, you know, we're fucking standing there on our own – fucking, you know, trying to talk to each other, but of course we both wanted to get stuck in and meet some other people and I was dying for a slash and Mari doesn't want to let me go and leave her on her own there, and all that, yeah?

But eventually we get talking to another couple, and a business guy I know comes in and it's warming up and I leg it down to the jacks and kind of – the way it goes, you know, I don't see Mari until everyone sits down later on for something to eat, 'cause when I'm coming out of the toilet and I'm going through the kitchen I meet a few other people who are there, and then I meet this… this woman that I'm talking about…

Her name is Vivien…

And I stop and say hello and, you know, we're standing there at the… you know, in the middle of a kitchen, sometimes in those big houses…

IAN. An island.

JOHN. Yeah, and there were these stools and it was like we were sitting at a bar somewhere, you know? The champagne keeps coming round, and it's great, you know? Because not only is this woman so beautiful to look at but we're having a brilliant chat, you know? 'Cause I had been in hospital for a few days having this thing done on my sinuses and it was weird because she was asking me about it and no one had asked me anything really, you know, not even Mari, although she had been great and everything and she came to see me every day – but I'd felt just this… just this real lonely feeling when I was in there, you know? I don't know why, or what happened but when I was in there, I just felt a bit scared and… and em…

But I'd had these feelings and anyway, for some reason I mentioned this to… to Vivien, and you know, God it just felt like I was being taken seriously. You know, and the champagne is coming round and it turns out that Vivien was in hospital at nearly the same time, you know? And she starts telling me that… she'd had… a miscarriage, you know? And she's telling me all this and she already has four kids who are teenagers and this pregnancy was out of the blue, and there'd been all this going on, and it hadn't worked out, and all this had… you know brought up, a lot of things for her about many things in her life and it's all this and, so like we're having this big talk, and then, you know, it's an hour-and-a-half later, and we're all being called in to sit down at this huge dinner… and on the way in, she… she takes my mobile number and puts it in her phone. And although in one way it just seemed like a normal thing to do, in another it was… you know… and I didn't really… let on to Mari that I'd only been talking to Vivien all that time when I got back, you know, I played up the other people that I'd only seen or just said hello to.

So we're there and we don't have a great time, because Mari is pissed off that I'd left her talking to these fuckers she didn't really know, and of course, about twelve o'clock, she says she doesn't feel so good, so great! We're the first ones to leave and we're not talking in the car and it's basically just one of those, and I'm kind of used to it, you know?

But Christmas, you know, we go over to her folks' house and do the whole bit, and when I get home, bit tipsy, I'm upstairs getting changed and I see on my phone, I have a text. And it's from Vivien and it's, 'Great to see you the other night. Happy Christmas.'

So I'm like standing up there in the bedroom, in my socks, you know, and I'm like some youngfella, and I text her back, 'It was great to see you too,' you know, 'Happy Christmas.'

And some part of me knew, you know? That I was sort of going into something… you know? And…

Pause.

But, you know there were no more texts and… but, something had… I mean whatever it triggered off… you know… here I was all of a sudden, just really thinking about this woman. Who… in many ways was different to what I knew, you know? And probably the big one was… you know… that… She was a mother.

Whatever that… means, you know? But anyway, Christmas was gone, and the new year and all that bollocks, which is a very depressing time of the year as far as I'm concerned and there were no more texts… and… I don't know what I was expecting to happen but I just got more and more into a filthy mood, over those days. And Mari was asking me what was wrong with me, and I was bulling because I'd erased Vivien's text, and I wanted to look at it again as something to hang on to, which was you know, whatever.

But as usual, Mari dragged me into the Christmas sales because I needed new clothes and we were in fucking… Roches Stores or somewhere and… I got a text… from Vivien, and it was just like, 'How are you?' You know? And man, it was like someone had thrown me a rope, you know? I was like, 'Thank God!' You

know? There's someone in the world who actually cares about
how I'm getting on, you know? Like, this was what that meant to
me. Crazy fucking shit, you know?

So I slipped off and said I wanted to have a look at some shoes or
something, and I texted her back, quickly just saying 'Post-Xmas
blues,' or something and bang! She texted me right back like,
'Hang in there,' or something and that's, it's so fucking stupid, but
that's how it continued then all day really.

IAN. Your wife didn't hear all these texts going off?

JOHN (*shakes his head*). No, I had the phone on silent, vibrate, in my
pocket, you know? I mean, you know? I was already… you
know…?

IAN. Mm. Yeah I know.

JOHN. And of course, suddenly I'm all chipper then, and I take Mari
for her lunch in the Westbury! You know, I'm all cheered up. That
morning she'd seen this bright red coat in one of the designer
shops in Brown Thomas or somewhere. Reduced from like three
grand to two grand or something, and of course it was still too
dear and all that, but after lunch I took her down and bought it for
her, you know? The fucking guilt, you know?

I mean, this is the terrible side of it. That coat was then, like her
good coat from then on, you know?

Pause.

She was wearing it, you know, the night she was… the night she
died, you know?

Pause.

She had it on when I saw her, you know? Behind the door there.

He exhales deeply.

So, but, you know, we went home, life continues. Back to work,
which I was glad about, because, you know, it gave me more time
to myself. You know? Texting Vivien? You know?

IAN. Mmm.

JOHN. And then of course…

IAN. What were the texts?

JOHN. Ah, it was just normal stuff, you know? Nothing. 'How are
you doing?' 'Back to work today.' 'Ah well, keep your chin up!'
You know? Nothing – except that it shouldn't have been
happening... you know, so... so then, of course, as time goes on,
that's, that's not enough for me...? So... I, I text her and say,
'Let's have a coffee sometime.' And that's opened it up, because,
at first I hear nothing, and I think, 'Woah, I've gone to far... ' But
then bang! Like a day later... She fucking rings me! Right in the
middle of a meeting with these two business guys down in
Longford, in the Longford Arms Hotel. And I see her name come
up on the phone – so I'm like, 'I have to take this.' So I go outside
and it's like, 'God it's great to hear you', you know? It was just...
it just felt like such a fucking relief, you know?

And she's on for like a big chat on the phone, but I'm like... I can't
do it, so I kind of cut to the chase, and I say, 'Let's meet up!' you
know? And she's, you know, suddenly I sense a kind of reluctance,
like she's not saying no, but... I can just... [sense it.] But I drive it
on and I say, 'Let's meet on Friday, get some lunch, just get a quick
sandwich somewhere', or something, and she's like, 'Where?' And
so like, without either of us acknowledging it, I say, 'The Killiney
Court Hotel', because it's really miles out of the way for both of us,
and no one would see us, you know, but of course I don't say that,
but I figure she gets it, and I say I'm going to be out that way and
so on. All very innocent, like – (*Sarcastic.*) 'Yeah, right!' But my
heart was pounding while I'm talking to her, you know? And I
could... like the stakes were really going up!

IAN (*affirmative*). Well, yeah...

JOHN. And... I mean, I don't know if you know what it's like, but...
Having a secret like that from your wife... Nothing is as strong as
a secret like that, I mean for binding two people. In my *mind*
anyway! As far as I was concerned, we were already like two
fugitives or something, you know? So, but, we made this
arrangement. And of course, the next few days was kind of mad,
like, 'What am I doing?', 'This is crazy.' I was... I was just like an
actor, or something, in my own life, just playing this part in
something that just didn't seem real, you know, or as real as... I
mean, crazy, you know? Like I felt I could just look behind
everything because it was only scenery, everywhere I went.
Because, I suppose in a mad way I believed that *something else*
was my reality! And that all this other shit – my life! – was... Like
I found myself looking at Mari while she was prattling on and

thinking, 'Who the fuck is this fucking woman?' What's
happened? That we live in the same house? There's been some
fucking... mistake, you know?

IAN (*affirmative*). Mmm.

JOHN. So a few days later, Friday, you know, I had cleared the decks,
I had nothing else to do so I was over there in Killiney at like
twelve o'clock, you know? And it was a horrible day, you know?
It never really got bright – didn't rain, but it was... almost like
GOD KNOWS WHAT YOU'RE DOING... you know?

They both laugh a little.

And eh... we met, you know? (*Suddenly without any defence or
guile.*) I couldn't believe it when I saw her coming through the
door. I just could not fucking believe it, you know? I was like,
Thank God, you know? Like how can this beautiful woman be
coming in here to be with me? You know? This is *real*, you know?
God. And she just came in there and she sat down where I was
sitting. And she was really nervous too, you know? And she just
starts talking, talking, talking. Her kid is in this new school and all
this, and her husband is going through this huge deal at work
and he's in Japan all the time and she's getting this work done by
these builders, and basically all this bollocks that I realise I have
no interest in at all! And there was this horrible feeling that all this
going on and on was just really a bit annoying, you know? This
just wasn't... I was selfish basically, and I... I wanted this to be
more about me, you know?!

They smile.

So we got a few hot whiskeys and after I feel like I've been
politely listening to all this shite for long enough, I started to move
it around more to... us being there, and... and I knew I was
rushing it but... I was really just, trying to move it on to the next
stage. Because I didn't want the whole... illusion of it... wrecked.
I mean, I was putting everything into this – the whole lot – all the
eggs in the one basket, I mean, insane, you know?

And I mean, madly, I just said to her, 'Look I need to... be with
you, you know? And hold you and...' Crazy.

And she just went so quiet then that I thought, okay, I've fucked it,
you know, she's... you know, she thought this was something
else... like we were going to be just friends in some... bizarre way

I don't fucking… relate to, you know? And it was three o'clock now and I'd have to start heading soon now anyway, but then she goes, 'Yeah, okay, let's…' But then I'm like slightly, like 'Don't just do this for me!' You know, like, don't kill yourself… But sure, I didn't even know what I was doing, you know?

I was like a robot. But everything I was doing was wrong so nothing made sense, like I got the key, and I was convinced your woman behind the desk was going to call the fucking guards, you know?! And this was before that place closed down, it was between when they had sold it and when they closed it down, there was hardly anyone around. Going up to the room, you know? And we didn't say anything. It was just, it was just… frightening really. And we go in and the room was like… it was like walking into one of the rooms in Fawlty Towers or something, like it was straight out of the 1970s. All brown and pink flowery patterns everywhere. And it was freezing. It was… it was horrible.

But. We sat on the bed. And we… started… sort of… kissing, but, I wasn't… it was just so obvious that this wasn't what she wanted. And to tell you the truth I was completely out of practice and I… tried to put my hand up her skirt and… you know, but she just stopped me. And neither of us were… it was just a huge mistake. I had fucked the whole thing to hell, really, you know? And I wanted to just go back to before, when we were just going to meet, you know?

But I didn't… I wasn't able to… quite express that, so… I was just sort of apologising, and really, we both had to go then and…

It was just fucking awful to tell you the truth, and there didn't seem to even be time to… make it… like, to have a drink and work it out or make it okay again. It was just over and we just, said goodbye in the car park, you know? Brilliant.

And of course when I got home, just the distance that I felt between me and Mari, I realised that whatever about the way we might have been before, it was nothing compared to this. This was like the Grand Canyon opening up, you know? I knew that I'd driven an unbelievable wedge… between us.

And of course, Mari can tell there's something wrong and she's… asking me, is there anything she can… She came and started stroking my back saying, 'God, those are big heavy sighs, John.' You know? So I just said, 'Ah it's a thing at work, don't worry about it.' Whatever, you know?

But seriously, you know, as the days went on, I mean I wasn't getting any sleep, and I was getting up in the middle of the night and just sitting in the kitchen, and then, not able to go into work.

Pause.

It was just so… I just felt like a piece of shit, you know?

I mean, I had gone from sharing this – I suppose it was a dream – of a… special communication or a secret… relationship that… and now it was, I mean I just felt like some sort of criminal. And I really felt so isolated and cut off and like there was nothing in my life to look forward to. And I just felt like, I knew then that something bad was going to happen, because I deserved it, because there was like some kind of evil in me, that I did.

IAN. Mari didn't… you didn't…

JOHN. Well, she just didn't know what to do, because I was just only, barely communicating with her. Because I fucking hate myself by this stage, you know?

And when I think about what I must have done to her. With all the silence and…

Pause.

I started pretending I had to stay down the country, for work, you know, overnight, but I was really just staying in places just so that I didn't have to deal with the terrible *pressure* of going home, you know? And facing that, and facing myself, and, you know?

I'd just be sitting there in some hotel bar in the midlands, you know? Just smoking cigarettes and looking at football or Man United or whatever – just unable to deal with anything, really. And I just, I had been staying in this place in Kildare and I had to leave and come back to Dublin, because I could only ever justify staying away for a night or possibly two at a push, and I was having a cup of coffee before I hit the road and I picked up this magazine, in a whole rack of old magazines, and I saw an ad for like, an escort service, a brothel. I knew what it was. And… I just needed to… connect with something, or someone, you know? When you're so alone like that… and when you feel… you know… I just… I just dialled the number and this woman answered and she sounded so nice, and you know, she told me where to go. To this place on the South Circular Road. And I fucking drove there, you know? I just…

Long pause.

IAN. Are you okay?

JOHN. Yeah, it's just, this is terrible.

IAN. No.

JOHN. I just find it so fucking hard...

IAN. You're doing so well, John. This is such important work, you know?

Pause.

Do you want to leave it there? We can just sit for a while...?

JOHN. How's the time, are we finished?

IAN. No we have time, but maybe you'd just prefer to...

JOHN. Well... No, I'll, I'll finish what I... I came... today to... you know...

IAN. Okay.

JOHN. Yeah, so I eh... anyway, I went to this place. Which was something I had never done. And this woman answered the door, and I was hoping the minute I saw her that she wasn't, I mean, she was a bit older now... And she brought me into this room. And there was just a couch there, and a shower over in one corner and some towels on a chair, and she says that this girl, Jeanette, was going to come in in a minute. And she says it's thirty euros to be there and then whatever I work out with Jeanette is between ourselves. And I mean, I'm already like, God this is, I haven't even met this girl, you know, but I give this woman thirty euros and she tells me to relax and take a shower and Jeanette will be in in ten minutes.

So I'm there in this room. And I can hear people in the house, talking or moving around or whatever, and it's a bit, you know... but I was hoping that whatever was going to happen was going to give me some relief, you know? Not a sexual thing, I don't... [think.] Just some... I mean, I know it sounds... 'Oh that's what everybody says... ' but you know...

IAN. No, I know.

JOHN. So I just, fuck it, I took a shower in there... in the corner. And I dried myself and... then I put my clothes back on!

They smile briefly.

And I'm in there maybe fifteen minutes and nothing is happening, you know, so I stick my head out the door, but I don't see anyone, and I decide to wait. And the doorbell goes and I hear the woman bringing in some other guy and she takes him off somewhere. And by this stage… I'm like… this is just freaking me out, really, but at the same time, like I say, I'm hoping for some… you know, I'm hanging in there. So I wait and I hear a bit of movement, and I hear someone leaving so I think maybe it's going to happen now, but then twenty minutes go by so I just, I'm like, forget it.

So I put on my coat and I open the door to go and the woman who let me in is coming down the hall going like – (*Strong Dublin accent.*) 'What are you doing? Go in and have a shower!' and she comes right up to me and the smell of drink off her, you know? And I'm like, 'Look I'm going to leave it.'

And then this guy appears, you know? Like a total skanger. Just with these really dead eyes, you know? And he's like, 'What's going on?' And they're much louder than they have to be, if you know what I mean.

And for some reason I… just… decide. That… I'm not gonna take this fucking shit any more, I've just had enough so although I'm probably definitely on a hiding to nothing I say, 'Give me my thirty euros back…' which of course, is madness, you know? But of course this *is* fucking madness, you know?

So she shouts, 'We don't owe you any money – we provide the amenities and that's what you were charged for. We don't owe you a fucking penny!' And your man is like, 'Come on now, you're either going to have to go in and have a shower or you're going to have to go.' But by this stage I suppose these two people represent everything that's wrong with the world to me and it's like I'm… I just refuse to accept this, you know? And I'm… *demanding* my money back! I just want to have a transaction where some normal rules apply again, you know? And look where I was trying to fucking achieve that! You know?

They smile.

And then, I just, before I know it, your man just hits me right in the stomach! And I mean, I'm not fit, and I haven't been in a fight since I was maybe ten or something! But that feeling of being completely winded, of not being able to breathe and being completely paralysed – it just… I just bent over slowly and I could hear this awful groan coming out and it was me making it – you know – completely out of my control. And I just went down and down until I was on my knees on the floor. And I hear your man going, 'Now you brought that on yourself.' And he was so fucking right, you know?

And then they sat me on the stairs, you know? They were getting a bit worried, because I just could not breathe. She's going like, 'What did you hit him for?' And he's saying to me, 'You'll be alright, you'll be alright…' And I felt fucking grateful! It was so stupid but in a mad way, that's what I wanted! I wanted someone to tell me that things were going to be okay. I mean I was really clinging to the fucking wreckage here now, you know?

He sighs deeply.

And… I went home. Still completely able to… I went in and Mari had my dinner there on the table, you know, chops and peas and potatoes. And the pain in my stomach was… I could barely fucking walk, you know? And, of course she… the minute she sees me she just… she was like 'Oh my God, John, what's happened? Are you alright?'

And I… (*Almost starts crying but keeps it together.*) I just turned on her, Ian, you know? I just… exploded. And I ate the head off her. I was like an animal. And it was just so… sudden. She looked so frightened, I had never seen that look, of real fear, and I was doing it! You know?

He starts crying.

And, I pushed her up against the wall and I told her, 'You're fucking killing me.'

And I… grabbed her by the shoulders and I shook her. I shook her so hard. I could feel how small and helpless she was. It was a terrible feeling. And I said to her, 'Don't fucking speak to me any more. Don't you dare fucking speak to me.' And she just cowered down on the floor – nothing like this had ever happened between us before, you know? And she curled herself up into a little ball there down beside the bin. And the sobs just came out of her, you know? Just the total… bewilderment, you know?

Pause. JOHN *is in the deep pit of his self-loathing.*

And after that, like from then on, I couldn't… And I just don't understand. How, why I just couldn't have talked to her? She only wanted to help me. But it was like… (*Short pause.*) I was in a kind of a storm, you know? You're only just barely hanging on, just hanging in there. And I was frightened that she'd, or anyone would… see how weak I was. And how… disgusting I was. And she'd hate me, you know? Everything just developed into a kind of paralysis. That's the only way I can describe it. You just can't fucking move, you know?

Because, I think I killed her that day, you know? I mean, I didn't kill her. But I might as well have.

I mean, I don't even know where she was going the night that… or where she had been. We didn't even speak to each other before she died, she was on her own, you know? I just feel like I just fucking left her alone in the world, you know? If I could have even slept in the bed beside her, maybe that might have even been enough! You know, I… I probably didn't even have to say anything… And now I can't go back!

Long pause.

I just… I believe in a way that I probably did it to her, Ian, you know?

IAN. No.

JOHN. And that's probably why I've seen her, you know?

IAN. No. I don't…

JOHN. Like she only wanted to fucking help me, you know?

IAN. But it was an accident. She was in an accident.

JOHN. But I… I mean I think about it. Where would she have been going? She wouldn't have been out on her own in town if… you know… And she was so kind, you know? I… I mean, is it…? Is it that, in some way, she… Is she trying to…

IAN. I really don't think that…

JOHN. Is she trying to hurt me? Or I mean…

IAN. Well, you see I'm not convinced that…

JOHN. Or maybe I've got it wrong. You know? Maybe I've got the whole thing arseways.

Pause.

Maybe she's… Maybe she's just trying to save me, you know?

Lights down.

Scene Four

A church bell strikes twice in the distance. It is night. The office is in darkness except for what light spills in from the street. We hear someone coming up the stairs. The door opens and IAN *comes in and switches on a lamp or two.* LAURENCE *comes in and hovers near the door. He is skinny and wears sports gear and runners. It is hard to tell if he is thirty and looks much younger or twenty and looks much older. He has a nervous, twitchy energy and seems like he lives from minute to minute. He has a dirty bandage on his right hand.*

IAN. Come in. Come in. It's okay. There's no one else. There's no one in the whole building. This is… where I work.

LAURENCE *shuts the door. They stand there,* IAN *doesn't seem to know what to do.*

Let me eh… I think I have eh… would you… drink a glass of wine?

LAURENCE (*shrugs*)…. Yeah.

IAN. Okay… Let me, eh… Let me…

He bustles about and finds the bottle NEASA *brought in Scene Two. He finds two mugs.*

I say 'glass'… but… I'll just… Eh…

He motions to LAURENCE *that he wants to get past him and he goes into the little toilet to wash the mugs. We hear him in there while* LAURENCE *stands alone in the room. He comes back out with the mugs and stops abruptly.*

Corkscrew. Didn't think of that. Didn't think of it. Em.

LAURENCE. You can push it in.

IAN. The…

LAURENCE. You can push the cork down. If you have something to…

IAN. Like eh…

LAURENCE. Just a knife.

IAN. I have a knife. (*Goes to a box which has a few kitchen things.*) Just a cutlery knife…

LAURENCE. Yeah, just anything…

IAN holds up an ordinary 'knife and fork' knife.

Yeah, you…

He goes to IAN who takes the bottle up and they awkwardly jockey for position.

IAN. Will I… or…

He hands the bottle to LAURENCE.

LAURENCE. Yeah, you just… you push it down. My… (*Gestures with his bandaged hand.*)

IAN. Oh yes, you just…

He takes the bottle and attempts to push the cork in.

LAURENCE. If you, just… if you take that, tear off the…

IAN. Oh yeah, yeah. (*Uses the knife to cut the seal away from around the cork.*) Actually I'm going to put it on the… Just…

He puts the bottle on the floor and pushes the cork down with the knife.

It's going down.

LAURENCE (*indicates toilet*). Is that the jacks?

IAN. Oh yeah, go ahead.

LAURENCE goes into the toilet. IAN struggles on the floor. Finally the cork goes in.

(*Calls out.*) I've done it, it's gone in!

He pours two mugs of wine. He stands there, waiting. He seems disconnected for a moment, almost not part of his own life. The toilet flushes. LAURENCE emerges. IAN hands him a drink.

Now. God, the things we do, ha? Well, cheers.

They drink.

God, it's alright. Here. (*Gives LAURENCE another drink.*) Is your hand alright?

LAURENCE. Ah yeah. It's wrecked.

IAN. What happened to it?

LAURENCE. Ah, a banger. I was eh… I was letting off a banger, with my son, on Hallowe'en. Sometimes my eyes aren't that good. And the fucking thing nearly blew my fucking hand off.

IAN. Oh my God. Is it alright?

LAURENCE. Ah it's wrecked. I can only move these two fingers.

IAN. Oh no.

LAURENCE. Yeah, it's a fucking killer, you know? I can't work, you know?

IAN. Oh no. What, what do you, what, what are you working at or…

LAURENCE. Ah, I was lined up to get a job driving a van, but…

IAN. Oh no.

LAURENCE. Yeah.

Pause.

IAN. Is it… is it healing or are you getting treatment for it or…

LAURENCE. Ah, I'm supposed to keep… to go in for physiotherapy but, it's, it's tricky 'cause I'm trying to keep a few things organised at the moment and I, sometimes… the appointments don't suit me, then, you know?

IAN. Right…

LAURENCE. Because of the times. But this fucking thing is filthy, I need to… but they keep you waiting for so long in there, though, you know?

IAN. God, well… God, well you… you don't want to let it get infected.

LAURENCE. I know. I know. But, yeah, you know, I have to do it. You know?

Pause.

IAN. Are you cold? Do you want me to turn that, turn that on?

LAURENCE. Yeah, I'm freezing. Are you not cold?

IAN. Oh sure, I'll... (*Goes and turns on an electric heater.*) This heats up real fast.

Pause.

I'd say it gets pretty cold when you're... up there just...

LAURENCE. Yeah, it's... you know... but sometimes you just fucking have to, 'cause...

IAN. Yeah... Yeah... (*Pause.*) I've never eh... I've never gone up there, before, you know? I've never... this is the... I mean... Do you, do... I, do you, do I pay you now, or do I...?

LAURENCE. Yeah, well, whatever. If you want to get it out of the way, you don't have to think about it then, any more, you know?

IAN. Yeah, yeah, that's... okay, let's... okay. (*Counts out some money from his pocket.*) Em. (*Hands it to* LAURENCE.) That's...

LAURENCE. Yeah. You don't have to be so nervous.

IAN. Yeah. I know. I'm sorry. I just, em... I've never...

LAURENCE. Because you're making me nervous.

IAN. Oh no, I don't want to, I'm sorry.

LAURENCE. Yeah, no, it's just, I get, like I just...

IAN. I know, I know, it's contagious. I know. I've never...

LAURENCE *indicates sound system.*

LAURENCE. Do you want to turn on some music or something?

IAN. Yeah! Yeah, I'll...

IAN *goes over to the stereo and starts looking through some CDs.*

God, what'll I put on?

LAURENCE. Just whatever you want.

IAN. Yeah, but em... Do you like the Eagles?

LAURENCE. Don't know them.

IAN. No. Hold on, someone burned this for me...

He puts on a CD. It is slow, mellow country rock.

This is, you know, it's quite laid-back.

LAURENCE *makes a slight move as though he may be coming towards* IAN. IAN *halts him with his voice.*

You have a son?

LAURENCE. Yeah.

IAN. Is he... How old is he?

LAURENCE (*without much enthusiasm*). He's six.

IAN. Wow, is he...

LAURENCE. He's with his ma. She's nuts, you know, her mother looks after him more.

IAN. Right.

LAURENCE. Yeah, but look, I don't really wanna...

IAN. Yeah, of course, I'm sorry.

Pause.

Are you a bit warmer?

LAURENCE. Yeah, yeah.

IAN. God... I'd say it's cold up there, though, when you're waiting around, is it?

LAURENCE. Yeah it's weird, you know? I mean, it's a bit...

IAN. Mmm.

LAURENCE. Yeah, I got the shit kicked out of me one time up there, you know?

IAN. Oh no...

LAURENCE. Yeah, ah it was my own fault. I wouldn't even be out there tonight only, I've been staying with my cousin in this flat in town. But this young one came to stay there, and she said there was some money gone out of her bag, and... it wasn't me, like, but... now... I have to try to...

IAN. Yeah...

LAURENCE. Get a few quid together.

IAN. I know.

LAURENCE. So I can go back and...

IAN. Yeah...

LAURENCE. I don't even want to go back, though, but I need an address.

IAN. Yeah.

LAURENCE. This is where you work, yeah?

IAN. Yeah, well, yeah... I've been here for a few months, you know?

LAURENCE. What do you work at?

IAN. Well, I'm a therapist, you know?

LAURENCE. A therapist?

IAN. Yeah, you know...

LAURENCE. What, do you...

IAN. Well, you know, people can come, and... talk to me, or...

LAURENCE. What, like mad people?

IAN. No, not mad... Just maybe... people who might just feel a little bit... stuck, you know? And maybe they... just need a... just another point of view on what's going on, if they're carrying, you know, a big burden, you know? Of some guilt maybe. You know? Or where they might feel it's hard to go on because they've got themselves just in a bit of a corner, because they're worried about other people, or maybe it's just that they have some old feeling... Maybe even from years ago, just even sometimes things can happen to us when we're children, and that, you know, maybe that sets the tone for how people get on later. Where maybe they get a bit stuck. And maybe I can just invite them to consider something that maybe they didn't think was that important before, but, you know, maybe it was... and...

LAURENCE. Do you ever hypnotise people?

IAN. No, no I don't. We... no, it's, it's all fully conscious. It's... about perceiving reality, I suppose.

Pause. LAURENCE *puts his drink down as if to move towards* IAN.

I have a daughter. That I haven't seen... either... you know, much... She's with her mother... I mean, I know what you... when you say...

LAURENCE *moves towards* IAN. IAN *stands very still.*
LAURENCE *puts his hand on* IAN's *arm and gently moves him closer.*

LAURENCE. It's alright. Don't be frightened.

LAURENCE *takes* IAN's *drink and puts it down.* IAN *is shaking.*
LAURENCE *pulls* IAN *towards him and holds him, swaying to the music.* IAN *tentatively puts his arms around* LAURENCE.
Suddenly the music breaks into faster, wholly inappropriate hillbilly fiddle/banjo music.

IAN. Sorry!

He goes to the stereo and turns it off.

God, that's look, em... when I say that I haven't, you know, done this, or gone up to the park before, I don't mean that I haven't just gone up to the park at night, you know... I mean. (*Pause.*) I mean I've never been with a man. (*Pause.*) Do you understand me?

LAURENCE (*shrugs*). That's alright. The men who go up there are all fucking married, you know? Loads of them are! That's why... they... (*Pause.*) What difference does it make? (*Pause.*) You should just do what you want to do, you know? (*Pause.*) Put on the other music. Put on the music that was on before. (*Reassuringly.*) I have nowhere else to go.

IAN *goes to the machine and puts on the other music again. He goes to the bottle and pours them both another drink. He hands a mug to* LAURENCE, *avoiding eye contact.* LAURENCE *takes his hand.* IAN *looks into* LAURENCE's *eyes.* LAURENCE *returns his gaze, and then places* IAN's *hand against his crotch, holding it there.* IAN *starts to caress* LAURENCE's *crotch and they move closer together.*

Lights down.

Scene Five

It is daytime. Bright sunlight streams into the room. As the scene progresses, the room should become more dusky. There are dust sheets on the desk and most of the furniture and books are gone. There are boxes all around the office, and IAN *is there packing books, files, etc. away. There is a little transistor radio on the floor and indistinct daytime radio is playing while* IAN *packs. The intercom buzzer goes off and* IAN *goes to answer it, maybe a bit pissed off, he doesn't expect anyone.*

IAN. Yeah? Hello? Hello? Yeah, hold on. (*Presses the buzzer to release the door.*) Hello? Are you in? Hello? What? Hello? (*Presses the button again.*) Hello? Are you there? What?

There is a knock at his door, IAN *opens it to reveal* JOHN, *carrying a present.*

Oh, hello!

JOHN. Sorry, I'm barging in on you.

IAN. No! No! I just I couldn't hear... come in, come in!

JOHN (*coming in*). No, I just... I've had this, fucking... I've had it in the car and I, 'cause I wanted to get you something.

IAN. Oh no!

JOHN. And then, of course, I've been driving around with it in the boot for the last six weeks, you know what I mean?

IAN. Oh no...

JOHN. It's nothing.

IAN. Oh no...

JOHN. It's a lamp, it's nothing.

IAN. Oh but still, thanks, you... come in, sit down, there's nowhere to sit.

JOHN. And I was going by, and I thought... God, I should just call in, and I thought, well, it's lunchtime, he probably won't have anyone there, and...

IAN. No, no, I'm...

JOHN. Janey Mack, you're...

IAN. Well, no, it's lucky you... I'm moving! I'm going, you know?

JOHN. You're moving your office?

IAN. I'm, well, no, I'm moving. I'm, I'm going down to Limerick, believe it or not.

JOHN. Limerick?

IAN. Yeah, my fiancé is there and... (*As though these are tedious little details that are too boring to go into.*) with our... baby, and some... friends of hers have lent her a house there, so...

JOHN. Yeah.

IAN. I'm going down... and I've, you know, I'm applying for a... I've an interview down there. For a post so...

JOHN. Yeah.

IAN (*doesn't understand* JOHN'S *reference*). Mm. You know, so... it's time, and...

JOHN. Yeah, well, great! That sounds good. Dublin's... you know...

IAN. Yeah.

JOHN. It's a tough town.

Pause.

IAN. Yeah, well, look, let me, move some of this stuff. Sit down!

IAN *bustles around.*

JOHN. Ah, I'm not gonna stay, really.

IAN. No, no! Look, the kettle is still... on the go, we're still... Let me...

IAN *disappears into the toilet with the kettle.*

(*Off.*) So, how are you keeping?

JOHN. Yeah. You know, I'm good! You know, I have to say, I'm good. Thank God, you know? I'm getting there, you know, definitely, and I really, you know...

IAN *re-emerges and plugs the kettle in.*

I just wanted to say thanks, because, you know...

IAN. No, no. You did the work, you know?

JOHN. Yeah, no, but, you know, I mean... I wanted to, you know...

IAN. God, well, you didn't have to. And you shouldn't have. Really, you know?

JOHN. Yeah, well...

IAN. No, well, thank you, I mean... will I open it?

JOHN. Yeah, yeah! Go ahead, open it, it's nothing, you know? It's really, it's not...

IAN *opens the paper.*

I mean, I have no eye for these things. The girl in the shop, you know, I – it was her really. I mean, I said it was a present and she said, who is it for, and then of course I realised, 'God, I know nothing about this man!' You know?

They laugh.

Because I don't! I mean, it's weird, isn't it?

IAN. Well, it's, you know, it's... [normal.]

JOHN. So I said, it was just a thank-you present really.

IAN. Tch, God, no...

JOHN. And she...

IAN *produces a stunning antique lamp from the box.*

IAN. Oh my God!

JOHN. Ah, no, sure...

IAN. This is too much.

JOHN. No, it's nothing.

IAN. Is it, it's... an antique, or...?

JOHN. It's, ah, it's from the thirties or fucking something, I don't know.

IAN. No, well that's, it's too much...

JOHN. Please, no. Do you like it?

IAN. It's beautiful, really...

JOHN. Well, you know, thank you, you know, that's… [why I'm here.] I…

IAN. Thank you, really, thanks, God…

JOHN *produces a card in an envelope from his pocket.*

JOHN. And this is just a little card. You know, to go…

IAN. Oh, God… God, thanks, thanks, John, really.

IAN *reads the card.*

JOHN (*interrupting* IAN *reading it*). Ah, read it later.

IAN. Tch. God, no, well. I don't know what to say now.

JOHN. Ah there's… [nothing to say.]

IAN. God, well, let me make you a cup of tea. Here, sit down, take off your coat.

JOHN. I'm grand, really.

IAN *produces an old stool from somewhere.*

IAN. No, sit down there, here.

JOHN *sits a bit awkwardly.*

So, God, how are you keeping?

JOHN. I'm good, you know? I'm good. I'm… I've just bought an apartment.

IAN. Oh wow, so we're both…

JOHN. We're both moving. Yeah… nearly finished the, the legal… which can be a nightmare… but it's… it's…

IAN. If it's what you've got to do, that's right, I know…

JOHN. Yeah, it's lovely. It's down there on the seafront, just there near St Anne's Park.

IAN. Oh very nice, yeah, I know there.

JOHN. Yeah, it's those ones there…

IAN. They're nice, yeah.

JOHN. Yeah, so whole new…

IAN *finds teabags and cups.*

IAN. And you're… You're good… in yourself, and…

JOHN. I'm… really good, Ian, you know? I have to say. I'm looking forward to the move. And I've… actually been in the house again, this last month, you know?

IAN. Oh right! God, that's… do you take sugar?

JOHN. No, no, it's fine.

IAN. Good, because I don't eh…

They laugh a little.

JOHN. No I don't, anyway, so… and eh, yeah, I've been there, in the house. And I mean, there was a time, as you know, I couldn't even have envisaged myself spending even one night there, so, no I'm…

IAN. But you're going to move on and…

JOHN. I'm moving on… It's, it's just… It just feels right. It just feels like that's, that's what… I… what I… that's just what I want to do! I mean, I don't want to be some old guy on his own in there. You know? That house is all to do with me and Mari, and it's even too big for two people – it was too big when we moved in. I mean, if there had been kids, okay, but, you know, that didn't happen and… I mean, I just feel like my life isn't over, you know? Like why should I stay in the house out of some kind of mad fucking duty to fucking… you know… I mean…

IAN. I know, you're right, I know. I mean it's so…

JOHN. I mean we create these fucking…

IAN. I know, I know…

JOHN. These mad…

IAN. I know. I know. But that's, you know, that's great, you're…

JOHN. Yeah… I'm… you know, I'm getting on with it, and I really see it now like a… like a new chapter is opening up, and like *you* know, there was a time I could never have thought that that was even possible! You know, I mean…

IAN. Well, that's great, I mean, that's…

JOHN. And that's why, I mean, I want to thank you really, because…

IAN. Yeah, well, like I say, you did the work.

JOHN. …I don't know what I… would've…

IAN. Well, look I'm... I'm glad. I'm happy for you, I mean that. And, you know, I hope, you know, you...

JOHN. My fucking brother introduced me to a woman, there, you know?

IAN. Oh...?

JOHN. Yeah, I mean, he's a prick. He can be a bit of an arsehole. But he's, you know... he's alright, you know, really.

IAN. Yeah, I know what you mean.

JOHN. Yeah, him and his missus were killed asking me over for some dinner there four or five weeks ago. I was like... (*Sarcastic.*) 'Yeah, right... ' you know. Because I can sometimes do without that, you know what I mean? But I... went over. There were a few people there. This girl was there. I knew her, though, slightly, from before, she used to work where I – she used to work there, coincidentally, and she's... she's a bit younger than me now, you know, but...

IAN (*shrugs*). Well...

JOHN. Yeah, sure, what fucking difference does it make? I agree. Although... if she was a good bit *older* than me now, the shoe might well be very much on the other fucking foot now, you know what I mean?

They laugh.

No, but, she's a nice girl, you know? Sure, I'm not... we just went to the pictures and had a drink, you know, just... (*Short pause.*) We're going to the theatre tomorrow night.

IAN. Oh!

JOHN. I know! (*As though the theatre is rubbish.*) 'Good luck!' Ah, but, sure...

IAN. Yeah, well, that's... (*Short pause.*) Don't feel that you have to rush into anything, John, you know?

JOHN. No, no, no, no, I'm not, no. I'm, it just feels like it's just a part of... just a new... it's all just a new... it's good, you know? Don't worry.

IAN. Yeah, yeah, no, I'm...

JOHN. But Jesus! Do you know who I saw?

IAN. Yeah?

JOHN. Vivien.

IAN. Yeah?

JOHN. Vivien, the…

IAN. Yeah.

JOHN. The object of my… my downfall. The big…

IAN. Yeah.

JOHN. Yeah, saw her there at a do. God, it was weird, you know? I mean she had great sympathy for me and everything, but it was really like nothing had ever happened? Between us? Weird, you know? And do you know what was really weird? I realised we had *nothing* in common. What about that, you know?

IAN *nods.*

Serious. Serious fucking shit. I came away thinking, 'I don't even like this woman', you know? Bizarre. When I… (*Short pause.*) Mad.

Pause.

IAN. God, John. Well, you know, it sounds like you're doing really well though, you know?

JOHN. Well, I'm, you know…

IAN. But you're getting out, you're meeting people… and…

JOHN. Ah, I'm just, I'm just taking it handy. And… it was a great help, you were a great help, Ian, to me, you know? I mean it and… I wish you all the best, you know?

IAN. Well, look, I wish you all the best too, John. I really do, you know, and… you know, it makes me feel good to see you… that you're, you know…

JOHN. Well, thanks. Thank you. You know? (*Short pause.*) And I'll… I only came to… I better let you…

IAN. Well, I'm, yeah… I said I'd drop the keys back this afternoon and… I'm…

JOHN. Do you want a hand with anything?

IAN. No, no, no…

JOHN. Are you sure?

IAN. Really, don't… I'm, I'm nearly there now.

They are standing. JOHN *picks up his coat.*

JOHN. Okay.

IAN. So, no ghosts.

JOHN. No. No ghosts. (*Exhales.*) But, I'll tell you, you know, even if I saw one, Ian, it's not… I mean, seeing something is one thing but… it's how it makes you *feel*, isn't it? It's how that makes you feel. That's what's important. Someone could see something and it doesn't really matter. Someone else'll see it and… it's the end of the world, you know?

IAN (*affirmative*). Mmm.

JOHN. That's the reality, you know? What it *does* to you is the reality.

IAN. I know.

JOHN. But you don't believe in ghosts anyway, Ian. You've got it sussed.

They are moving towards the door.

IAN. John, there was a time I would've given anything to see one. Just to know that there was… something else. Do you know what I mean?

JOHN. Sure.

IAN. Just something else, besides all the… you know… the pain and the confusion. Just something that gave everything… *some* meaning, you know? I'm talking about God, really, you know?

JOHN. I know. Where is he?

IAN. I know. But don't get me wrong. I think you had a real experience. I think you really experienced something – but I think it happened because you needed to experience it.

JOHN. Yeah, I know…

IAN. You were pulling all this… you felt maybe you couldn't move on without being… punished somehow and…

JOHN. I know.

IAN. It happened! But... I don't believe you saw a ghost. Does that make sense?

JOHN. Well, yeah, it makes sense to me now, but there was a time it really wouldn't have, you know? (*Pause.*) But that was a different time.

IAN. Yeah, it was.

JOHN *opens the door.*

JOHN. I'll tell you, the mind, it's mad isn't it?

IAN. John, we know nothing. We just know nothing really.

JOHN. We're just barely fucking hanging in there, really, aren't we?

IAN. Well, some better than others. But you're doing good, John, you know? Considering, I mean, you know?

JOHN. I know. I know that. But I had to fucking go there to find that out. Do you know what I mean?

IAN. I do. I know.

Pause.

JOHN. Look, I'll love you and leave you. Good luck with everything, alright?

IAN. Well, you too, and thanks, for the present. It really is so thoughtful...

JOHN (*interrupting*). Ah, it's nothing, good luck.

They shake hands.

I'll see you.

IAN. Well... Actually, I'll wait here till you get out down there. And I can buzz it if... 'cause it's still...

JOHN. Oh, nothing changes! I'll see you, Ian, good luck.

IAN. I'll see you, John, bye now.

IAN *hovers near the open door while* JOHN *goes down. He picks a flyer up off the floor at the threshold and crumples it up. He picks two books off the floor and looks at the back of one of them. We hear the outer door slam shut. In the distance we hear the faint sound of an ice-cream van's music.*

(*Calls out.*) Did you get out?

There is no answer.

IAN *throws one of the two books in a box near the door. He shuts the door and crosses the room to throw the other book in a different box.*

In the darkening gloom of the afternoon, we see that MARI's *ghost has appeared behind the door. She is looking at* IAN, *just as* JOHN *described her; she wears her red coat, which is filthy, her hair is wet. She looks beaten up. She looks terrifying.*

IAN *has his back to her at his desk, going through some old post. But he seems to sense something and turns.*

Lights down.

THE SEAFARER

> *He knows not*
> *Who lives most easily on land, how I*
> *Have spent my winter on the ice-cold sea*
> *Wretched and anxious, in the paths of exile*
> *Lacking dear friends, hung round by icicles*
> *While hail flew past in showers...*

> Anonymous. *The Seafarer,* c.755 AD,
> translated from Anglo-Saxon by Richard Hamer

The Seafarer was first performed in the Cottesloe auditorium of the National Theatre, London, on 28 September 2006 (previews from 20 September), with the following cast:

MR LOCKHART   Ron Cook
IVAN CURRY   Conleth Hill
JAMES 'SHARKY' HARKIN   Karl Johnson
NICKY GIBLIN   Michael McElhatton
RICHARD HARKIN   Jim Norton

Director   Conor McPherson
Designer   Rae Smith
Lighting Designer   Neil Austin
Sound Designer   Mathew Smethurst-Evans

The play received its American premiere at the Booth Theater, New York, on 31 October 2007, with the same artistic team. The cast was as follows:

IVAN CURRY   Conleth Hill
MR LOCKHART   Ciarán Hinds
NICKY GIBLIN   Sean Mahon
JAMES 'SHARKY' HARKIN   David Morse
RICHARD HARKIN   Jim Norton

Characters

JAMES 'SHARKY' HARKIN, *erstwhile fisherman/van driver/chauffeur, fifties*
RICHARD HARKIN, *his older brother, recently gone blind, late fifties/sixties*
IVAN CURRY, *old friend of the Harkins, late forties*
NICKY GIBLIN, *a friend of Richard's, late forties/fifties*
MR LOCKHART, *an acquaintance of Nicky's, fifties*

Dialogue in square brackets [ ] is unspoken.

Setting

The action takes place in a house in Baldoyle, a coastal settlement north of Dublin City. It is an old area which could hardly be called a town these days. It is rather a suburb of the city with a church and a few pubs and shops at its heart. From the coast one is looking at the north side of the Howth peninsula. Howth Head (Binn Eadair) is a hill on the peninsula which marks the northern arm of Dublin Bay. Due to its prominence it has long been the focus of myths and legends.

Act One takes place on Christmas Eve morning and late afternoon.

Act Two takes place late on Christmas Eve night.

ACT ONE: THE DEVIL AT BINN EADAIR

Scene One

The grim living area of a house in Baldoyle in Dublin. The house seems to be built into a hill. The main entrance is down a flight of stairs from the ground floor, giving a basement feel to the room. There is a window with a net curtain and threadbare heavier curtains drawn over it. At the back wall is an opening to a passageway giving access to a yard. Off the passageway are a mostly unseen kitchen and a toilet.

The place lacks a woman's touch. It has morphed into a kind of a bar in its appearance. Those who live or pass through here are so immersed in pub culture that many artefacts in the room are originally from bars: a big mirror advertising whiskey, ashtrays, beer mats, a bar stool or two somewhere. There is a cold stove. The furniture is old and worn. An armchair, a couch, mismatched chairs, a dresser with very old mugs, cups and various chipped plates, a little table more suited for playing cards than for eating at...

As the play begins the room is more or less in darkness. Some light seeps through from the kitchen, from the door to the yard, from down the stairs and through the threadbare curtains. There doesn't appear to be anyone here. An old stereo plays low music. A scrawny artificial Christmas tree haunts a corner.

SHARKY *comes down the stairs, pausing to tap a red light under a picture of the Sacred Heart which has gone out. It flickers to life for a second but goes out again as he descends and surveys the scene. He is in mismatched pyjamas with a sweater over them and wears a pair of runners. He is not a big man, but is wiry and strong. A very tough life is etched on his face. His eyes are quick and ready. He has a small plaster at the bridge of his nose and a few plasters on the knuckles of his right hand. He opens the curtains to let in the morning light which reveals the squalor. He goes to the stereo and shuts it off. He then realises the phone is ringing. He lifts the receiver.*

SHARKY. Hello? Hello?

He hangs up. As he does so, RICHARD, *his older brother, stirs awake. He has been asleep (passed out) on the floor where we*

*didn't notice him or took him for a bundle of rags. He wears a
black suit, one slipper, an ancient baseball cap and a filthy white
shirt. He is unshaven and looks terrible. He has recently gone
blind. He rises up behind* SHARKY...

RICHARD. Who's that? Sharky?

SHARKY (*startled*). What are you fucking doing?!

RICHARD. What happened?

SHARKY. Nothing – I just turned off the radio. I thought you told me
you'd go up to bed!

RICHARD. Yeah, I meant to, but I'd no one to help me up the stairs!

SHARKY. Where was Ivan?

RICHARD. I don't know! He must've gone home.

SHARKY. I thought you said you could feel your way up!

RICHARD. Ah, Sharky! Not when I'm jarred!

SHARKY (*going to* RICHARD, *picking up a slipper*). For fuck's
sake, Richard...

RICHARD. Ah, don't be at me now, I'm not able for it. What time is
it?

SHARKY. It's half ten.

RICHARD. Oh God, I'm bursting... give us a hand, where's me stick?

SHARKY, *slipper in hand, looks around for* RICHARD's *stick,
while* RICHARD *shakily holds on to the chair, one slipper on, one
slipper off.*

Sharky!

SHARKY. I'm here!

RICHARD. God, it's freezing! Where's me stick?

SHARKY. I don't know! Where did you put it?

RICHARD. If I knew where I put it, I'd have it!

SHARKY. Ah, don't fucking start, I'm looking for it, if you'd've let
me bring you up to bed last night you'd have everything...

RICHARD. Ivan was here! What was I gonna do, leave him sitting in
here on his own?

SHARKY. No, you were too busy drinking your fucking brains out.

SHARKY *goes towards the kitchen.*

RICHARD. Hark at you! Hark at Sharky! That's a good one! 'The hypocrite's voice haunts his own den!'

SHARKY *returns with the stick.*

SHARKY. Here, I have it.

RICHARD. Where was it?

SHARKY. It was outside the jacks door. Where it was yesterday as well.

SHARKY *gives* RICHARD *the stick and crouches to help* RICHARD *get his slipper on.*

RICHARD. Would you give me a hand and bring me through!!

SHARKY. I am! What do you think I'm doing?

SHARKY *lifts* RICHARD'*s foot into his slipper.*

RICHARD. Alright! I'm just asking… Jaysus, who got out of bed on the wrong side this morning?

SHARKY (*helping* RICHARD *towards the passageway*). Good fuck, Richard, you absolutely stink again, do you know that?

RICHARD. Yeah, happy Christmas to you as well!

SHARKY. Would you not let me put you in the bath? I'll give you a nice shave.

RICHARD. I told you! Tomorrow! Christmas morning! What's the point doing it today? I'll only stink the place out for Santy!

SHARKY. Alright! Relax! You have me going deaf in that ear!

SHARKY *opens the toilet door.*

Ah, Richard, who did that all over the floor?

RICHARD. Well, I don't know!

SHARKY. Come on, let me bring you upstairs I'll give you a shave, come on.

RICHARD. I said tomorrow! Would you let me do my toilet please, Sharky? For… Jaysus' sake will you come out of me road?

SHARKY (*off*). I am! Let me just wipe the seat…

RICHARD (*storming in and ejecting* SHARKY). Come out of me road!

The toilet door slams. SHARKY *tidies up a few things, finding a bottle of Powers whiskey under a chair with about a quarter left. He goes to the stove and pokes around in there.*

(*Off.*) Sharky!

SHARKY. What?

RICHARD (*off*). Is there not any jacks roll in here?

SHARKY. I don't know! You're in there!

RICHARD (*off*). Well, there's none on the holder and I can't feel on the floor…

SHARKY. Hold on!

SHARKY *goes into the kitchen and takes a roll of tissue paper to the toilet.*

RICHARD (*off*). Don't come in!

SHARKY. Well, what do you want me to do?

RICHARD (*off*). Just hand me in some!

SHARKY. There's only kitchen roll here, okay?

RICHARD (*off*). Just hand it in to me.

SHARKY. Here…

RICHARD (*off*). Where's your hand?

SHARKY. Here! Here!

SHARKY *slams the toilet door.*

RICHARD (*off*). Don't slam the door!

SHARKY *reappears and begins laying the table for some breakfast, bringing out a bowl of mandarin oranges, and a Kellogg's variety pack of various cereals in small boxes. He goes back into the kitchen.* IVAN *appears at the top of the stairs. He is a big burly man with a red face and curly hair. He wears a shirt tucked into his pants, the back sticking out. He feels his way gingerly down.* SHARKY *comes back with some milk and two bowls.*

IVAN (*sheepishly*). Morning, Sharky.

SHARKY. Ivan! Did you stay over?

IVAN. Yeah, no, I couldn't get a taxi. (*Hands shaking...*) Oh God, I feel terrible.

SHARKY. Have some breakfast.

IVAN. Oh God, I don't know. Let me just... get my bearings for a minute, is that okay?

SHARKY. You don't have to ask me that, Ivan. Sure, do whatever you...

IVAN. Yeah, no, I... can't find my glasses. You didn't see them?

SHARKY (*looking*). Em... Where did you... did you get a good kip?

IVAN. Yeah, yeah... I was dead to the world just then. What was all the shouting?

SHARKY. Ah, that was... (*Signals 'Richard'.*)

IVAN. When did you get back?

SHARKY. I got back three... four days ago.

IVAN. Yeah?

SHARKY. Sure, I was talking to you last night!

IVAN. Were you here last night?

SHARKY. Yeah, I made yous hot whiskeys...

IVAN. Oh yeah...

SHARKY. Do you not remember?

IVAN. No yeah, no, no I do. Just I wasn't even... sure I was only on my way home. I was only calling in to see if your man was alright... I certainly didn't mean to still fucking be here! Jaysus...

SHARKY (*laughs*). Yeah, well... Listen, thanks for all the... calling in on him and... he's... eh...

IVAN. Yeah, yeah, no, no bother. God, I'm gonna be killed...

SHARKY. Are you?

IVAN. No, there's still a few Christmas bits I have to do. God, I'm gonna be killed now.

SHARKY. How is Karen keeping?

IVAN. Don't talk to me.

SHARKY. Yeah?

IVAN. Don't talk to me.

SHARKY. And the kids?

IVAN. Ah, they're great, yeah. They're grand, you know yourself.

SHARKY. Yeah, well that's…

IVAN. Yeah…

Pause.

SHARKY (*calling off*). Are you alright there, Rich?

RICHARD (*off*). What's wrong with ya?

SHARKY. No, I was just seeing if you were alright?

RICHARD (*off*). Would you leave me alone? I'm trying to go to the fucking toilet in here!

SHARKY. I'll just grab the… the tea…

IVAN. Yeah, yeah, work away.

SHARKY *goes into the kitchen.* IVAN *moves through the room a little, throwing his eye around quickly for something to drink. He can't see anything.* SHARKY *comes back with a pot of tea and some cups then he goes to put some briquettes in the stove.*

SHARKY. Here, were yous out the back last night?

IVAN. What? Oh! Yeah… Oh no, it was… [stupid.] Did you hear him?

SHARKY. Ah yeah, I heard him, I heard yous. I rolled over, I tried to just ignore it. Sure that's…

IVAN. Yeah…

SHARKY.…that's a regular…

IVAN. I know, mad!

SHARKY. What was it? The winos out in the lane?

IVAN. Yeah! We were sitting there at the fire and bang! Suddenly he gets up! I'm like, 'What are you doing?' He's like, 'Them winos are out in the lane again! I'm gonna kill them!' he says, waving the fucking… stick around!

SHARKY. I know!

IVAN. Nearly took my fucking head off with it, and out he runs, *off* on out through the back there, it was nearly like he could see! You know?

SHARKY. I know!

IVAN (*rubbing his elbow gingerly*). And I... fucking went over, smack!... on them newspapers all in the back door there, trying to stop him! And then out in the garden or...! I didn't know where I was!

SHARKY. I know. He's a mad bollocks, Ivan.

IVAN. Ah no, he's alright. He's just... (*Beat.*) So, here, did I ask you this last night? How did you get on down in... Where was this you were?

SHARKY. I was down in Lahinch, in County Clare.

IVAN. Yeah?

SHARKY. Yeah, it was, it was, it was... it was great.

IVAN. You got on well?

SHARKY. Yeah, got on great. Down the country is great, you know...

IVAN. Ah, down the country's smashing. Were you on the boats or...?

SHARKY. Nah... Can't get a job on the boats. But the people I was working for were spot on...

IVAN. What were you doing? Chauffeur?

SHARKY. Yeah, I was doing a bit of driving for this developer guy... and his wife there and eh... (*Short pause.*) But I had to get back up because...

He signals 'Richard'. They hear an attempt to flush the toilet.

IVAN. Ah yeah, no, fair play, Sharky. Oh here, Nicky Giblin was telling me, how's the...

They stop to listen to RICHARD's attempts to flush the toilet.

SHARKY (*calling*). Are you alright, Rich?

RICHARD (*off*). Ah, I can't flush this fucking thing!

SHARKY. Do you want me to do it?

RICHARD (*off*). Is that Ivan out there?

SHARKY. He's heard you.

IVAN (*going towards kitchen door*). Are you alright, Richard? Do you not want your brother?

RICHARD (*off*). No, Ivan, you're strong. Come here and give this yoke a yank, will ya?

IVAN goes off to help RICHARD. SHARKY continues to get the breakfast and tidy up while IVAN and RICHARD attend to the toilet.

(*Off.*) That's it – one more like that, Ivan…

IVAN (*off*). Here give us that till I stick it down the… hold on, come away…

The toilet flushes. IVAN leads RICHARD back out.

RICHARD. Well done, Ivan… sorry about that…

SHARKY. Lads, some breakfast.

IVAN (*unable to consider it*). Oh…

RICHARD. What is there?

SHARKY. There's toast, if you want, there's cereal…

RICHARD. What cereal?

SHARKY (*looking at variety pack*). There's Cornflakes, there's Frosties, there's Coco Pops, there's…

RICHARD (*gravely*). Em… Coco Pops…

SHARKY. Okay, and I've mandarin oranges, there's tea, Ivan.

RICHARD. Did you not get coffee?

SHARKY (*pouring out bowl of cereal*). No, I told you, I forgot, I'll get it today.

RICHARD. You know what I'd really like?

SHARKY. What?

RICHARD. Ivan? Irish coffee…

IVAN. Oh now…

RICHARD. Warm us up!

SHARKY. Yeah, well, we don't even have coffee so…

RICHARD. Well, then, we'll just have the Irish and no coffee – ha, Ivan?

SHARKY (*going to kitchen*). I'll put on some toast.

RICHARD. Well, Ivan, how's the head?

IVAN. Don't talk to me, Rich. I can't find my glasses. I'm like you, I'm feeling my way around.

RICHARD. Well, they have to be here somewhere. Did you have them when you got here?

IVAN. I'm assuming I did.

SHARKY *comes back.*

RICHARD (*of* SHARKY). Hey, check out Johnny Weismuller, off the drink for… what is it, Sharky? Two days?

SHARKY. What?

RICHARD. How long are you on the dry now? Two days, is it? I was just telling Ivan. The old delirium tremens must be fairly ramping up now, ha?

SHARKY *ignores him.*

IVAN. Yeah well, fair play. Hey, Shark, I was gonna ask you, how's the nose? Nicky Giblin was telling me.

SHARKY *signals to him not to continue with this line of enquiry.* IVAN *doesn't twig it in time.*

RICHARD. What's this?

IVAN. Did he not tell you?

SHARKY (*signalling to* IVAN *who finally sees him*). No, it was nothing…

RICHARD. Tell me what?

Pause.

What? Tell me what?

IVAN. No… eh… Nicky was… (*Dismissively.*) Ah, you know Nicky…

RICHARD. I know Nicky well! What happened to you, Sharky?

SHARKY. Ah, it was nothing, it was…

RICHARD. What? Ivan?

IVAN. Ah… (*To* SHARKY.) Nicky was saying, I was only asking to see if you were… (*To* RICHARD.) Nicky was saying that Sharky got in a spot of bother there off someone there outside the Elphin and I was just…

RICHARD. When was this?

SHARKY. Ah, it was… it was the other evening… the night I got here.

RICHARD. You kept that very quiet! What happened?

SHARKY. Ah, it was fucking… I got off the Dart at Howth Junction and I was…

RICHARD. What did you get off at Howth Junction for?

SHARKY. Ah, I meant to go to Bayside or Sutton Cross, and I mixed it up and I…

RICHARD. You blew it!

SHARKY. Yeah, well, I was walking all up there, up the coast, and…

RICHARD. Why didn't you get a taxi?

SHARKY. I had no cash!

RICHARD. Go on out of that, you were in the Elphin!

SHARKY. No, I went into the Elphin…

RICHARD (*sarcastically, as though he had failed to see a big distinction*). Oh!

SHARKY. I needed to make a phone call… my phone was…

RICHARD. Go on out of that! You were jarred from the train, you got off at the wrong fucking station…

SHARKY. I fucking…! I had two, three pints… (*To* IVAN.) 'cause young Cathy Wolfe was having her birthday in there and her da bought me one…

RICHARD. Oh… I see…

SHARKY. And then the end of the match was on and…

RICHARD. Ah, of course…

SHARKY. Ah, I'm not gonna fucking tell you if you're...

RICHARD. No, I'm only having you on! What happened?

Pause.

SHARKY. Ah... I was coming out and there was some lads
messing around, sitting on the bonnet of a car out there and...

Pause.

RICHARD. What happened?

SHARKY. Ah, I just said, 'Come up off of that...' as I was kind of
walking by...

RICHARD. What?

SHARKY. Just, only, not even that serious, you know...

RICHARD. You fucking eejit...

SHARKY. And next thing, I'm down at the corner, they're all around
me! And your man is, 'What did you fucking say?' And all this.
And I'm like, 'Ah, lads, I was only...' And then, one of them... he
just gave me this unbelievable kick in the arse, you know? And it
was so... it was so... the humiliation of it, like, and I...

RICHARD. Ah, Sharky...

SHARKY. I turned around and I threw a dig and I was... but there
was loads of them and I got an awful couple of smacks in the...
my nose was pumping, it's alright now, but I had to leg it back into
the Elphin. The fucking... streams of toilet roll I had stuck up my
nose... it was so... The Wolfes put me in a cab, gave your man
twenty euros to drop me up.

Short pause.

RICHARD. Why didn't you say anything? (*Short pause.*) You
fucking eejit!

SHARKY. Yeah, well, I'll get the toast.

SHARKY *goes into the kitchen.*

IVAN. Mmm...

RICHARD. I mean, what can you do with a fella like that?

IVAN. Yeah, it was... they were all... Nicky Giblin was telling me...

RICHARD. Yeah, well, Nicky means well, I'm sure...

Short pause. IVAN *checks to see if* SHARKY *is in earshot.*

IVAN. Does Sharky know that Eileen is with Nicky now?

RICHARD. What? Ah, yeah... no that's... Sure that's... she called into me here about two weeks ago, did I tell you that?

IVAN. Who, Eileen?

RICHARD. Yeah, she was here, she does a morning or two cleaning for the Franciscan monks up there in the Friary. She called in to see if I was... to see how I was. We had smoked cod and chips from the chipper and everything. Ah, it was great, we were talking about (*Re:* SHARKY.) Head-the-ball... and Nicky and... yeah, the whole...

IVAN. Ah, I'm kind of avoiding Nicky, to be honest with you, Dick.

RICHARD. Why?

IVAN. Ah, there's just always some fucking shite going on and I'm...

IVAN *clams up as* SHARKY *returns with some toast.*

SHARKY. Can you see there, Ivan?

IVAN. I can just about...

SHARKY. Would you... [help Richard]?

IVAN. Yeah, yeah, do you want some toast there, Dick?

IVAN *starts to very shakily butter some toast as* SHARKY *nips back into the kitchen to get some for himself.*

RICHARD. I tell you what I'd love. I'd love a big Irish breakfast! A big fry with all white pudding and a runny egg and all...

SHARKY *returns with his own toast and a carton of orange juice.*

Do you hear me, Sharky?

SHARKY. What?

RICHARD. We should be having a nice Christmassy breakfast. We have to get some decent grub in for tomorrow, Sharky, Christmas pud and the works. This is disgraceful!

SHARKY. Yeah, I'm going up now when I get dressed...

RICHARD. How will you go?

SHARKY. Do you have your car with you, Ivan?

Pause. IVAN *looks at him blankly.*

RICHARD. Do you have your car, Ivan?

IVAN. I can't... I don't know.

RICHARD. We'll go in a taxi.

SHARKY. Are you coming as well?

RICHARD. Ah, let me get out for a bit, for Jaysus' sake, Sharky, we might even get a Christmas pint...

SHARKY (*sighing*). Oh... well, wait now because if...

RICHARD. No, because we need to get a few bits in as well, Sharky, from the off-licence, in case anyone calls. We'll get a taxi back, because I want to be settled in here now for Christmas Eve...

SHARKY. Yeah, but wait a minute, because if I have to...

RICHARD (*suddenly despairing*). I have so little left to live for!

Pause.

IVAN (*reassuringly*). Ah now, Richard...

RICHARD. What?! Yous don't know. Yous don't know.

SHARKY. No we'll all... we'll all go... we'll get the few bits and...

IVAN. Sure you'll be grand, you'll have a grand Christmas here with Sharky here, and with you and all, and...

RICHARD (*dismally*). Yeah...

SHARKY. If we're going out... will you have a wash?

RICHARD (*shouting*). I'll have a wash tomorrow!! I told you! Now leave it!

Pause.

IVAN. God, I'll have to find my glasses. Karen'll kill me, God, what am I gonna say?

SHARKY. We'll find them, I'll have a look now in a minute before we go.

IVAN. Thanks, Sharky.

SHARKY. Tea, Rich?

RICHARD (*sheepishly*). Yeah, thanks.

SHARKY *brings him a cup of tea.*

I just don't want to be cooped up all over the...

SHARKY. Yeah, I know, we'll get out, we'll get you some fresh air.

RICHARD. Yeah...

IVAN. Hey, any sign of your money there yet, Sharky? From the bus people?

SHARKY. What? Aw... Well, the...

RICHARD. Get this!

SHARKY. Well, no, because the solicitor fucking... he misdated the statement I gave him. About the... the actual night I fell down the stairs...

IVAN. What, the bus went round the wrong corner, or a different corner or something, was it?

SHARKY. Yeah, he went around the wrong corner up there at Christchurch there, he went around too early, and I was getting up to get off... but that's... no one is disputing that, but the date, you see, on the... affidavit, it's the wrong date and...

IVAN. Can you not just...?

SHARKY. Nah, the courts are...

RICHARD. He put the wrong year on it!

SHARKY. The whole thing has been put right back now, I don't even know if...

IVAN. But can he not just change the...

RICHARD. It's a shambles...

IVAN. ...the year...

SHARKY. No...

IVAN. ...if it was just a mistake...

RICHARD. Ivan, the law... the law is the law. It has to be.

IVAN. Yeah...

SHARKY. So now I have to look at...

IVAN. Yeah, if you keep going with it…

SHARKY. No, if I want to start the whole thing off again…

IVAN. What?

RICHARD. Yeah. Seven-and-a-half years he's been…

SHARKY. Ah, it doesn't matter, it's too…

IVAN. Jaysus, that's a pain in the bollocks, isn't it?

SHARKY. Ah it's…

Waving it away.

IVAN. 'Cause I'd say you could've done with the few bob…

SHARKY. Yeah well…

IVAN. Nightmare…

RICHARD. Of course, he was using your man, that solicitor out of Kilbarrack.

SHARKY. Yeah, alright, Rich…

IVAN. That drinks in *The Fox & Hound*?!

RICHARD. Yeah, your man that does be falling around the car park!

SHARKY. Ah no, see it was him that…

RICHARD (*shaking his head*). Sharky…

SHARKY. I was never even gonna take a case! It was him that… I mean…

RICHARD. What a shambles…

SHARKY. Yeah, well…

IVAN. Aw well, I'm sorry to hear that, Shark. I only saw your man the other week there actually, and the Baker, and Steady Eddie and all them lads were down in Grainger's, do you know what they were talking about? Do you remember Maurice Macken?

RICHARD. That used drive the milk lorry?

IVAN. Yeah, and then he got into the electrical trade. Do you remember him, Sharky?

SHARKY. The skinny fella?

IVAN. Yeah, Maurice Macken used play a lot of cards all up around Sutton and Howth, you heard what happened him?

RICHARD. Oh yeah, I heard all about that.

SHARKY. Was this in the paper?

IVAN. Yeah it was all in the paper, you would've seen it. He was electrocuted up in a house where he was working in Santry. There was a tremendous bang! Blew him right across the room, I believe. One of his fillings ended up in his ear. Somehow he survived. They let him go home out of Beaumont Hospital, and then there was a fire in his house that night! And he was gone!

RICHARD. Gobshite…

SHARKY. Jaysus, that's mad.

IVAN. His number was up! His number was just up and he was going to have to go, one way or the other, you know what I mean, mad! Survived the electrocution only to be burned!

RICHARD. Fucking eejit…

IVAN. But listen, what the lads were saying up in Grainger's – two people, two different people, now, have seen him hanging around at the off-licence serving hatch round the side near the car park.

RICHARD (*incredulously*). Come on!

IVAN. Two different people saw him, Dick, on different nights. And apparently a barman tidying up after they were closed said he heard someone shouting in the jacks – and when he went in, there was no one there.

RICHARD. That's bollocks.

IVAN. Yeah, well, apparently he looks really white. He was standing near the hatch. Big Bernard's cousin saw him. Apparently he was just standing there looking out into the car park, like he was waiting on a lift or something.

RICHARD. Go on out of that! What's he waiting on? A few cans?

He laughs.

IVAN (*to* SHARKY). Spooky though, isn't it?

SHARKY. Yeah, well…

RICHARD (*mildly derisive*). Yeah, right…

Suddenly there are three loud bangs at the front door upstairs.
RICHARD *jumps with fright.*

Fucking hell! Who's that?

SHARKY (*going up the stairs*). Probably the postman…

RICHARD. We have a letter box! For the love of God…

Short pause.

IVAN (*sighing*). Yeah…

RICHARD. Ivan, quick, where did he put that Gold Label?

IVAN (*quickly squinting around*). I can't fucking see, Dick…

RICHARD. Have a look in the kitchen, go on, quick.

IVAN *strides purposefully towards the kitchen.*

On top of the fridge or in the press with the pots…

IVAN *disappears into the kitchen and returns quickly with the
bottle* SHARKY *put away earlier, unscrewing the lid…*

IVAN. Here, Rich, give us your cup.

RICHARD (*offering his cup of tea to* IVAN). Pour that out.

IVAN *takes* RICHARD's *cup and wildly looks for somewhere to
pour it out, deciding eventually to pour it on to the carpet nearby,
bending low so as not to make a splashing sound, he then rubs the
steaming carpet with his foot and pours a big dollop of whiskey
into* RICHARD's *cup, handing it to him.* RICHARD *raises it to
his mouth immediately.* IVAN *goes to the table to look for a cup
for himself, swigging a mouthful of whiskey from the neck of the
bottle as he does so.*

He grabs a mug and pours some whiskey, wheeling around to give
RICHARD *another shot, as* RICHARD *instinctively holds his cup
out for it. Both men are retching and making faces as though their
throats are burning. Their arms and legs undergo a rudimentary
stretch as they seem to come alive.* IVAN *pours some tea on top of
the whiskey in his cup and conceals the bottle while* SHARKY
*appears at the top of the stairs, descending with a tastefully gift-
wrapped box.*

(*Brightly.*) What was it, Shark?

SHARKY. Postman.

IVAN. Look at that!

RICHARD. What is it?

SHARKY. It's a… it's a present…

RICHARD. For who?

SHARKY. For me.

RICHARD. Who's it from?

SHARKY. Ah, the, the people I was working for down in Clare… His wife, Miriam, she's very… you know… (*To* IVAN.) She's a very nice lady, she's eh…

RICHARD. Woooooooooo! (*Childishly.*) The big birthday present!

SHARKY. It's a Christmas present, you dozy fucking eejit.

RICHARD. Oh! (*Same tone.*) A Christmas present! Anything good?

SHARKY (*handing* RICHARD *an envelope*). Here, there's a card here for you.

RICHARD. Who's it from?

SHARKY. The Department of Social Welfare.

RICHARD (*throwing it away*). Ah, that's only my balls!

SHARKY *opens the card that came with his present and stands there reading it.* IVAN *slurps his tea…*

Well? What is it?

SHARKY *looks at him as though coming out of a daze…*

SHARKY. What?

IVAN. Are you gonna open it up?

RICHARD. Yes! Cheer us all up! Presents arriving for Sharky! I mean, what next?

SHARKY *takes the wrapping off…*

What is it?

SHARKY. It's a few CDs.

IVAN. Nice one!

RICHARD (*childishly*). Wooooooo, music to put you in the mood…!
  For getting in your nude…!

IVAN. Hey, she knows her stuff! Some of these are classics! Here,
  put one on!

RICHARD. No! Later! We have to go and get the few bits for the
  Christmas! Come on…

IVAN. I have to find my glasses!

RICHARD. Sharky'll look for them. Sharky, have a quick look for
  Ivan's specs, will you?

SHARKY. Where would they be, Ivan? Where did you sleep?

IVAN. Eh, in the box room.

SHARKY. There's no bed in there!

IVAN. I slept on the rug.

SHARKY. The rug?

RICHARD. Ah, Ivan…

IVAN. Ah, no, there was towels, and there was…

SHARKY. I'll have a quick look. (*Going off up the stairs.*) You
  should've slept in the spare room…

IVAN. Ah no, I was grand I was fine…

RICHARD. Did you just sleep on the floor? Like an animal?

IVAN. No, I slept on the rug.

RICHARD. Ah, I don't even know what you're talking about. Give
  us a hand, Ivan, will you?

IVAN (*helping* RICHARD *up*). I thought Sharky was in the spare
  room.

RICHARD. I often just go off here at the fire. (*Coughs up some
  deeply embedded old phlegm and rubs it into the side of his
  armchair.*) You should have got into my bed.

IVAN. Nah, I wouldn't do that, Dick. Here, do you want your shoes?

RICHARD. Ah, sure we'll get a taxi, my slippers is grand. I don't
  expect we'll be walking the street like hobos. Just get us my
  anorak hanging up there behind the kitchen door.

IVAN *goes to the kitchen.* RICHARD *feels around for his cup.* IVAN *brings the anorak and starts looking for his own coat.*

Is that Gold Label dead? We have to make a list. We have nothing organised. That's your man, of course. He was supposed to get up to me weeks ago. His head is arseways. You're seeing him on the dry now, that's why he's running around in here like a fly in a bottle.

IVAN *finds his own coat which he puts on and goes to retrieve the bottle from whatever nook he hid it in. There is only a swig left in it.*

But of course then with jar on him he's worse! Throwing digs outside the Elphin! Or getting in mills outside the chipper on Kilbarrack Road the last time he was here! Getting arrested by the Guards up in Howth! I mean what am I going to do?

As IVAN *drains the last shot of whiskey straight from the bottle…*

Here, is there a shot left in that Powers, Ivan?

IVAN. Nah, we've had it. Here do you want your anorak, Dick?

RICHARD (*sighing heavily*). Yeah…

IVAN *helps* RICHARD *to put his coat on.*

Here, if you're gonna be round tomorrow, you should drop in, do you know what I have that I've been saving? A drop of Brigid Blake's poitín, that Big Bernard got me…

IVAN. Oh, look out!

RICHARD. That'll fucking…

He makes a high-pitched whistle, pointing to his head. IVAN *laughs.* SHARKY *descends. He has got dressed and wears his coat.*

SHARKY. Ivan, I can't see your glasses anywhere.

RICHARD. Ah, they have to be somewhere, Sharky!

SHARKY. Do you not have a spare pair at home'll do you till…?

IVAN. Yeah, I think I… they're an older prescription, if I can find them… Oh God, Karen is gonna kill me.

RICHARD. No, no she won't! I'll ring her, I'll say I had them here, it'll be grand. Sharky, get a pen, we need to make a list. Ivan, I expect we'll be seeing you over the Christmas, I'll be very disappointed if we didn't, so Sharky, Harp, what, four six-packs?

SHARKY (*grabbing a pen*). Yeah, Harp…

IVAN. Ah, don't just do that for me, Rich. Sharky, I'll drink whatever's going.

RICHARD (*pointing imperiously*). No. Sharky.

SHARKY (*writing*). Yeah, Harp. Stout, Richard?

RICHARD. Yeah and Paddy Powers. Get three bottles.

SHARKY. Three bottles? The off-licence is open again on Monday, Rich.

RICHARD. If we have visitors they may want a hot whiskey. It's called being festive. I know you may not comprehend it, Sharky, but some us like to be social. Ivan, Christmas? You have to!

IVAN. Ah, Christmas is great!

RICHARD. And Miller for Nicky.

SHARKY. For Nicky Giblin?

RICHARD. Nicky drinks Miller, Sharky. We all understand that you have issues with life and it's an endless struggle for you to grasp human relationships, but Nicky is a friend of mine. And a friend of Ivan's… and…

IVAN. Ah, he can be very messy, Richard.

RICHARD (*with finality*). The man is welcome here!

SHARKY (*writing*). Bottles of Miller.

RICHARD. Thank you.

SHARKY. What'll I get for tomorrow? A chicken?

RICHARD. Turkey! Turkey!

SHARKY. We won't get a turkey now at this stage, Rich…

IVAN. Karen is doing us a big turkey tomorrow, I could drop down with maybe a few…

RICHARD. No, no, Ivan, we couldn't do that to you, we'll get a turkey, don't worry about it…

SHARKY (*sucking his pen*). I mean we might be able to get a piece of em…

RICHARD. Look! Let's go!

SHARKY. Do you not want to make a list?

RICHARD. Yeah, yeah, we'll get all that when we're there. We'll see all that. Ivan, will you take me out the back way and we'll hail a taxi on the road, I want to check them awful fucking winos haven't been messing around at our laneway door.

IVAN is leading RICHARD out towards the yard.

Will you lock up, Sharky?

SHARKY. Yeah.

RICHARD. We'll see you out on the road. (*As they go.*) All the kids' presents got then, Ivan?

IVAN. Ah, yeah… I think they are.

RICHARD. Well, I hope so, says you!

As they leave through the back door, SHARKY folds up the list and puts it in his pocket. He takes out his keys and goes to lock the back door. He comes back into the silence and picks up the card he received. He looks at it for a moment, then briskly puts it in his pocket and leaves, running up the stairs.

We hear the wind and perhaps music plays as the lights slowly change from bright morning to a dusky feel and we slide into:

Scene Two

The wind is picking up outside as the sunlight fades and the temperature drops. The music dies away as SHARKY comes down the stairs with bags of shopping, mostly from the off-licence, which he takes into the kitchen. A church bell chimes solemnly somewhere off in the distance. He reappears, switches on a lamp or two, bends down under the scraggy old Christmas tree and plugs in some coloured fairy lights. He sees two little presents wrapped up there. He picks one up and looks at it for a moment, wondering about it before he puts it back. He goes back up the stairs, pausing to tap the extinguished light under the Sacred Heart. It doesn't come on and he continues up to the hall to get the rest of the shopping and reappears, carrying more bags. As he descends we hear RICHARD calling from off, up in the hallway.

RICHARD (*off*). What are you fucking doing?

SHARKY (*halting and turning*). What?

RICHARD (*off*). What, were you gonna just leave me up here?

SHARKY. I thought you could manage your way down!

RICHARD (*off*). Ah, not when I'm jarred, Sharky!

SHARKY. Just give me a second.

> SHARKY *carries the bags down, leaving them at the bottom of the stairs, and makes his way back up.*

RICHARD (*off*). I'm freezing!

> SHARKY *reappears, helping* RICHARD *down.*

You are in one foul humour today…

SHARKY. Richard, now, please don't start…

RICHARD (*warmly, paternally*). What's the matter with you?

SHARKY. Richard…

RICHARD. What…

SHARKY. Nothing's the matter with me.

> RICHARD *stands in the room rubbing his hands.* SHARKY *starts clearing a few things away, taking the breakfast things on a tray into the kitchen.*

RICHARD. God, it's freezing! Would you get the fire going for the love of Jaysus, Shark?

SHARKY. I am! I'm doing it! I've a million things to do here, just give me a second, would you?

RICHARD (*as though* SHARKY *has completely overreacted*). Okay! Okay!

> SHARKY *returns, goes to the stove, puts some peat briquettes in and sets about lighting it.*

God, I never seen such a Christmas wrecker! Would you not have left the old Kaliber out for today and had a drink with me and Ivan… and…

SHARKY (*working at the stove*). I'm pissed *off* with you, Richard.

RICHARD. With me? Why? What did I do now?

SHARKY. What did you have to go and invite Nicky Giblin up here for?

RICHARD. When?

SHARKY. When Big Bernard let you speak to him on his mobile.

RICHARD. Ah, that was only a happy Christmas, Jimmy, come on...

SHARKY. You told him to call in to us...

RICHARD. But sure, that's what you say! That's what everybody says!

SHARKY. You told him to call in to play cards!

RICHARD. That's... that's just what you say! Anyway – so what?! Would you stop being such a curmudgeonly old bollocks your whole life, will you?

Pause. SHARKY *works...*

(*Warmly, drunkenly conciliatory.*) Ah, Sharky... I only said to stick the head in if he was in the area...

SHARKY. You don't fucking say that to fellas like Nicky, Dick. He'll be in on top of us before you know it!

RICHARD. No he won't! He was elephants! He was down in the Brookwood Inn of all places! How the hell is he gonna rock up here? In a taxi? I don't think so! Hey, is there 'ere a Christmas drink going a-begging around here?

SHARKY. Yeah, well, I saw him the other day, and he was driving my car, Richard.

RICHARD. Who?

SHARKY. Nicky Giblin!

RICHARD. Yeah, well, you gave your car to Eileen!

SHARKY. I loaned it to her for the school run, Dick. I didn't ever expect to see that fucker driving around in it! I saw him pulling out of the shops down there in Bayside, and I was walking down to get the Dart in the pissing rain! And he was in my car!

RICHARD. Ah, grow up, Sharky! What do you want? Him and Eileen are together now, so get over it, 'cause that's life, okay?

Now would you ever give us a Jaysus fucking drink, you're gonna blow the whole Christmas atmosphere. This is all I have! And how many do I have left? Maybe only this one! Maybe that's it for me!

SHARKY. What are you talking about?

RICHARD. Ah! It's hardly even worth it!... What's the point?

RICHARD *turns away in disgust.* SHARKY *takes the rest of the shopping into the kitchen.* RICHARD *opens his coat and makes his way unsteadily towards his armchair and sits forlornly.* SHARKY *re-emerges with a glass of whiskey for him.*

SHARKY. Here... Richard...

RICHARD. What?

SHARKY (*putting the drink in* RICHARD*'s hand*). Here...

RICHARD. Ah, thanks, Sharky.

SHARKY *takes a festive-looking candle in a red glass holder from a bag. He is tearing the price and the cellophane wrapping off and bringing it to the windowsill.*

What's that?

SHARKY. Hmm?

RICHARD. What are you doing, there?

SHARKY. Ah, I'm just gonna put an old candle in the window.

RICHARD. Ah, that's nice. That's more like it, Sharky. I never like it when you're down. It changes the whole...

SHARKY. Would you like some smoked salmon and brown bread?

RICHARD. Oh, now, that sounds... Ah, thanks, Sharky... thanks. Delicious!

SHARKY. Keep us going anyway... Is that getting warm?

RICHARD. Oh, we're warming up now...

SHARKY *goes towards the kitchen.*

Oh, Sharky. Just one... just one small thing, quickly, before you do that.

SHARKY. Yeah?

RICHARD. You wouldn't take a basin of hot water down out to the back door at the lane…? Them filthy fucking winos have all puke and piss and everything else all down our step all up the fucking door out there…

SHARKY (*face dropping*). Are you serious?

RICHARD. Ah, it's absolutely disgusting. We can't leave it like that on Christmas Eve… It'll only take you a minute… Good man…

SHARKY goes unhappily to the kitchen to boil the kettle. RICHARD cosily raises his shoulders as though he is snuggling down into a lovely warm bed.

Now, this is nice now. It's getting nice and Christmassy now…

There is a loud rapping at the front door upstairs. RICHARD turns to profile. SHARKY steps back into the room…

Sharky!

SHARKY. I hear it.

RICHARD. Well, get it, will you!

SHARKY. I'm not gonna get it, I told you I don't want Nicky Giblin in here, I just don't want it.

RICHARD. What!?

There are more loud raps at the door…

SHARKY. I told you, Richard! Why do you have to do this to me?

RICHARD. What are you talking about? I'm not doing anything to you. Don't be a fucking child, will you, and get the door, for God's sake…

SHARKY just stands there looking at RICHARD. RICHARD suddenly bursts up out of his chair…

I'll get it myself!

With surprising speed, RICHARD darts towards the staircase. He hits the wall, collapses, bounces up again, grabs the banister and attempts to pull himself up the stairs…

SHARKY. Richard! Hold on, will you?

SHARKY runs across and grabs RICHARD. RICHARD stumbles and falls backwards into SHARKY's arms, the two of them sinking to the ground as the doorbell rings.

RICHARD. What are you fucking doing?!

SHARKY. What are you fucking doing? Come back over here and sit down, will you?

SHARKY *bundles* RICHARD *towards his chair...*

For fuck's sake...

RICHARD. Will you get the door?

SHARKY. Yeah, will you just sit down please?

SHARKY *storms angrily off up the stairs.* RICHARD *gets up and feels around for his glass which has fallen somewhere... We hear* SHARKY*'s voice off upstairs...*

(*Off.*) No, no, it's no problem! Don't be silly... come on, come on down to Richard.

IVAN (*off*). I'm sorry, Sharky.

SHARKY *leads* IVAN *down.*

I'm sorry, Richard, I'm sorry to...

RICHARD. Who is it? Ivan?

IVAN. Richard, I'm sorry, I'm barging in on you again... I'm sorry, Sharky...

SHARKY. No...

RICHARD. What's the matter with you?

IVAN. Karen's after completely doing her nut.

RICHARD. What? Why?

IVAN. Ah, even if I... I should've just gone straight home it might have been different. But after you left and I was gonna head, I was just standing outside Doyle's with Big Bernard having a smoke, she was coming out of the post office and I didn't have my glasses and I didn't see her and...

RICHARD. Did you not get your spare glasses?

IVAN. I didn't even get in the house, Dick! She fucking reefed me out of it! (*His face crumples in pain.*) The kids were there and... (*A sudden impassioned plea.*) I only went in to have that quick one with yous! I was on my way home! Yous know that! But sure then there was people buying me Christmas pints left and right – I couldn't even see who they were to say to say no! (*Sinks into a chair.*) This is a disaster!

RICHARD. Ah now, come on, Ivan…

IVAN. I hate it when the kids see us fighting and…

RICHARD. These things happen.

IVAN. Now I'm after ruining Christmas on them all – (*Beat.*) again!

RICHARD. No, you haven't! She'll calm down… Just take it easy… Sharky, where's your manners? Will you get poor Ivan something to drink?

SHARKY. I'll tell you what. I've a nice bit of smoked salmon we were gonna have, and there's little mince pies I was gonna heat up. Will you have one, Ivan?

IVAN (*rubbing his face*). Oh, I don't know…

SHARKY. Ah, it'll do you good, Ivan…

IVAN. I suppose… thanks, Sharky.

RICHARD. Yeah, great, and get him a drink, will you, Sharky? Good man.

SHARKY *goes to the kitchen.*

Now, not to worry, Ivan. The woman is being completely unreasonable, she'll come round, just you watch. And we'll be nice and cosy here now and we'll figure it out…

SHARKY *returns with some glasses, a can of Harp for* IVAN, *and a bottle of whiskey for* RICHARD.

Sharky. (*A little laugh.*) Excuse me, I lost my drink in the… in the confusion there…

SHARKY. I have one here for you.

RICHARD. Ah, thanks. Hey, I know! Sharky'll go back up with you, Ivan.

SHARKY *impotently shoots a look at* RICHARD.

Sharky, you'll explain! His glasses have to be here somewhere! And we can…

IVAN. Oh, I don't know, I wouldn't go up there now at the moment, Sharky. She absolutely now… she fucking reefed me out of it. There was people all standing there looking at us… even Bernard just went back in. It was awful. The kids were there…

RICHARD. No, no, we'll let her cool down, absolutely…

SHARKY *gives* IVAN *a glass of beer.*

IVAN. Thanks, Sharky.

RICHARD. Yeah, and get the mince pies, we'll get nice and Christmassy here now.

SHARKY. Yeah, I've the oven heating up.

RICHARD. Oh and listen, don't forget to wash that auld step and the door in the lane, will you?

SHARKY. Yeah, I'll do it…

RICHARD. Good man, Sharky.

SHARKY *goes.*

(*Raising his glass, brightly.*) Now! Happy Christmas!

IVAN. Yeah… happy Christmas…

RICHARD. Sure here we are, aren't we? Ha? We're having a nice Christmas drink. And we'll let the whole… Ivan, are you listening to me?

IVAN. Yeah. No, I am…

RICHARD. The whole situation will… (*Signals 'Settle down'.*) And we'll talk to her and… And we'll all be right as dodgers. Do you hear me?

IVAN. Yeah, I'm sorry, Richard.

RICHARD. No, no, no, no, no, no, no… Come on! When I used clean windows all up along, all up the coast all up into Sutton, I saw every conceivable kind of men and women all shacked up in myriad… (*With sudden force.*) myriad, states of confusion and banjaxed relationships. Believe me, she'd have been rid of you long ago at this stage if your marriage wasn't strong enough to weather a tiny little bump every now and again… (*Laughs.*) It's Christmas Eve! Ivan. Ivan…

IVAN *just looks up silently into* RICHARD*'s blind eyes. The doorbell rings, a loud cutting sound.* IVAN *looks up and then back at* RICHARD. *Pause.*

(*Calling.*) SHARKY! (*Pause.*) Ah, he's out the back. You wouldn't go up and answer that for us, would you, Ivan?

IVAN. Yeah, no…

He shoots his drink back and goes up the stairs.

RICHARD. Ah thanks, good man. (*Starts to sing tunelessly.*) 'Oh the weather outside is frightening, it's dark and there's thunder and lightning…'

He suddenly hunches and shudders, holding his shoulders as though someone has walked over his grave. We hear voices off and then see NICKY*'s legs descending. It is completely dark outside by now.*

NICKY (*off*). Oh yeah, yeah, yeah, yeah, yeah, no, yeah! (*In Irish.*) 'Is mise le meas, Sean Lemass!' (*Laughs.*) Did you see all the Christmas lights all up the… Aw no, no, no, no, no, no… We won't stay long if he's… Come down, Mr Lockhart!

NICKY *descends into the room followed by* IVAN *and* LOCKHART.

RICHARD (*rising*). Nicky!

NICKY. Happy Christmas! Happy Christmas! Happy Christmas!

NICKY GIBLIN *has a skinny, nervy appearance. He rarely seems in bad humour. He is about* SHARKY*'s age or maybe younger. He wears a tatty-looking anorak and threadbare grey slacks that are slightly too short for him, revealing white towelling sport socks in low-cut, dark, wine-coloured slip-on shoes.* LOCKHART *is a man in his fifties perhaps. He is well dressed with a camel-hair Crombie overcoat, a silk scarf, a fine trilby hat and an expensive-looking suit. He looks like a wealthy businessman and bon viveur. Both he and* NICKY *glow warmly with festive indulgence.*

RICHARD. And a happy Christmas to you, Nicky!

They embrace fondly. NICKY *produces a gift-wrapped bottle of whiskey from his anorak pocket.*

NICKY. And I brought you just a little…

RICHARD (*mildly remonstrating*). Ah, Nicky…

NICKY (*dismissive*). Ah, go on, would you? Sure where you would you be without the old Christmas, and I was just saying to… Sorry, this is… Richard, this is Mr Lockhart.

RICHARD. Mr Lockhart! Pleased to meet you. Season's greetings!

LOCKHART. And to you too, Mr Harkin. I hope you don't mind us crashing in on you here now…

RICHARD. What are you talking about? Not at all! Not at all! Of course not! Will you have a drop of… Nicky! We have Miller! Ivan, will you get a glass there for… I got Miller in especially for you, Nicky. Ivan, it's in the… it's probably in the kitchen there. Ask Sharky, will you?

NICKY. Is Sharky here?

RICHARD. Mr Lockhart? Will you have a drop? Is this what I think it is? Or a drop of stout or…

LOCKHART. I'll take a small Irish whiskey if you have it, Mr Harkin.

NICKY. And you do have it! Right there!

RICHARD. Ah, Nicky… And Mr Lockhart, please, call me Richard… Ivan, here will you…

He holds the bottle out.

IVAN. Ha?

RICHARD. Will you take this and… (*Thinks better of it.*) or actually, just bring me a glass for Mr Lockhart, and a bottle of Miller for Nicky out of the fridge there, or it should be… just ask Sharky. Please excuse me, Mr Lockhart. Unfortunately my sight is… I fell into a skip and I…

I have no sight.

IVAN goes to the kitchen.

LOCKHART. God help you.

RICHARD. And this is my, this is my first Christmas here in the dark, so to speak… so it's eh…

LOCKHART. Yes. But let me say, you have a fine holy glow off you, all the same.

RICHARD. I say me prayers!

LOCKHART. I can see it.

NICKY. And the old mind burns brightly, Richard, ha?

RICHARD. Ah, well, I don't know…

NICKY. No, no! To me, here now, sure you seem absolutely no different at all.

RICHARD. Ah, Nicky…

NICKY. No, it's true! So you got out for a Christmas drink?

RICHARD. Yes! We were down in Doyle's. Ivan was there and Big Bernard and Steady Eddie and the bouncy-castle fella was singing hymns and, ah, it was brilliant…

IVAN *returns with a drink for* NICKY, *a glass for* LOCKHART *and a glass for himself. The glasses are somewhat mixed and unsuitable but usable, e.g. perhaps he is using a little jug for himself…*

NICKY (*to* IVAN). Is Sharky here?

IVAN. I think he's out in the…

RICHARD. Ah, don't mind him, he's off the drink – for Christmas! – and he has all our heads wrecked. So tell us, where were you? (*Proffering bottle.*) Here, Mr Lockhart!

NICKY *takes the bottle from* RICHARD *to pour a drink for* LOCKHART.

NICKY. Where weren't we? Is the question! Good God – we've been… Well, what happened was, I'd a few bits to do with Eileen down in Killester, so she went off and I went into the Beachcomber – fucking nobody in it! (*To* LOCKHART.) What time was that at?

LOCKHART. About twelve?

NICKY. Twelve o'clock, nobody in there. I think, 'Right, I'll just have a quick pint and head on…' But then I see Mr Lockhart is sitting up at the bar, who I know from up in the Marine… Mr Lockhart, you'd do a lot of your drinking up in the Marine Hotel…

LOCKHART. I've been known to frequent the premises…

They all laugh.

NICKY. And we know each other from me calling up there to see my brother Eric… so we have a pint, but there was no atmosphere, so fuck it, we left – up to the Yacht.

LOCKHART. No, Harry Byrne's.

NICKY. Sorry no, Harry Byrne's…

RICHARD. Oh, very posh!

NICKY (*pouring drinks for* LOCKHART, RICHARD *and* IVAN). Oh yeah, they had the fires lit and then we were in the Yacht… which was hopping.

RICHARD. Jaysus, yous were getting around!

NICKY. That was only the start of it! The Yacht, the Dollymount House…

LOCKHART. The Raheny Inn…

NICKY. The Raheny Inn, the Green Dolphin, the Station House, the Cedars, the Elphin – your man – (*Indicating* LOCKHART.) won't let me put my hand in my pocket – this is taxis everywhere now!

RICHARD. Very wise… God yous were…

NICKY. Then back all the way up to Edenmore, Eugene's, the Concorde… the bleeding Brookwood Inn! (*Laughs.*) And then up here.

RICHARD. My God, that's a right Christmas drink, Nicky!

NICKY. Yeah well, Mr Lockhart had to say happy Christmas to a few people… (*Suddenly to* LOCKHART.) We never tracked them down!

LOCKHART. And I'm glad we didn't! Because we would never have made it up here! Anyway, as soon as a sing-along starts, I'm out of a place, that's just the way I am… But we're here now, and that's it!

RICHARD. Well, I'm glad you're here!

LOCKHART. Yes, and we'll say happy Christmas – (*Raises his glass in a toast.*) and we'll have a toast…

NICKY (*raising glass*). Yes.

IVAN *has just taken a big gulp of whiskey. His glass is empty, so he spits the whiskey back into the glass for the toast…*

LOCKHART. To old friends and old times!

RICHARD. And new friends!

NICKY. Exactly! Cheers!

RICHARD. Happy Christmas!

NICKY. Happy Christmas!

They all drink deeply.

(Taking the bottle to give refills.) So where's Sharky? God, I haven't seen him in ages...

RICHARD. Ivan, get Sharky there, will you?

IVAN. Yeah, I'll...

He goes out through the kitchen.

RICHARD. There's a good man.

NICKY. How is he doing? Alright?

RICHARD. Ah, Nicky, sure you know yourself. This is my brother, Mr Lockhart. He claims he's here to look after me, but between ourselves, he's an awful useless fucking eejit, God love him. I don't know who's looking after who!

NICKY. Sure you'd be well able to look after yourself, Dick...

RICHARD. This is it. If they can get me one of those dogs that bring you your meals... or even someone just to do a tiny bit of shopping. Sure all I really need is the bit of company really.

NICKY. Well, I knew you'd up for a bit of companionship and when I mentioned to Mr Lockhart that there might be an old game of cards on the horizon, he was very, eh...

LOCKHART. Well, there's nothing like a game of cards at Christmas.

RICHARD. You're so right! And you're welcome, Mr Lockhart. We're only amateurs now you understand.

NICKY. Go on out of that! You'll have to watch yourself, Mr Lockhart, you'll be fleeced for Christmas!

RICHARD. Yeah, right!

LOCKHART. No fear! I'm not a big gambler myself necessarily. To be honest with you I just like the social... ness and the crack.

RICHARD. Well, this is it! There's no big gamblers here, Mr Lockhart. Why can't a game of cards be just for fun? You know what I mean?

SHARKY and IVAN appear from the kitchen. SHARKY is wearing an apron and rubber gloves and carrying a filthy cloth. Pause.

NICKY. Ah, there you are, Sharky! Happy Christmas!

NICKY goes to him to shake hands. SHARKY removes a glove to shake his hand dutifully.

SHARKY. Yeah, happy Christmas, Nicky.

NICKY. Eileen sends her regards. We hope you'll pop in over the…

SHARKY. Yeah, sure…

NICKY. This is Mr Lockhart.

LOCKHART. Sharky. A pleasure.

SHARKY. How do you do.

As they shake hands, SHARKY is wondering where he knows LOCKHART from.

NICKY. Mr Lockhart said he'd pop in to help us make up the old numbers for a game of cards…

LOCKHART. I hope you don't mind, Sharky…

SHARKY. No. I just didn't know we were playing cards.

NICKY. Ah, it's a tradition, Sharky! Ivan, you'll play…

IVAN. Well, yeah, I'll… No, I've no… I've no money on me 'cause…

RICHARD. Don't worry about that, Ivan. Of course he'll play, we'll all play!

SHARKY (*to RICHARD*). How will you read your cards?

RICHARD. Ivan and me'll play together! Ivan, you can read our cards and I'll bankroll us. How does that sound?

IVAN. Yeah, that's… that'd suit me…

RICHARD. And we'll split our takings fifty-fifty. Sure, I'm probably gonna have to bankroll Sharky anyway!

NICKY. Ivan'll be the eyes and Richard'll be the ears!

RICHARD. And the brains!

LOCKHART. Now, you're sure I'm not barging in on your…

RICHARD. Not at all! Not at all! You're welcome. We'll take all of Nicky's money. Do you have any collateral, Nicky?

NICKY. Always. Feel that.

He holds out his arm for RICHARD.

RICHARD. Feel what?

NICKY. You feel that fabric?

RICHARD *feels the arm of* NICKY*'s anorak.*

RICHARD. Oh, nice!

NICKY. This is a Versace jacket.

RICHARD. Yes…

IVAN. Is it?

NICKY (*to* IVAN). Feel that.

RICHARD. It's nice…

NICKY. You feel that? It's dog's skin.

IVAN. What?

NICKY (*laughing*). No, it's not dog's skin. It's called dog's skin. It's German. Right, Mr Lockhart?

LOCKHART. Yup.

RICHARD. It's nice, Nicky.

IVAN (*incredulous*). That's a Versace jacket?

NICKY (*defensively*). Yeah… Well… no, like it needs a wash for Christmas, only 'cause I wear it all the time, but it's eh… yeah, you know?

RICHARD. You might tell Sharky where he'd get a nice jacket like that, Nicky.

NICKY. Jacket like this? Two, three grand, Richard.

IVAN. What?!

NICKY. Oh, big time! Oh here, Ivan, are you still driving that old orange Ford Fiesta?

IVAN. Yeah…

NICKY. 'Cause didn't we see, Mr Lockhart? There was a load of old winos out there sitting on it, you don't want that.

IVAN. What? Is my car here?

NICKY. Yeah. (*To* LOCKHART.) Didn't I point it out to you? And I fucking said it...

LOCKHART. Yeah, it's parked up around the other side of the green out there sort of half up on the path on the corner.

RICHARD (*springing into action*). Them fucking winos!! Come on, we can go out this way! Ivan, give me a hand. Show us where, Nicky.

SHARKY. Richard!

RICHARD *goes towards the kitchen, taking hold of* IVAN'*s arm.*

RICHARD. We won't be long, Mr Lockhart. The winos are always scared of me. Drinking that old meths always has them nervy, you see. Sharky, you look after Mr Lockhart. Come on! We'll have them gone out of it now, lickity spit.

NICKY. We're not gonna be getting in a fight, are we?

RICHARD. No, no, they'll run off immediately. We'll be back in a minute. Come on, Ivan! Nicky, hit that light out there for yourselves.

NICKY. Yeah, I got it.

NICKY *hits a switch as* IVAN *opens the back door and leads* RICHARD *out, followed by* NICKY. SHARKY *and* LOCKHART *are alone.* SHARKY *shakes his head at* LOCKHART.

LOCKHART. I know. Family, ha?

SHARKY. Yeah, don't talk to me. Are you okay for a drink there or...

LOCKHART. Yeah, I'm grand. You not having a drink yourself?

SHARKY. Nah... I'm... trying to... not drink.

LOCKHART. If you can just beat Christmas, ha?

SHARKY (*with a little laugh*). Yeah...

LOCKHART. If I can just beat Christmas I can achieve anything!

SHARKY. Mmm.

LOCKHART. But it's so hard. 'Cause the old drink stops the brain cranking. Stops the mind going into the forest.

SHARKY is looking at LOCKHART, wondering about him.

(*Knowingly.*) Oh yes, I've seen you on your travels. You don't remember me, Sharky...

SHARKY (*trying to place him*). No, I... I do...

LOCKHART. Yeah, I've seen you. On your wandering ways. I've seen you going down Wicklow Street, and halfway up Dame Street, down Suffolk Street, Grafton Street, Dawson Street, round and round, back up, back down, am I right? (*Pause.*) I've seen all those hopeless thoughts, buried there, in your stupid scrunched-up face.

SHARKY. What are you talking about?

LOCKHART. Oh, come on, Sharky! You don't remember me?

SHARKY. No, I... I do. But where did we...?

LOCKHART. We met in the Bridewell, Sharky.

Short pause.

Remember? We were locked up in a cell together. You'd had a bit of bother the night before...? You were waiting to go up before the judge in the morning... We played cards!

SHARKY. Yeah... no... I remember you, but...

LOCKHART (*brightly*). So how have things been with you?

SHARKY....Okay...

LOCKHART. Not great though...

Pause.

SHARKY. You've a good memory.

LOCKHART. Old as the hills, Sharky. You know I was sure I'd run into you today. (*Laughs.*) But you're off the drink! Now that completely threw me, I have to say! Do you know how many pubs I was in?

SHARKY. What, were you looking for me?

LOCKHART. Well, it's just that matter we discussed back then, in the Bridewell that night.

Short pause.

SHARKY. This has to be what? Twenty years ago!

LOCKHART. Twenty-five years ago. But I'm still surprised you don't know why I'm here.

SHARKY. Yeah, well, I don't.

LOCKHART (*disappointed*). Ah, Sharky... We had a deal. (*Short pause.*) No?

SHARKY. Look, I don't know what's going on here, or if Nicky's put you up to this, but I have to say I don't know what you're talking about.

LOCKHART. Are you serious?

SHARKY. Do I look like I'm telling a joke?

LOCKHART. No, hold on. You're seriously standing there telling me that it's never struck you as odd, down all these years, that you just walked out of jail? After what you did? Ah, that's brilliant, Sharky!

SHARKY. What do you mean 'after what I did'?

LOCKHART. Oh, come on, now...

SHARKY. What? What did I... I can't even... What? I got into a fight with some wino in the back of a shebeen up in... Francis Street or... somewhere, was it? I can hardly even remember! So what?

LOCKHART. Well, no, not quite. His name was Laurence Joyce. He was sixty-one. He was a vagrant. He said he was trying to get to Cardiff...? Said he had some family there...? Said his wife was once the Cardiff Rose? You beat him up in the back of O'Dowd's public house in the early hours of the twenty-fourth of December 1981. You killed him. (*Short pause.*) I let you out. I set you free.

Pause.

SHARKY. No, here, wait a minute...

LOCKHART. Come on, you remember. Remember in the morning, that moment when the guards opened the door, and told you to get your stuff and get lost?

SHARKY. ...Yeah?

LOCKHART. I organised that. Because you won that hand of poker we were playing.

SHARKY. Wait a minute. That fella didn't die!

LOCKHART. Oh no. He did. What, are you trying to tell me you don't see him in your nightmares?

Pause. SHARKY *doesn't respond.*

God, the poor old brain hasn't aged too well, has it, Sharky? Look at you. Twenty-five years on the lash like some old borderline wino yourself. What chance haven't you fucked up? Driving the van for those English fellas? Or when you blew that nice cushy security job on the building site in Naas? You make me laugh, Sharky. Tell me, are you still in the wars with Dublin Bus about the night you were pissed and you fell down the stairs? How much are you looking for? For that twinge in your back?

Pause. SHARKY *is staring at* LOCKHART, *dumbfounded.*

You even blew that chauffeur job down in Lahinch! (*Darkly.*) You fancied your man's wife, didn't you?

SHARKY. Who are you?

LOCKHART. Ah, Sharky… don't say you don't know who I am. (*Short pause.*) Or what I want.

SHARKY. Well, I don't know!

LOCKHART. You don't remember we played cards?

SHARKY. No, I kind of do but…

LOCKHART. Poor Sharky. It's always a bit hazy, isn't it? (*Short pause.*) I want your soul, Sharky.

SHARKY. What?

LOCKHART. I want your soul.

SHARKY. What the hell are you talking about? Is this some kind of stupid fucking joke of Nicky's?

LOCKHART *just looks at him.* SHARKY *seems to feel queasy and then enters the grip of some greater pain. It's so excruciating that he starts to sink pathetically to his knees. He tries to get a grip on something but ends up on all fours fighting the urge to pass out, so great is the agony – both physically and deep within his mind.*

LOCKHART. I'm the son of the morning, Sharky. I'm the snake in the garden. I've come here for your soul this Christmas, and I've been

looking for you all fucking day! We made a deal. We played cards
for your freedom and you promised me, you promised me, the
chance to play you again. So don't start messing me about now.
(*Short pause*.) Of course, after you skipped merrily off to some
early house in the morning you probably never even thought about
it again, did you? Ha? You think I'm just farting around? You think
you're better than me? Pig. Well, think again. Because we're gonna
play for your soul and I'm gonna win and you're coming through
the old hole in the wall with me tonight. Now get up.

SHARKY *is silently crying as he staggers back to his feet.*
LOCKHART *suddenly bursts towards* SHARKY, *as though about
to beat him.*

No crying! Don't do a Maurice Macken on it! I'll fucking batter
you! Do you hear me?

SHARKY *flinches backwards, blinking, a hand feebly raised.*
LOCKHART *laughs.*

(*With disgust*.) Don't make me puke…

There is a commotion outside as NICKY *helps* RICHARD *back in
through the back door, followed by* IVAN.

RICHARD (*on his way in*). Them friggin' winos! They do my head in!

NICKY. You should've seen it! They ran for their lives!

RICHARD. Good Jaysus, would someone please give me a drink, for
the love of God?

NICKY (*grabbing the whiskey bottle to give* RICHARD *a drink*). He
blew them out of it! They flew off up the coast! You should have
seen it!

IVAN *comes in from the kitchen with a Miller for* NICKY *and a
can of Harp for himself.*

RICHARD. But was your man there? My little friend that I fucking
hate, with the navy anorak and the big black head of hair on him?
He's the worst…

NICKY. Yeah, I think there was one like that. He fucking legged it!
(*To* SHARKY *and* LOCKHART.) The roars out of this fella…

RICHARD. Ah, you have to…

NICKY. And then Ivan!

RICHARD. I have Ivan well trained! You see, they're so shaky and nervy when they get that old meths into them, you can destroy them with a good scream. They think it's the banshee, God help them.

NICKY. Did you see that one was going to the toilet down behind the car?

IVAN. I thought I saw one down in behind…

NICKY. That was a woman!

IVAN. Was it?!

RICHARD (*with disgust*). Oh, don't…!

NICKY (*bursting out laughing*). It was all going down the back of her leg when she ran and fell over the bin!

RICHARD. Ah stop, will you? They're awful…

LOCKHART (*to* IVAN). Is your car alright?

IVAN. Ah… it… it wasn't my car! I don't have my car with me. I forgot I walked up here in all the excitement.

RICHARD. Ah well, all's well that ends well! Are we gonna play cards?

NICKY (*to* IVAN). Can you see to play cards?

IVAN. I can see to about here. (*Holds his hand up about ten inches from his face.*) After that, it's your guess is as good as mine!

RICHARD. Yeah, you can see the cards…

IVAN. I can read the cards…

RICHARD. Hey, Shark! Where's all the goodies you promised us that you were banging on about earlier? Get the smoked salmon and the mince pies out and all the Christmas goodies and the crisps and all… Are you hungry, Mr Lockhart?

LOCKHART (*looking at* SHARKY). I wouldn't say no.

NICKY (*making a face and touching his stomach*). Them cocktail sausages they were handing out earlier down in Raheny were gone off…

RICHARD. Well, Sharky'll get the grub organised. Ivan, pull out that table into the middle, the cards is on the windowsill.

NICKY *and* IVAN *begin to bustle about getting the table ready for cards.*

Another beer, Nicky?

NICKY. I have one, I'm good, Richard...

RICHARD. Mr Lockhart? Another drop of Irish? Is it there? You can help yourself.

LOCKHART. I'm grand. Sharky's looking after me...

NICKY. I'm bursting for a slash, will I run in quickly?

RICHARD. No, run up. There's a better one, Nicky. Sharky! Is that upstairs loo in tip-top condition?

SHARKY. Yeah, you know where it is, Nicky.

NICKY. Yup, end of the landing.

NICKY *runs up the stairs.*

RICHARD. Ivan, there's stout there if you want a stout. I think I might have a stout actually.

IVAN. Good idea.

He goes towards the kitchen.

RICHARD. And don't mind Matt Talbot on the Kaliber there, he can look after himself. Is the table out?

LOCKHART. Here, Richard...

LOCKHART *helps* RICHARD *to the table.*

RICHARD. Ah, thanks, Mr Lockhart, you're a real gent. And don't mind Sharky's bad humour, he came out backwards and his head has been arseways ever since. Here, give us the cards till I give them a shuffle.

LOCKHART *hands the cards to* RICHARD. LOCKHART *and* SHARKY *stand looking at each other from opposite ends of the room.*

(*Shuffling cards.*) When Ivan comes back now he can cut them for me. (*Laughs.*) I don't know whether these are up or down! I'm in total space here, Mr Lockhart. Wheeee! And when Sharky has the grub for us and Nicky's back down we'll get going. God, I haven't played an old game of poker in so long! I'm really looking forward to it now. Ivan!

IVAN (*off*). Yeah?

RICHARD. Come on till we sort out this money!

IVAN (*off*). I'm coming, Dick! I'm just going to the jacks!

RICHARD. Come on, Nicky! Sit down, Mr Lockhart, sit down. Sharky! Where's Sharky? Sharky, come on! Sharky!!… Let's play!!

Blackout.

ACT TWO: MUSIC IN THE SUN

It is many hours later. The room is darker, seemingly lit only by a few lamps, candles and the glow from the stove. The wind is howling outside as a storm lashes the coast. The card game is in progress. RICHARD sits in his armchair which has been pulled nearer to the centre of the room, closer to the table. He has a big box of chocolates nearby and munches one from time to time. To his left sits IVAN, who is at the edge of the table where he can play but also turn easily away from the others to consult strategy with RICHARD. SHARKY sits to IVAN's left and NICKY sits to SHARKY's left. LOCKHART sits at the far end of the table. They are coming to the end of a round of heavy betting. The biggest piles of money are in front of IVAN and LOCKHART. A lot of drink has been consumed; bottles, cans and empty plates are strewn around. IVAN's intoxication is constant, he coasts along, veering neither up into euphoria nor down into depression. It is his efficient life-state, removed, yet heavily present. NICKY, on the other hand, is a euphoric drunk. His genuine love for friends and comrades is freed. While he plays cards he wears wraparound mirror shades like a poker pro. When not playing he sits them on his head. RICHARD, as we have seen, can lurch from sentimentality to vicious insults within seconds. But while all inhibitions may be gone, he remains alert, quick-witted and deeply interested in what goes on around him. LOCKHART is a philosophical drunk, yet prone to deeper maudlin feelings. SHARKY has thus far managed to remain sober...

IVAN. Nicky...

NICKY. I'm thinking. I'm thinking.

RICHARD. I know. I can hear your brain crunching in your head from over here.

NICKY. Yeah, well, don't be rushing me. What is it again?

RICHARD. Mr Lockhart raised it twenty. We're in. Sharky's bailed.

IVAN. You have to put in forty.

NICKY (*takes a long sharp inhalation and thinks*). Yeah, well, you're bluffing 'cause I saw Richard telling you...

RICHARD. Would you go on out of that!

NICKY. Mr Lockhart is being cautious, he raised it twenty, but he's on a roll anyway so he's battering us from a position of strength. (*To* IVAN.) You have nothing.

IVAN (*ironically*). That's right.

NICKY. You have nothing! So stop with the… If you didn't have that pile in front of you, I'd have your guts for garters.

RICHARD. Why, what have we got?

NICKY. You've about two hundred and fifty fucking euros in front of you there, Dick.

RICHARD. Yo ho! Santy's come early!

IVAN (*playing down their success*). We're doing alright. We're doing nicely.

NICKY. And half of that is mine. (*With sudden confidence.*) You have fuck-all there, Ivan.

IVAN. Well, why don't you make sure?

NICKY. Mr Lockhart has two pair or something.

RICHARD. Well, come on then!

NICKY. I am! (*Seeing and raising.*) Here's your forty. And twenty now to show yous a statement of intent.

RICHARD. Oh ho…

NICKY. Now, that shook yous.

IVAN. Mr Lockhart?

LOCKHART. I'll stick around.

He sees NICKY*'s twenty.*

IVAN. And we'll have a look.

He sees it too. Pause. NICKY*'s courage seems to wane.*

NICKY (*to* IVAN). What do you have?

IVAN (*to* NICKY). What do you have?

RICHARD. What do we have?

IVAN (*to* NICKY). What do you have?

NICKY (*to* LOCKHART). What do you have?

LOCKHART. Threes.

NICKY. Threes of what?

LOCKHART (*shows his hand*). Three nines.

NICKY. Three nines! You stuck it out with three nines?!

LOCKHART. I enjoy playing. Isn't it worth a go?

NICKY *bursts out laughing.*

RICHARD. What have you got, Nicky?

NICKY. Christmas present. Full house. (*Shows his hand.*) Fives and kings.

IVAN (*showing his hand*). Kings and sevens.

NICKY. Bollocks!

RICHARD *whoops.*

Ah, that's fucking…

LOCKHART. Hard luck, Nicky…

NICKY (*to* LOCKHART). What were you doing driving the pot up the wazoo with three nines?! These lads are cleaning me out here!

RICHARD. Ah, Nicky…

NICKY. Look at me! I'm like Sharky here. I've about thirty-five euros to me name. This is to do me all through January.

NICKY *gets up and walks over to the stove, restlessly.*

IVAN (*counting his winnings*). Well, Sharky had the right idea. He bailed. He knew.

RICHARD. He has no money!

IVAN. Do you want a stout, Rich?

RICHARD. Sure! Hey! You know what I have in there of course, beside the boiler? There's a drop of Brigid Blake's famous Antrim poitín in there.

IVAN. Oh ho!

RICHARD. Do you ever take a drop, Mr Lockhart?

IVAN *heads towards the kitchen.*

LOCKHART. I will! Why not? Sure I might as well be shit-faced as the way I am!

IVAN (*on his way into the kitchen*). Yo ho!

RICHARD. Good man!

NICKY. Yeah, well, leave me out of it… Grab us a Miller there, Ivan, would you?

IVAN (*off*). Yeah!

NICKY. Ah, well… it's only a game. It's only money, that right, Rich?

RICHARD. Yeah… Your money!

NICKY *sighs heavily, looking to* LOCKHART *in a silent appeal for understanding.*

NICKY. So, Sharky! You're back! (*Drunkenly placing a hand on* SHARKY*'s shoulder.*) We've missed you! D'you know that?

He turns to LOCKHART, *pointing at* SHARKY *meaninglessly then turns back to* SHARKY.

RICHARD (*insincerely*). Yeah… we've all missed you…

NICKY. So tell us! Where's this you were working?

SHARKY. Ah, down in Lahinch, County Clare.

NICKY. On the trawlers?

SHARKY. No.

NICKY (*surprised*). No?

SHARKY. No, I was eh… (*Glancing at* LOCKHART, *who is smiling at him broadly.*) I was doing a bit of driving for a fella down there.

NICKY. Lahinch? Was I reading somewhere or where was it? That Lahinch is the gay pick-up capital of Europe?

SHARKY. What?

NICKY. So I believe…

IVAN *returns with a whiskey bottle full of clear liquid.*

SHARKY. No…

RICHARD. Ah, Nicky, Lahinch is only a small town, how could it possibly be the gay capital of Europe?

NICKY. Well, I don't know!

RICHARD. The gay capital of Europe is Cork City!

NICKY. Is it?

RICHARD. It very probably is. Are you pouring us a drop of that Moon Juice, Ivan?

IVAN. Will I open it?

RICHARD. Yes.

NICKY. Did you get me a Miller?

IVAN. Did you ask me for one?

NICKY. Yes!

IVAN. Oh sorry, I didn't hear you.

IVAN *goes off towards the kitchen.*

NICKY. Thanks, Ivan. I wouldn't touch that brain blower now if you paid me… Look out, Mr Lockhart, you'll be bollixed.

RICHARD. No, he won't! It'll help him play!

NICKY. It will in my arse! Sure Steady Eddie was hallucinating that traffic wardens were coming to arrest him in the snooker club in Harmonstown one morning after he'd been skulling that shite the night before!

RICHARD. Ah, he's a child! Don't mind him, Mr Lockhart.

LOCKHART. No, I'll have a drop.

RICHARD. Good man.

NICKY. Well, I don't mind if you all start losing!

IVAN *returns, making his way to the table to pour some drinks.*

Thanks, Ivan. Good to see you, Shark. Of course you know I'm in a totally new line now myself?

SHARKY. What, you're not doing the babysitting?

NICKY. No, I'm out of the babysitting. I'm out of that this long weather now. Too many trust issues, essentially. Not on my part. No, I'm gone into the cheesemongering business.

SHARKY. Cheesemongering?

IVAN *is pouring some poitín for* RICHARD *and* LOCKHART, *bringing it to them.*

NICKY. Yeah, I've me own counter down the back of Thrifties.

SHARKY. Have you?

NICKY. Yup. I'm only started it, but it could be a whole new empire.

SHARKY. Do you not have to study for years to do something like that?

NICKY (*incredulously*). What!?

SHARKY. I thought you had to study to do cheese and wines and all… to do it properly…

NICKY. No, you don't! Who told you that?

SHARKY. I don't know. No, I just thought…

NICKY. No, you don't! (*Laughs.*) Whoever told you that now is… Ah, poor Sharky!

SHARKY. How's the car?

NICKY. What car?

SHARKY. The Peugeot.

NICKY. Eileen's car?

SHARKY. Well, it's my old car actually.

NICKY. Oh, is it?

SHARKY. Yeah.

NICKY. Did you get a new one?

Pause.

RICHARD. No, he didn't! Sure where would Sharky get a new car? (*Raising his glass of poitín.*) Your health, Mr Lockhart!

NICKY. Say goodbye to it!

LOCKHART. No, this is smooth!

NICKY. Yeah, you think…

LOCKHART. You know this is the only time of the year I really enjoy? A game of cards on Christmas Eve, sure where would you get it?

RICHARD. Absolutely!

IVAN. You play a lot of cards, Mr Lockhart?

LOCKHART. Well... I do at Christmas! Boys, I've played cards in
public houses, shebeens, hotel bar rooms, suburban boozers –
anywhere! Three, four in the morning, nobody there, only a few
auld lads in their shirt sleeves, tidying up while they watch some
poor fucking eejit play it all away... Houses! Little houses... on
Christmas Eve... in the middle of nowhere I've played. Out on the
western seaboard, but mostly in the east. Ah, I've played
everywhere! You name it! In Garda barracks... Sharky. Up in
amazing Georgian rooms with wonderful evocative gilt mirrors and
beautiful windows towering out on to bountiful trees – in the middle
of Dublin, or London, in the city, yup. A school or two I've played
in. In my time. Always late. It's always so late... Time deepens and
slows down somehow in a card game. It could be any moment. It's
always the same moment... Where do I know you from, Ivan?

IVAN. Ha?

LOCKHART. Have we played cards?

SHARKY. No, I don't think you have...

IVAN. Yeah, we might of...

LOCKHART. You're the fella won the boat that time in a card game,
Nicky was telling me...

NICKY. Yeah.

IVAN (*modestly*). Well...

RICHARD. No, he did, that's right.

IVAN (*to* RICHARD). Do you remember that, Dick?

RICHARD. I sure do! *The Briquette Queen.*

NICKY. Forty grand's worth of boat, Mr Lockhart!

IVAN. Yeah, but I sold it for twelve. I didn't want it! What would I
want with a fucking boat?

NICKY. It only would've cost him money anyway...

IVAN. I sold it for twelve grand up in the Cock tavern in Howth – Do
you remember, Richard? Best Christmas ever!

RICHARD. Ah, brilliant. It was brilliant!

NICKY. You could never top that!

IVAN. I lost it all in three weeks, Mr Lockhart. Betting in the bookies in Baldoyle and practically living in Doyle's Lounge. I was eating so much fish and chips and battered sausages at all weird hours and I saw fuck-all daylight…

NICKY. This is all true!

IVAN.… that I ended up getting the runs so bad and I was so dehydrated the doctor wouldn't let me out of the house for four whole days!

RICHARD, NICKY *and* IVAN *are laughing…*

It was unbelievable! It was an absolutely unbelievable Christmas. Do you remember all the stars we saw that Stephen's Night, Nicky?

NICKY (*too beautiful to describe*). Aw!

IVAN. Yeah, but you panic though when it starts to run right down. Oh Jaysus, if Karen had've known I'd had all that… Oh! (*Shudders.*) Had to get rid of it.

LOCKHART. Yeah, and you won it just in a card game in a house?

IVAN. Yeah, won it off a total nutcase that killed himself not long after. He drowned after driving his lorry off the end of the pier in Howth.

NICKY. *The Briquette Queen.*

IVAN. He had a business delivering peat briquettes…

RICHARD. Oh, he was a nasty piece of work, Mr Lockhart…

NICKY. Aw, he was a real bollocks!

LOCKHART. Yeah? God, that's a great story. But you know what I was wondering, after Nicky told me about it, I wanted to ask you… Look at Sharky looking at me suspiciously there… no, I was just wondering, with the stakes so high – a forty-grand boat, like – I was wondering what you had in the pot that he was betting his boat against you?

IVAN. Ha?

LOCKHART. No, just what did you have in the pot to put up against his boat? I'm assuming there couldn't have been forty grand in the pot. In a card game like the way we're playing now… What did you have, that he wanted…?

IVAN *looks at* NICKY. *Pause.*

SHARKY. Here, look, are we gonna play here?

LOCKHART. You don't have to tell me…

RICHARD. It was stupid! Your man was out of it! They were all elephants!

NICKY. He was a lunatic! He was acting the bollocks. Ivan took him down fair and square and…

LOCKHART. It was something to do with that hotel down in Wicklow, was it?

Long pause.

SHARKY (*to* LOCKHART). What are you doing?

LOCKHART. You told me something about that, Nicky, didn't you? About Ivan and what was it? The Ardlawn Hotel?

NICKY (*guiltily*). No…

RICHARD (*disappointed*). Nicky…

NICKY. I didn't…

SHARKY. Let's just play, will we? That's got nothing to do with anything.

LOCKHART. What was the name of those two families?

IVAN (*in a dark place*). The Murdochs and the Kavanaghs.

LOCKHART. That's right…

RICHARD. That was all in the news. Ivan was completely exonerated…

NICKY. It was inconclusive…

SHARKY. Yeah. Hey, look… Can we just get on with the…

SHARKY *takes a sharp intake of breath and puts his hand to his head in sudden, immense pain.*

NICKY. Are you alright, Shark?

SHARKY (*blinking*). Yeah, no, I'm…

RICHARD. Leave him alone. He just needs a drink. That whole thing was an open and shut case, Mr Lockhart…

LOCKHART. What happened? There was a fire…?

IVAN. Yeah, well… It was twenty odd years ago. It was more…

NICKY. Ancient history…

IVAN. I was working in the Ardlawn. I was doing a bit of portering and bit of night-portering…

RICHARD. Ivan was completely exonerated.

NICKY. There was no blame.

IVAN. No, they had to investigate it. I had… you see I had burned my hand on the ring of the cooker when I was… I was heating some beans… it was very late and… (*Pause.*) This was all in the papers!

LOCKHART. Yeah… but it can really hang over a man, something like that…

IVAN. Well, yeah, the… this fella with the boat, the briquette king. He wanted to play for…

NICKY. He was a wanker.

IVAN. The bet was that he could… if he won, he wanted to ask me… about it. I don't know…

LOCKHART. To give him the truth.

Pause.

IVAN. Yeah…

NICKY. It was a ridiculous fucking bet… He was a sick fucking eejit and that's all that was going on. And he got his comeuppance!

RICHARD. He's gone and good luck to him. He was a bully.

LOCKHART. High stakes, Ivan…

IVAN. Yeah… well, I'd a strong hand.

LOCKHART. Yeah. I knew there had to be something… You don't mind talking about it…

Pause.

NICKY. I hate that fucking poitín! The fucking smell of it, even!

RICHARD. Ah, stop giving out! Are we gonna play cards? There's too much Auld Lang Syne going on around here and not enough cards!

NICKY. Yeah, well, let's play, come on!

RICHARD. Whose deal is it? Sharky! You deal!

LOCKHART. Yes! We haven't hardly had a burst out of Sharky tonight at all!

RICHARD. Ah, Sharky could never play cards!

NICKY (*gathering up the cards to give* SHARKY). I've seen Sharky win.

LOCKHART. Maybe he's preoccupied.

RICHARD. Ah, he's always preoccupied...

NICKY. Come on. Two euros to play. Maybe this is Sharky's hand.

RICHARD. Give us a drop of that holy water, Ivan, till we bless ourselves.

NICKY. Little threes is all I need.

SHARKY *shuffles the cards to deal. Everyone puts in two euros.* IVAN *puts in four, to cover himself and* RICHARD, *then he gets up to pour a drink for* RICHARD.

IVAN. Richard...

RICHARD (*to* IVAN). Good man. (*Raising glass.*) Mr Lockhart?

LOCKHART. I will! Thank you, Ivan.

RICHARD. Hey, Mr Lockhart...

LOCKHART *looks at* RICHARD *who points to his head and makes a whistling sound to indicate the effect of the poitín.*

LOCKHART. I know! I'm fucking slipping in and out of time zones here. I thought it was last Christmas there for a minute!

RICHARD. Yes! That's right!

IVAN *goes to pour a drink for* LOCKHART.

NICKY. Yeah, well, leave me out of it. I want to stay here in this Christmas and beat the shite out of yous now with this hand. I can feel it in me waters. Little threes there now, Sharky. Get us a Miller there, Ivan, will you?

IVAN *goes to get a beer.*

IVAN. Do you want another 7 Up, Shark?

SHARKY. Nah, I'm alright…

RICHARD. Oh, threes is a beaut…

NICKY. That's my killer hand, is three threes.

RICHARD. Yeah: I love three tens. Three tens is my…

LOCKHART. Ah, a ten is like a shining tower. It's like the twentieth century. It's solid. It looms at you, yeah?

RICHARD. Absolutely.

NICKY. Well, I also like to see an eight. Give me a pair of eights for starters and I'm…

RICHARD (*dismissively*). Ah, eight! Eight is sneaky… Look at it! What is it? Eight! It's not a ten, it's almost as bad as a nine…

LOCKHART. Well, nine can have a certain symmetry to it.

NICKY. Oh, three threes is a lovely little hand. It's like a little grenade.

RICHARD. And seven…

LOCKHART. Oh, seven is deep.

NICKY (*to* IVAN, *who has returned with beers for* NICKY *and himself*). We're talking about numbers.

IVAN (*unconvinced*). Ah, seven is only my hole. Give me a four.

SHARKY. Yeah…

IVAN. Four is where you build your house.

They have all picked up their cards and peruse them.

LOCKHART (*to* IVAN). Do you not have two fours in front of you there?

IVAN. That's a secret, Mr Lockhart.

NICKY. Ah, nice try! Mr Lockhart is no slouch!

RICHARD. Well, neither is Ivan! How are we doing? Who's it to?

SHARKY. Ivan?

IVAN. Ah, check…

SHARKY. Nicky?

NICKY. Eh… I'll check for a minute.

SHARKY. Mr Lockhart…

LOCKHART. Ah, sure we'll make it interesting anyway. (*Putting in coins.*) Three euros.

RICHARD. Will we stick around for three euros, Ivan?

IVAN. We'll see what happens.

He puts in coins.

SHARKY. Nicky?

NICKY. Ah, we'll hang around.

Sees the bet.

SHARKY. And I'll have a look. (*Sees it and picks up the deck to deal.*) Ivan?

IVAN. Eh… Three please, Sharky.

SHARKY *deals him three cards.*

LOCKHART. Little pair of fours there, Ivan?

RICHARD. Don't tell him nothing!

IVAN. I'm not…

SHARKY. Nicky.

NICKY. Eh… two…

SHARKY *deals him two cards.* NICKY *suddenly throws down one more card.*

No, three…

SHARKY. You sure?

NICKY. Yeah, three, thanks.

SHARKY (*deals another card to* NICKY). Mr Lockhart?

LOCKHART. Just one, please, Sharky.

Reactions to this around the table. SHARKY *deals him a card.*

RICHARD. Just the one, Mr Lockhart?

LOCKHART. Just the one…

NICKY. Ah, he's on a kamikaze. What is it? A run? Flush? Did you get it?

LOCKHART. Maybe it's four of a kind.

RICHARD. Maybe it's total bollocks.

LOCKHART. Maybe…

SHARKY. And I'll take three. To you, Mr Lockhart.

LOCKHART. Ah, we'll keep the dream alive. Sure, five euros.

Puts in money.

RICHARD. Oh, look out…

SHARKY. Ivan?

IVAN. Ehm… We'll hang on.

Sees the bet.

RICHARD. We'll hang on for a minute…

SHARKY. Nicky?

NICKY. Ah, we'll go along for the ride. (*Sees it.*) And we'll make it interesting. Ten euros.

He raises the bet. Reactions around the table…

RICHARD. Oh, now!

SHARKY. Mr Lockhart?

LOCKHART. I'll see you… With ten.

Raises the bet further still.

RICHARD. Oh now, here! What are we doing? Ivan!

NICKY (*to* LOCKHART). You fucker…

IVAN *leans over to whisper to* RICHARD, *who listens intently…*

RICHARD. Ah, fold, for fuck's sake! Would you? Jaysus…

IVAN (*throws his hand in*). We're gone.

SHARKY. Nicky?

NICKY (*considers* LOCKHART). I'll see you.

Puts in ten.

RICHARD. You're a fucking eejit…

NICKY. Hold your horses. Stranger things have happened at sea...

RICHARD (*dismissively*). Yeah, right...

LOCKHART. Sharky?

RICHARD. Don't be a hero now, Sharky...

SHARKY (*considering his hand*). So what is it?

NICKY. It's twenty-eight for you to play, Shark. And I'd advise you to tread warily against what I have here now...

RICHARD. Easy now, Sharky. I'm not keeping you in pocket money for the whole of next month now, right?

SHARKY. Twenty-eight. (*Sees it and reaches into his pocket, taking some money out*). With twenty-five.

RICHARD. What!?

IVAN. Ah, let him play, Rich.

LOCKHART. Brave man...

NICKY. To you, Mr Lockhart...

LOCKHART. I'm in.

He sees the bet. NICKY *looks at his cards...*

IVAN. Nicky...

NICKY. I'm thinking. I'm thinking. I'm thinking. I'm thinking.

RICHARD. I thought I smelled something burning...

NICKY. Ha ha... (*To* LOCKHART, *putting money in.*) Come on! What do you have?

Pause.

LOCKHART (*showing his hand*). I've nothing.

NICKY. You bastard! What were you doing?!

LOCKHART. I'm playing the game!

NICKY (*derisively*). The game! You fucking eejit. That's that poitín. I told you...

IVAN. It could be yours, Nicky...

RICHARD. It better not be!

IVAN. Go on, Nicky! What do you have?

Pause.

NICKY. Ah, I've even less nothing. I've a hand of feet. Half a run. (*Re:* LOCKHART.) I knew he had nothing. I thought it'd be too pricey for Sharky. I thought he was having us on. What have you got, Shark, two pair or some fucking thing...

SHARKY. Not even. One pair.

NICKY. One pair?! (*Grabs* SHARKY's *cards.*) Two fucking fours!?

IVAN. It still beats you.

LOCKHART. Nicely played, Sharky...

NICKY *throws the cards on the table and stands up.*

NICKY. A hundred euros with two fours!

He paces around, going towards the stove.

SHARKY. Your deal, Nicky...

NICKY *kicks a pile of newspapers.*

NICKY. Bollocks!

RICHARD. Oy! Oy! Nicky, don't destroy the place.

NICKY. No, no. I'm sorry, Richard.

IVAN. Nice one, Sharky...

NICKY (*taking money from his wallet*). What were we all doing? (*To* LOCKHART.) You had nothing!? I had fuck-all! And Sharky wins a hundred euros with two fucking fours!

LOCKHART. Luck of the draw.

NICKY. What were you doing raising all the time?

LOCKHART. You were raising as well.

NICKY. Ah, I was only having a go! Here, give us some change there, Ivan.

LOCKHART. It's only money...

NICKY *goes to* IVAN's *pile to get some smaller denominations, throwing two twenty-euro notes down.*

RICHARD. Ah, hard luck, Nicky, sure it's only a bit of fun...

NICKY. I won't be having much more fun at this rate…

RICHARD. You could never bluff, Nicky. That's just something you can't…

IVAN (*pointing at* SHARKY). You see him? King of the bluffers.

RICHARD. Who, Sharky?

IVAN. Yeah.

RICHARD. Yeah, well, that's only because he has a recklessness in his heart which is the undoing and ruination of his whole life.

IVAN. Not tonight.

RICHARD. Yeah? Just wait. Ah, cheer up, Nicky.

NICKY. Yeah, well, give me a few minutes…! That's a harsh lesson there now.

LOCKHART. Only kind that works, Nicky.

IVAN. Well, Sharky's around for another few hands in anyway…

RICHARD. He should quit while he's ahead.

LOCKHART. Don't worry, Nicky. I'm gonna take Sharky down.

NICKY. Can I bet on it?

LOCKHART. Nothing surer.

RICHARD. Ah, would you come on and deal the cards and stop moaning. You'll probably trounce us all this time out.

NICKY (*taking the cards to give them a shuffle*). I hope so!

RICHARD (*handing box of sweets to* IVAN). Here, Ivan, pass them around.

IVAN. Oh, nice one!

A mobile phone is ringing somewhere…

RICHARD. What's that music?

NICKY. Oh bollocks! That's my phone!

RICHARD. Oh, here's trouble…

IVAN. I'm not here…

NICKY goes to his jacket and rummages for his phone…

NICKY. It's Eileen!

IVAN. Well, whoever it is, I'm not here.

They all wait as NICKY *stands looking at his phone.*

NICKY. I'm gonna have to answer this, Dick.

RICHARD. Well, would you answer the Jaysus thing and stop driving us all around the fucking twist!

NICKY *answers it.*

NICKY (*very innocently*). Hello?

The others are listening.

Hi, hon. What? No! No, I'm just visiting poor Richard to see if he… No. No, Sharky's here. Yeah, no he's here. He's not even drinking. And I'm only… I'm just having a very quick bottle of Miller. No, I swear to God, he isn't! What? Yeah, no I'll be back. No, don't try lifting it down yourself… No, no I'll do it! (*Drifts upstage towards the staircase and upstairs out of earshot of the others.*) No, I'll be there! What's wrong with you? It's Christmas, Eileen! What? Hold on, just let me…

He is gone.

RICHARD. Trouble in paradise.

IVAN. Don't talk to me about trouble in paradise! Here, will I put on some music?

RICHARD. Oh yes! Good idea! Good idea!

IVAN *wanders over to the stereo…*

LOCKHART. Hey, hold on, are we not gonna… [play]?

RICHARD. Music to soothe the soul. What kind of music do you like, Mr Lockhart?

LOCKHART. I don't really like music.

IVAN *surfs up the dial on the tuner and finds some softly-played, festive, perhaps choral, music…*

RICHARD. How can you not like music? Any music?

LOCKHART. I don't like any music.

RICHARD. Do you hear that, Ivan? Mr Lockhart doesn't like any music!

IVAN. Sure, that's impossible.

RICHARD. That's what I would've thought.

LOCKHART. No, you see... I can't hear it.

IVAN. What, are you tone-deaf?

LOCKHART. No, no, I just don't like the sound. You see, to me it's just an ugly noise.

RICHARD. Dear God! That's a terrible affliction. Sure you can hardly escape music!

IVAN. What? Like, do you want me to turn it off?

LOCKHART. If you don't mind.

IVAN *stands there, hoping* LOCKHART *will relent.*

That would be most agreeable.

IVAN *goes and turns off the music. Pause.*

RICHARD. Lordy, lordy, lordy, lordy, lordy, lordy, lordy, lordy, lordy, would you listen to that wind? God, I had an awful dream the other night. I dreamt I could see. I dreamt that I woke up and I could see and that being blind had been a dream. And I dreamt the sun was shining in through the window there, and there, just sitting on the windowsill, was a bluebottle looking at me. You ever notice about those things? The whole head is nearly their eyes. Two big black footballs on the whole two sides of their head. And I was just staring at him and he was just staring at me – as much as you can tell if he's 'looking' at you at all... 'What does he think of me?' I was wondering, as we were kind of... communing with each other there. And there was such... comfort, in his blank unseeing regard for me, Mr Lockhart. You just know that God is in a fly, don't you? The very existence and the amazing design in something so small and intricate as a bluebottle – it's God's revelation really, isn't it? Don't you feel that?

LOCKHART. Well... except that they seem to like the taste of shit so much, don't they?

RICHARD. Ah, that only adds to their intrigue...

LOCKHART. If you say so.

RICHARD. Well, I do! I do say so! And... But then I had the terrible misfortune to wake up and... and I realised I couldn't see. And I kind of... I kind of panicked. I didn't know if it was night, or day, or what the hell it was or where I was. And I didn't want to call out to Sharky, because in case I woke him, his moods do be bad enough! And I... or turn on the radio in case I woke him, but I got my bearings. I was down here and I thought, 'If I can get a drop of whiskey, the old panic may subside.' But then, of course, I fell in the fucking kitchen door and I made such a clatter that Sharky woke up anyway! Didn't you?

SHARKY. Yeah, well, I wasn't asleep. But Jaysus... I thought someone was breaking in. Bottles smashing all over the floor...

RICHARD. Yeah! What was it? It was...

SHARKY. It was five o'clock in the bleeding morning.

RICHARD. Yeah, well, we were up then, weren't we?

SHARKY. Yeah.

RICHARD. Then your man (*Re:* SHARKY.) wants to give me a bath! (*Pronounced 'bat'.*)

LOCKHART. A what?

IVAN *goes round with the poitín topping up their drinks...*

RICHARD. A bat! He wants to wash me! And bathe me, the fucking... [*eejit*].

LOCKHART. Well, he's trying to be what's known as 'a good person'.

RICHARD. Well he should give up! (*Laughs.*) Hey, Sharky, (*Touching his groin.*) what about that...

SHARKY (*remembering with disgust*). Oh...!

RICHARD. Ivan, there was a... what would you call it, Sharky?

SHARKY. I don't want to talk about it.

RICHARD. It was like a lump of... up here at the top of me leg where the crease meets the...

SHARKY. Aw, would you fucking stop, Richard?

RICHARD. It was hard, now. And deeply... embedded in the...

SHARKY. Ah, Richard!

RICHARD. Like either congealed... or... The smell when Sharky started rubbing it!

NICKY *descends.*

SHARKY. Richard!

RICHARD. And the fucking pain of it… Sharky going at it with the nailbrush! And the smell!

NICKY. What's this?

RICHARD. Nicky, you'd be interested in this, I had this…

SHARKY. No, come on, that's it now. Jesus Christ!

RICHARD (*angrily*). Ah, I'm only trying tell a fucking story here, Jim, what's the matter with you, for Jaysus' sake?! (*Short pause, to* NICKY.) I'll tell you later…

Short pause.

NICKY. Well, I've got about an hour's parole, so let's get on with the cards because if I want to have any chance of…

There is a sudden loud bang at the back door out in the kitchen. They all fall silent, listening.

What was that?

RICHARD (*getting up*). That's them fucking winos! Where's me stick? Ivan!

SHARKY. Ah, Rich, come on… don't be…

NICKY *goes into the kitchen, peering out the back door into the gloom.*

RICHARD. Don't fucking start now, Sharky! You don't know what I have to live with! I'm sorry, Mr Lockhart, we have an awful problem with these winos out in the lane, come on, Ivan!

IVAN. They're probably gone, they just…

NICKY. I think they must have thrown something or…

IVAN. Put the light on out there, Nicky.

RICHARD *has a hold of* IVAN.

RICHARD. Come on, Ivan. Come on, Nicky. Open that back door for me.

NICKY. Hey, hold on, is there something I can…?

RICHARD. There's an old golf club in there beside the jacks door, Nicky.

IVAN. Put the light on out there, Nicky, will you?

NICKY *finds the golf club and hits a light in the back garden.*

NICKY. Hold on now, Rich, now I don't see anyone.

RICHARD. Come on, we'll get them in the lane.

SHARKY. Richard, put your coat on, will you?

RICHARD. Ah, we're alright, we'll just chase them off.

IVAN. They'll be gone I'd say anyway.

NICKY *opens the back door and goes out into the wind,*
RICHARD *and* IVAN *following.* RICHARD *does a native Indian*
whooping sound by vibrating his open palm in front of his mouth
while letting out a high-pitched shout.

RICHARD (*going*). Keep a hold of me now, Ivan!

NICKY (*off*). Hey, mind with that stick, will ya?

RICHARD (*off*). Sorry, Nicky!

The back door shuts. SHARKY *and* LOCKHART *are alone.*
Pause.

LOCKHART. Well, Sharky. You ready to come with me?

SHARKY. You haven't beaten me yet.

LOCKHART (*getting up to pour himself more poitín*). No, not yet,
I'm enjoying myself too much! I'll hammer you now in this next
hand. And then I'll take you right through the old hole in the wall.

As LOCKHART *pours himself a drink, he sways and steadies*
himself against the table.

Whoops.

SHARKY. Mind you don't fall.

LOCKHART. Well, to tell you the truth, I never drink this much.

SHARKY. Yeah, well, welcome to our house.

LOCKHART. Mmm. Your brother… He's a real… believer, isn't he?

SHARKY *shrugs.* LOCKHART *stands with his drink and raises*
his free hand to look at it in the light.

I hate these stupid insect bodies you have. (*Switches his drink from*
one hand to another). This fucker is left-handed! (*Looking down at*
his legs.) I mean, what is it? What are human beings? Two balloons
– that's your lungs and an annoying little whistle at the top where

the air comes out – that's your voice… (*Pause. Bitterly.*) I mean
what have you got that I haven't?! (*Short pause.*) I'm talking to
you, Love's Young Dream! What have you got? Ha? You all age
and wither before me like dead flowers in a bright window! You're
nothing! Me? I live in the stars above St Anne's Park! Thousands
of Christmas Eves I've seen! I'm so old… and thousands more I'll
see; maybe millions! I'm the very power that keeps us apart! Isn't
that worth saving? (*Beat.*) Evidently not. No, he loves you. He
loves all you insects… (*Lost and distant.*) Figure that one out.

Pause.

SHARKY. What'll to happen to me? If I lose.

LOCKHART. When you lose.

SHARKY. If I lose.

LOCKHART. You're going to Hell.

Short pause.

SHARKY. What is it?

LOCKHART. What's Hell? (*Gives a little laugh.*) Hell is… (*Stares
gloomily.*) Well, you know, Sharky, when you're walking round
and round the city and the street lights have all come on and it's
cold. Or you're standing outside a shop where you were hanging
around reading the magazines, pretending to buy one 'cause
you've no money and nowhere to go and your feet are like blocks
of ice in those stupid little slip-on shoes you bought for
chauffeuring. And you see all the people who seem to live in
another world all snuggled up together in the warmth of a tavern
or a cosy little house, and you just walk and walk and walk and
you're on your own and nobody knows who you are. And you
don't know anyone and you're trying not to hassle people or beg,
because you're trying not to drink, and you're hoping you won't
meet anyone you know because of the blistering shame that rises
up in your face and you have to turn away because you know you
can't even deal with the thought that someone might love you,
because of all the pain you always cause.

Well, that's a fraction of the self-loathing you feel in Hell, except
it's worse. Because there truly is no one to love you. Not even Him.
(*Points to the sky.*) He lets you go. Even He's sick of you. You're
locked in a space that's smaller than a coffin. And it's lying a
thousand miles down, under the bed of a vast, icy, pitch-black sea.

You're buried alive in there. And it's so cold that you can feel your angry tears freezing in your eye lashes and your very bones ache with deep perpetual agony and you think, 'I must be going to die…'

But you never die. You never even sleep, because every few minutes you're gripped by a claustrophobic panic and you get so frightened you squirm uselessly against the stone walls and the heavy lid you've banged your head off a million times and your heart beats so fast against your ribs you think, 'I must be going to die…' But of course… you never will. Because of what you did. And what you didn't do.

Pause. SHARKY *stares into his bleak eternal fate.*

That's where I am too, Sharky. I know you see me here in this man's clothes, but that's where I really am… Out on that sea. (*Short pause.*) Oh, you'd have loved Heaven, Sharky. It's unbelievable! Everyone feels peaceful! (*Laughs.*) Everyone feels at such peace! Simply to exist there is to know an exquisite, trance-like bliss, because your mind is at one with the infinite!

(*Darker.*) At a certain point each day, music plays. It seems to emanate from the very sun itself. Not so much a tune as a heartbreakingly beautiful vibration in the sunlight shining down on and through all the souls. It's so moving you wonder how you could ever have doubted anything as you think back on this painful life which is just a sad distant memory. Time just slips away in Heaven, Sharky. But not for you. No. You are about to find out that time is more measureless and bigger and blacker and so much more boundless than you could ever have thought possible with your puny broken mind.

SHARKY *looks down forlornly.*

Poor old Sharky. You've really got it for her, haven't you?

SHARKY. Who?

LOCKHART (*derisively*). Who! The wife of that fella you were working for down in Lahinch.

SHARKY *looks away.*

…That sent you all those CDs this morning! (*Derisively.*) 'Who…?' Trust you to blow it, Sharky. Trust you. That's how I know you'll be coming with me tonight. I know you'll lose this next hand. Because you always make a pig's mickey of everything.

SHARKY *seems to ponder his whole life for a moment, then goes to the bottle of poitín and pours himself a huge measure. He begins to drink it perfunctorily with one hand on his hip...*

That's it, Sharky, good man. Drink yourself up on to the next shelf in the basement. Drink to where possibility feels infinite and your immortality feels strong.

SHARKY, *having drained his glass, joylessly pours another.*

That's it... Genius! You poor, stupid bastard.

SHARKY. Why don't you give it a rest?

LOCKHART. The condemned man's last meal. A big glass of hooch!

SHARKY (*snapping at* LOCKHART). I said, give it rest, will ya?

LOCKHART (*fumbling towards* SHARKY, *holding out his glass*). Here, give me one.

SHARKY (*shuffling away*). Get it yourself.

LOCKHART. Oy, oy, oy oy!

SHARKY *drinks while* LOCKHART *looks at him, unsure for a moment... We hear a commotion as the others return to the kitchen through the back door. They are laughing.*

NICKY (*wandering in to get a drink*). They'd scarpered! They were gone!

RICHARD (*coming through with* IVAN). We chased them off! Another battle to us. The generals prevail! Ivan, would you please pour us a sharpener to warm us up? Mr Lockhart? Are you alright for a...?

LOCKHART. I don't know... This poor brain can't cope, I don't think!

RICHARD. Would you go on out of that? Have a stout! Ivan, are you alright? Ivan fell.

NICKY (*laughs*). Ivan wrecked himself!

IVAN. Ah, I walked right into the basin of dirty water Sharky left out there! Me socks are ringing!

RICHARD. You fucking eejit!

IVAN (*going towards kitchen*). Ah, I'll take these off. I'll deal with it later...

RICHARD. You gobaloon... And Sharky, what were you doing leaving a basin of water in the laneway? (*Imploring the heavens.*) Lord, I'm surrounded by ninnies! Deliver me!

NICKY. Oh, I'll tell yous, Richard's blood is up!

RICHARD. What?

NICKY. He's missed his mill with the winos!

RICHARD. Excuse me?

NICKY. You were gunning for a fight, so you were, go on out of that!

RICHARD. Yeah, right! Sure, how could I be? I'm blind, Nicky, actually, you know?

NICKY. Go on out of that! That never stopped you! (*Spies SHARKY pouring a drink.*) You having a Christmas nip, Sharky?

RICHARD (*ears pricking up at this*). Ha?

IVAN falls in the kitchen door with a crash, trying to get his socks off.

NICKY. Wo! Easy there, Ivan! Are you alright?

IVAN (*off*). Yah...

RICHARD. So... Is Sharky back among the living, yeah?

LOCKHART. He's just trying to kill the pain.

RICHARD. Mr Lockhart, take it from me, Sharky will never kill all that pain. He'd have to drink Lough Derg dry, God help him!

They all laugh except SHARKY, who continues to drink perfunctorily... IVAN wanders back in, barefoot, from the kitchen, drinking a beer. NICKY brings RICHARD a drink.

Ah, at last! Hey, cheers, Sharky! (*Raises his glass, needling SHARKY.*) Welcome back!

SHARKY just looks at RICHARD darkly. NICKY, IVAN and LOCKHART look at SHARKY.

SHARKY. Yeah, Cheers, Richard...

NICKY and IVAN relax but...

RICHARD. Ah, clink me glass, will ya?

SHARKY *reluctantly goes and clinks his glass against* RICHARD*'s.*

Good man. Drink up. Mr Lockhart, it's a well-known fact in this whole area that my brother has that rare gift which is, unfortunately, the opposite to whatever the Midas touch was.

NICKY. Ah, Richard...

RICHARD. No, no... I'm going to say something positive. I believe that Sharky has potential. Yes. I believe he can change.

LOCKHART. Ah, well, that's sweet... Isn't that nice, Sharky?

NICKY (*moving to the table*). Yeah, lovely. Come on, are we gonna play cards?

RICHARD. You ever see an old couple going down the street, Mr Lockhart? An old couple who've been married for a million years, going along the road to the shops or to mass, with their grey, dead faces?

LOCKHART. Yes.

RICHARD. Like some ghastly ancient brother and sister. Nothing to say to each other any more or ever again except to snap the fucking head off each other for not putting the jelly back in the fridge or some fucking shite, you ever see that? Don't tell me they were always like that! Don't tell me they haven't changed! 'Cause I won't believe it! No, I believe in Sharky. He can change. I believe that he can change back to...

SHARKY. Back to what?

NICKY. Will I deal?

IVAN. Yeah, go on, Nicky, deal...

LOCKHART. Hold on, Sharky wants to ask something...

RICHARD. What did you say?

SHARKY. Back to what? I can change back to what?

NICKY. Ah, lads...

RICHARD. Well... How about back to the little fella that always had a tune on his lips and had integrity, and wasn't a sneaky little fucker who broke his mother's heart. How's that for starters?

NICKY. Ah, Richard, come on...

RICHARD. Back to that! You see, I remember, Mr Lockhart, when it was all fields all's around here... all around all up to Donaghmede, all up to Sutton, all up to Howth. All fields, Mr Lockhart. All farms, Nicky.

NICKY. Yeah, well, my roots are in Ballyfermot.

RICHARD. Our mother was a wonderful woman! (*Suddenly stands to attention.*) Our father was a fine man. A tough man. He was devoted to his greyhounds! He lived for them! Great with his fists.

LOCKHART. That's fascinating...

RICHARD. Yes. No, our mother, God rest her, she only ever had one problem in her life. Sharky. Yes...

NICKY. Ah, Richard, come on, that's the poitín talking. Sharky, sit down till we play...

RICHARD. He upset her that much, she hit him with a chair and broke it one night, Mr Lockhart. I witnessed it.

NICKY. Ah, come on, Dick, come on, Sharky... let's not have the yearly...

SHARKY. What's your point, Richard?

RICHARD. Ha?

IVAN. Come on, Shark...

SHARKY. What? Did you want me to stay? And live here with you and them? And all the fucking rows all the time, and all the fucking drink?

RICHARD. You never needed anyone to show you how to drink!

SHARKY. 'Cause would you have got the house then?

RICHARD. What!

NICKY. Ah, lads, for fuck's sake...

LOCKHART. No, wait, let Sharky finish.

SHARKY. I am finished.

RICHARD. What do you mean would I have got the house then? How dare you?

SHARKY. You think you've always got it all figured out. Look at you.

RICHARD. What do you mean 'Look at me?' Look at you!!

SHARKY. Yeah well, don't worry about it. Because you know what? You're gonna get what you want.

NICKY. Ah, lads…

SHARKY. 'Cause I'm leaving here tonight and I'll be gone and that'll be the end of it.

NICKY. Ah, Sharky…

SHARKY (*forcefully*). And you can walk into the walls and spill Paddy Powers all down your horrible filthy whiskers and sit in your own stink 'cause you don't even know what day it is or what time it is. And then they'll stick you in some home out in Blanchardstown or somewhere where you won't even get a drink, how does that sound?

RICHARD. You're being completely unreasonable!

SHARKY. Am I? Just watch!

NICKY. Come on, Sharky, you don't mean it…

SHARKY. Yeah? Tell them, Mr Lockhart, or whatever your fucking name is, go on, tell him! Tell him!

NICKY *is on his feet, trying to pacify* SHARKY.

NICKY. Sharky… come on… it's alright…

SHARKY. Take your fucking hands off me, I'll give you such a box in the fucking head!

IVAN. Wo, wo… Sharky…

NICKY. Hey, easy, Shark…

SHARKY. You're only a fucking scumbag.

NICKY. What?

SHARKY. You heard me, you sponger.

IVAN *is also on his feet.*

IVAN. Ah, Sharky, now, come on…

SHARKY. Eileen is far too good for a fucking scumhead like you. Always on the mooch…

NICKY. Hey! Don't be having a go at me! (*Rolls up his sleeve to show* SHARKY *a tattoo.*) Read that! What does that say! Eileen! And that? Eileen! I look after Eileen and the kids!

IVAN. Ah, lads!

NICKY. At least I don't be getting into mills all the time and getting barred out of pubs all over the place! At least I don't be waking up screaming and roaring at all hours of the night having bad dreams and freaking the kids out and waking the whole place up!

RICHARD. That's right!

SHARKY. What?

NICKY. Sure everybody knows! You're a nutcase, Sharky! Everybody knows!

SHARKY *enters an inarticulate rage and throws a punch at* NICKY. NICKY *defends himself, pushing* SHARKY *backwards.* IVAN *manages to get a hold of* SHARKY *and restrains him.*

RICHARD. What's going on? Sharky! Calm down!

SHARKY *tries to escape* IVAN's *grip, dragging him over to* LOCKHART.

SHARKY (*shouting at* LOCKHART). Come on! You and me! Outside! Let's finish this for once and for all!

IVAN. Come on, Sharky. Come on…

IVAN *bundles* SHARKY *towards the kitchen.*

SHARKY (*turning to shout at* LOCKHART). You fucking bastard!

IVAN *gets him into the kitchen and shuts the door. We hear* SHARKY's *muffled cries for a moment and* IVAN's *soothing voice.*

LOCKHART. What did I do?

RICHARD. No, no, Mr Lockhart, you didn't do anything. What did any of us do, sure? I can only say I'm terribly sorry… for his behaviour…

LOCKHART. Not your fault, Richard.

NICKY (*picking up an overturned chair and a glass*). He's renowned for that temper. Renowned. He can't drink! He never could! He's barred out of… Richard?

RICHARD. Ah, he's barred out of nearly everywhere. He can't even get a job on the fishing boats any more... They won't have him.

NICKY. Yeah! Like, he had a go at all of us there! You know what I mean?

RICHARD. That's what I live with! That's what we all had to live with, with him.

NICKY *shakily pours them all a drink.*

If our poor old ma said left, Sharky said right. If our da said up, Sharky went down. They'd send him out on a message, maybe to get a few bottles of stout or whatever, he just wouldn't come back! He was like a stray cat in a sock, God help him. Always. And you also have to excuse that he hasn't had a drink in a couple of days, Mr Lockhart. And I don't know why he bothers. That's like running into a brick wall at full tilt there now tonight again, the fucking eejit... What's he drinking?

NICKY. He's drinking that fucking poitín shite you got from the north!

RICHARD. Yeah, I should have known... But, this is the mad thing, he'll be grand now in a minute, watch! Won't he, Nicky?

NICKY. Oh yeah, he'll calm right down now, wait till you see... I should probably be heading on soon anyway or we won't get a taxi...

RICHARD. Ah, Nicky...

NICKY. Fucking... Sharky's left hook is nothing compared to Eileen's, I'll tell you!

RICHARD. She wouldn't hit you, Nicky...

NICKY. It's the force of her words, Richard! Fucking pin you up against the wall...

They laugh. The kitchen door opens and a sheepish SHARKY appears with IVAN. They are both holding cans of beer. Pause.

SHARKY. I'm sorry, Nicky.

NICKY. Yeah, no worries, Shark...

Pause.

SHARKY. I'm sorry, Richard.

RICHARD (*grandly*). Apology accepted.

They are silent while the wind continues to blow outside.
SHARKY stands near his chair. NICKY sits, IVAN sits...

Are you not going to apologise to Mr Lockhart?

Pause.

LOCKHART. No need. No need. No need.

RICHARD. No, Mr Lockhart, I think he should...

LOCKHART. No, no! I perfectly understand. It was only the old
drink talking. Sure I'm full of it myself. I'll tell you what: the only
reparation I'd require, if no one objects is... let's all finish up like
friends and play the last hand and we'll call it a night. How does
that sound?

NICKY. Good idea!

IVAN. Ah, I don't know if maybe this is such a – [good idea].

NICKY. Yeah! It's alright for you there with a big pile of money in
front of you!

RICHARD. No, no, don't worry, Nicky, we'll play, we'll play, won't
we? Sharky? A last hand now and no digs flying, alright?

Pause.

LOCKHART. Okay, Sharky?

SHARKY (*looking at* LOCKHART). Okay...

RICHARD. Will someone pour Sharky a drink there, calm him
down...

IVAN. He has one...

LOCKHART. Will I deal?

He expertly shuffles the cards like a dealer in a casino.

RICHARD. Fire away, Mr Lockhart!

LOCKHART. I'll give 'em a good shuffle...

NICKY. You alright, Shark?

SHARKY nods.

I'm sorry as well, okay?

He offers a handshake. SHARKY *shakes his hand, watching*
LOCKHART *shuffle.* NICKY *and* IVAN *put two euros each in the*
pot.

RICHARD. He's grand! Leave him alone. I live with that silence!

LOCKHART (*proffering deck to* SHARKY). Cut the deck, Sharky?

A little pause before SHARKY *leans forward and taps the deck*
with his knuckle to indicate that he is satisfied with the cut.

(*Taking the cards and dealing.*) Right!

RICHARD. I feel a big win in me waters!

NICKY. That's my big win!

RICHARD. Then why am I feeling it in my waters?

NICKY. Your waters is warning you.

RICHARD. Oh, I don't know about that. I heard a little whistle from
Santy down the chimney, Mr Lockhart…

LOCKHART. Well, last hand! I feel something's really gonna
happen…

NICKY. Something's got to give…

They all collect their cards and peruse them.

Well…

RICHARD. Anything interesting, Nicky?

NICKY. A card or two of note…

RICHARD. Ivan?

IVAN. We're doing alright…

LOCKHART. Care to open the betting, Ivan?

IVAN. Ah, last hand, we'll open it with five euros.

He puts five euros in the pot.

NICKY. Five euros?

RICHARD. Easy now, Ivan!

NICKY. Here, wait! Who's shy?

SHARKY. Oh, sorry…

SHARKY *puts two euros in the pot…*

LOCKHART. I'd hate for you not to be in this hand, Sharky.

SHARKY. Yeah…

RICHARD. So five to play, lads.

NICKY. I'll hang around.

He puts in a fiver.

LOCKHART. Sharky?

SHARKY *considers…*

Ah, you're not gonna go without a fight?

RICHARD. Sharky's had more than enough fights! You should sit this one out, Shark, hang on to your few shekels and don't have me be bailing you out…

LOCKHART. Ah, it's the last hand…

RICHARD. Exactly!

SHARKY. No. I'm in. (*Puts in five and then throws in another note*). With twenty.

The table reacts.

RICHARD. With what? Twenty? You fucking berk!

NICKY. Ah, now, here! Hello…

RICHARD. What are you doing?

IVAN. Let him play, Rich…

RICHARD. Ah, this is mad! How are we doing? What have we got?

IVAN *leans over to confer with* RICHARD, *whispering in his ear.*

NICKY. God, Shark! I thought we were quits… the punishment continues!

LOCKHART. It's only a game!

NICKY (*sarcastically*). Oh, is it?

LOCKHART. Are you in or out, Nicky?

NICKY. Ah fuck it, come on!

He puts in twenty euros.

LOCKHART. Ivan?

IVAN. We'll see it…

LOCKHART. And so will I.

IVAN and LOCKHART *put in twenty.*

RICHARD. You're some bollocks, Sharky.

IVAN. Let him play, Dick.

LOCKHART. Ivan?

IVAN (*throwing a card in*). Just one please, Mr Lockhart.

LOCKHART. One…

He deals him a card.

NICKY (*incredulous*). One?

RICHARD. Yes, Nicky, one.

LOCKHART. Sharky?

SHARKY. One.

NICKY (*downbeat*). One as well?

RICHARD. Ah, he's having a laugh, don't mind him.

NICKY. And what are yous doing?

RICHARD. We're not messing about. We're playing for keeps.

NICKY. Great… Give me three.

LOCKHART (*dealing him three cards*). Three.

NICKY looks at his cards.

RICHARD. That made you go quiet.

NICKY. No, it didn't.

RICHARD. What suddenly happened?

NICKY. No, nothing…

RICHARD. Go on out of that. Nicky suddenly has a hand.

NICKY. Why don't you play me and find out. With your pathetic
   little run up to a six or whatever it is.

RICHARD. Don't worry, we will. How many did you take,
   Mr Lockhart?

LOCKHART. I'm happy.

NICKY. You're happy?!

LOCKHART. No cards. I'll stick with these.

NICKY. Oh bollocks.

LOCKHART. The bet's to Sharky.

RICHARD. Throw 'em in, Shark. Don't lose it all on a bluff now.

Pause. SHARKY *considers* LOCKHART.

SHARKY. Fifty.

NICKY. Oh God…

RICHARD. Sharky!

IVAN. No, let him play, Dick!

LOCKHART. Nicky?

NICKY. Oh God…

NICKY *gets up and walks away from the table.*

RICHARD. Where's he going?

NICKY. I'm thinking!

RICHARD. God help us!

Pause. NICKY *comes back, taking some money out of his pocket.*

NICKY. Come on! It's Christmas. Fifty. I'm in. And I'm fucked now.

LOCKHART. Ivan?

NICKY. Sure he (*Re:* SHARKY.) has nothing.

IVAN. Yeah. (*Puts in fifty.*) Fifty.

RICHARD. Jaysus, you're very *flathulach* [*Irish for 'generous'*] with my money there now, Vano.

IVAN. Hey, I won some of this too, Rich, don't forget.

RICHARD. Yeah well, easy come…

LOCKHART. And I'll see Sharky's fifty. With fifty.

NICKY (*throwing in his hand, then standing up*). Ah here! If yous are…

RICHARD. With what?

IVAN. With fifty…

NICKY. 'Cause if yous are…

RICHARD. With fifty?!

IVAN (*trying to keep* RICHARD *committed*). No, hold on… hold on…

NICKY. This is just too expensive! I mean I can have fun for nothing, like!

RICHARD. You out, Nicky?

NICKY. I'm gone! I'm out…

NICKY *goes and grabs his jacket.*

(*Almost mumbling.*) This is fucking crazy…

LOCKHART. Ivan?

IVAN *turns to whisper to* RICHARD. SHARKY *sits watching* LOCKHART, *who returns his gaze.*

NICKY. Lads, I have to shoot. 'Cause we won't get a taxi…

RICHARD. Yeah, hold your horses…

NICKY. Yous have all me money!

RICHARD (*to* IVAN). Go on, go on…

IVAN. We're in.

He puts in fifty.

NICKY. Jaysus…

LOCKHART. Sharky.

SHARKY. Here. (*Raising.*) And whatever else this is… eighty…

LOCKHART. With eighty?

RICHARD. Sharky, what are you doing? You mad bollocks?

LOCKHART. Ivan?

NICKY. Lads… don't blow a good evening now…

IVAN. No, we'll see it…

RICHARD. Ivan…

IVAN. To you, Mr Lockhart.

LOCKHART. Well, I've no change so I'll just throw in a hundred.

IVAN. So twenty to play.

He puts in twenty to see the bet.

RICHARD. Ivan!

IVAN. We're alright, Dick.

RICHARD. Speak for yourself!

LOCKHART. Sharky?

SHARKY. Em…

NICKY. Sharky's busted. You're gone, Shark, you're out…

LOCKHART. Well, if he wants to play… I know he's good for it.

RICHARD. Good for it?! He is not!

SHARKY. Richard, I have it.

RICHARD. Where? Under the mattress down in Lahinch?

SHARKY. Yeah, just not… I have it.

RICHARD. Where?

NICKY. Ah, he's good for it, Rich.

LOCKHART. I'll play him.

RICHARD. What the fuck is this, the Credit Union? Sharky, if we win, you've to cook that coddle I been asking you for, right?

SHARKY. Yeah, alright, I'll do it!

RICHARD. With the black pudding?

SHARKY. Yeah, alright!

NICKY. He'll do it…

RICHARD. Yeah, but what if Mr Lockhart wins? Who's gonna pay him for Sharky?

SHARKY. I'll pay him myself.

RICHARD. With what?

IVAN. We'll give it to him!

RICHARD. We'll have nothing left!

LOCKHART. We'll go up to the hole in the wall, sure. Isn't there one up there by the off-licence?

RICHARD. The hole in the wall? (*Laughing.*) Sharky has no bank account!

SHARKY. I have it, Rich, alright? Just let me play.

RICHARD. Do you have a sneaky bank account? Are you putting all my change from the shopping in there?

SHARKY. Richard! Would you give it a rest?

RICHARD. You're gone mad!

LOCKHART. I'm happy to play him, Richard. And I'm happy to go up to the hole in the wall with him if I win.

IVAN. Let him play, Rich…

RICHARD. Okay! But this is… I give up. I fucking give up!

LOCKHART. So? We're all in? Show our hands?

NICKY. Yous probably all have nothing, have yous?

Pause. SHARKY *takes a long drink.*

LOCKHART. Sharky?

SHARKY. I have a poker. Four eights.

SHARKY *and* LOCKHART *sit watching each other.*

NICKY. Four fucking eights? Bang!

IVAN. Yous are not gonna believe this…

RICHARD. I'm sick…

NICKY. What have you got, Ivan?

IVAN. We had a poker as well! Four fours!

RICHARD. Ah, this is a disaster!

NICKY. No!

IVAN. Four fours…

He throws his cards face down with disgust…

NICKY. Sharky wins! What a hand, though! Both of yous!

RICHARD. That is a total killer now…

LOCKHART. Well, one moment, gentlemen, please…

Pause. He lays his hand down for them to see. SHARKY *closes his eyes when he sees it.*

NICKY. Four tens!!! What are the chances?!

RICHARD. What?

IVAN. Four tens…

NICKY. Sharky…

RICHARD. Did Sharky blow it?

NICKY. Sharky, you're beaten…

RICHARD. Sharky, you fucking eejit!

NICKY. You had to play it.

RICHARD. What were you doing?

IVAN. He had to play with a hand like that, Dick, come on…

RICHARD (*angrily*). Ah!

NICKY. Well, you certainly cleaned us all out, Mr Lockhart.

LOCKHART. A pleasure, gentlemen…

IVAN. Hard luck, lads…

NICKY. Look, I'm gonna have to see if I can grab a taxi. (*Remembering he is broke.*) Eh… D'you want to share one, Mr Lockhart?

LOCKHART (*rising, collecting his money*). No, I'm going to walk, Nicky.

NICKY. All the way up to Howth?

LOCKHART. I always like to savour the last few hours of dawn before the Child arrives. I never have too long, you see. Sharky'll keep me company as far as the hole in the wall anyway.

NICKY (*baffled*). Eh… well, whatever you want… I'm gonna…

He zips up his jacket.

LOCKHART. Sharky?

SHARKY. Yeah.

RICHARD. Here, take it from me, Mr Lockhart, what do we owe you, twenty?

SHARKY. Nah, it's alright, Dick, I'll go with him...

RICHARD. But we have it here! Give it to me later!

SHARKY. Nah, I should give him my own... what I owe him.

RICHARD. Don't be ridiculous! It's the middle of the night!

SHARKY. No, it's fine. Really...

RICHARD. Talk about contrary! Sharky, come on...

NICKY. Here, Ivan, do you want a lift if I can grab a taxi out on the street?

IVAN. Oh, I don't know if I'd be welcome now at this hour...

NICKY. Would you not chance it? What time is it? It's a quarter to seven?! Oh bollocks!! How did that happen?

IVAN. What? Oh God, okay, let me have a slash quickly!

IVAN *jogs into the kitchen to use the toilet.* NICKY *runs up the stairs.*

NICKY. I'll see if I can grab a jo. I doubt it though... Bollocks!

He is gone.

LOCKHART. Well, Richard. It was very nice to make your acquaintance.

RICHARD. Yes! Well, thank you for calling.

LOCKHART. I hope you're not too sore about losing.

RICHARD. No, I'm just annoyed that I can't see and I can't play properly for myself. Or do anything that I'd really want. But we must do it again. Are you around?

LOCKHART. Oh I'll be gone now... till Good Friday anyway.

RICHARD. Well, maybe around then. And please excuse my brother and his... behaviour. Please, let me give you the twenty euros. I'm nervous about him going off out now at this hour... I just... he's had a few drinks and you've seen that he can be… Sure, you'll nearly have to go all the way up to Sutton Cross! The cash machine at the shops has been empty for days now coming up to Christmas!

LOCKHART. I'd be happy to oblige you, Richard. But Sharky seems to feel he should pay me himself.

RICHARD (*groping for money, holding out whatever he has grabbed*). Jaysus, Sharky, I'll give it to you, alright? Happy Christmas, okay? Are you happy?

SHARKY. I have to go, Richard. I have to do it myself. I'm sorry.

RICHARD. Ah, I give up! Come straight back now, won't you?

Pause.

You promise me?

Short pause.

SHARKY. Yeah.

NICKY *reappears, coming down the stairs.*

NICKY. Where's Ivan? Is he coming? I have a jo! It's Mungo Mickey's brother, whatshisname… He's on his way home, so come on! Ivan!

IVAN *reappears from the toilet, wearing a big pair of spectacles.*

IVAN. I found me glasses!

RICHARD. Well, thank fuck for that!

NICKY. Come on, do you want to chance it, I'll bring you home?

IVAN. Oh, I don't know… I'm really after blowing it now sure, it's the fucking morning!

RICHARD. Look, hang on here with me, Ivan, we'll give her a ring, alright? And smooth the passage…

IVAN. Yeah, maybe… (*Defeated.*) Oh… Sure, I'm jarred, Nicky…

NICKY. Okay, well, look, I'll see yous. Good luck, Richard.

NICKY *comes and shakes hands with* RICHARD. IVAN *sits at the table and takes a drink.*

RICHARD. See ya, Nicky, me old flower!

NICKY. And I'll be in to see you now over the Christmas. And we'll have a nice, proper Christmas drink…

RICHARD. Absolutely. You'll have to rescue me.

NICKY. Would you go on out of that, you don't need rescuing, Dick! (*Hurrying towards stairs*.) Lads, I'll see yous. You sure yous won't take a lift?

IVAN. Here, hold on…

He picks up his hand from the game…

These is four aces!

NICKY. What? (*Goes to look*.) It is! Yous had four aces, you dozy fucking eejit!

RICHARD. What's he saying?

NICKY. Yous had four aces!

IVAN. I thought they were fours, I couldn't…

NICKY. Yous won it! (*Turns to* LOCKHART.) They beat you, Mr Lockhart…

LOCKHART. No…

NICKY. No, they did.

LOCKHART. Let me see…

NICKY *brings the cards to* LOCKHART.

IVAN. I thought they were… you see I fucking thought they were fours! They were aces!

RICHARD. Well, happy Christmas!

IVAN. I just couldn't see them!

RICHARD. Here, hold on, how many other hands did you balls up on me?

NICKY. Well, that saves you an auld trip to the hole in the wall, Sharky…

SHARKY *and* LOCKHART *look at each other.*

RICHARD. Let's have a drink! I knew that hand was ours! I could feel it in me waters! I told yous! Woo hoo!

IVAN. I'm sorry about that, Mr Lockhart...

NICKY. Oh, that's a pain in the hole, Mr Lockhart. Lads, I have to run, I can't believe none of yous is coming with me! Come on, Mr Lockhart, you might as well take a lift now... Come on!

LOCKHART *stands there looking at them, then he takes the money from his pocket and puts it on the table.*

LOCKHART. Well, what can I say? Somebody's done you a big favour, Sharky.

RICHARD. Hey, this is a square house, there's no cheating or favours being done when it comes to playing cards in here!

LOCKHART. I'm not saying it was anyone here...

RICHARD. What in the name of God are you talking about? It was just a mistake. People make mistakes, Mr Lockhart. It's not the end of the world...

LOCKHART. No...

IVAN. I just couldn't see! They looked like fours... I didn't look at them properly, I'm sorry.

RICHARD. Hey, you owe me that twenty euros now, Sharky.

NICKY. Come on, Mr Lockhart, I'll drop you at Sutton Cross, you can stroll up from there. Sharky. I'll see you, right?

SHARKY. Yeah, I'll see you, Nicky.

They shake hands.

NICKY. Call in over the Christmas, say hello, won't you?

SHARKY. Yeah.

NICKY. Good man. Ivan, I'll see you up in Doyles no doubt, have a good one, right?

IVAN. Yeah. Cheers, Nicky.

NICKY. And don't spend all that wonga until you get me a pint of Miller, or three, right? I'm gone! Come on, Mr Lockhart, if we lose this lad we're goosed!

NICKY *runs up the stairs.*

LOCKHART. Well then... I'll say goodnight.

RICHARD. Yeah, good morning! Happy Christmas! I hope Santy brings you what you want!

LOCKHART (*buttoning up his coat*). I only want what yous fellas have.

RICHARD. Yeah? What's that, then?

LOCKHART (*putting on his hat*). Peace of mind.

RICHARD *and* IVAN *burst out laughing.*

RICHARD. What? Are you fucking joking me?

LOCKHART. No. Goodbye, Richard. Goodbye, Ivan. See you again.

IVAN (*pouring a drink for himself and* RICHARD). Yeah, good luck.

LOCKHART. Goodbye, Sharky.

SHARKY *doesn't answer him.*

Perhaps we'll play again some time, when my luck changes. Or yours does.

SHARKY. Nah, you're alright.

RICHARD. Sharky!

SHARKY. I just don't want to play any more.

LOCKHART. Well, you should think about it. Somebody up there likes you, Sharky. You've got it all.

LOCKHART *unsteadily mounts the stairs and goes off. The light under the Sacred Heart blinks on. The first rays of dawn are seeping into the room. The front door slams.*

RICHARD. Well, Jaysus! That is one maudlin fucker! Talk about a poor loser!

IVAN. Where do I know him from?

RICHARD. Ah, he's one of Nicky's strays. Jesus Christ, it's freezing in here!

SHARKY. Yeah, let me just…

SHARKY *goes to the stove and puts fuel in.*

RICHARD. Good man, Sharko! Hey, do yous know what we should do? The monks do have an early mass in the Friary. Do yous feel like it? Because then – this is brilliant – we'll get one of them to run you up home, Ivan, soothe Karen's temper – they love her up there – and be an honest broker. How's that for genius?

IVAN (*considers, not too convinced*). Well, I don't know…

RICHARD. And you know of course that they brew their own ale up there? I was there when they started doling it out one Christmas. It's strong stuff. Two or three jugs of that after mass and you'll be whistling Dixie for the whole afternoon! What do you think, Sharky?

SHARKY. Yeah, I suppose we could walk up if it's not still raining…

RICHARD. Hey, Sharky…

SHARKY. Yeah?

RICHARD. Go over to the tree.

SHARKY. What?

RICHARD. 'What?' he says! What, did you think I didn't get you anything? What do you think I am? An ogre? Hey, Ivan, check out bah humbug over here! Go on, Ivan, get yours as well. He knows what it is. He wrapped them for me, didn't you, Ivan?

IVAN *lets out a loud snore…*

SHARKY. He's having a nap.

RICHARD. Ah, leave him. Yours is there. It has your name on it. It doesn't matter. They're both the same.

SHARKY. Ah, Rich, are you serious?

RICHARD. Yeah, well, you don't deserve it now after your disgraceful behaviour. But sure, it's Christmas. All is forgiven. What do you say?

SHARKY *goes to the tree and picks up one of the presents.*

Open it, you berk!

SHARKY *opens the wrapping.*

You see what it is? It's a mobile phone!

SHARKY. Oh yeah. Thanks, Rich… it's…

RICHARD. Yeah, well, that old 088 you were using, sure that's practically obsolete! No one can ever get you! I just thought that if

you were gonna get back to the driving or if I ever needed to…
that I could get you, you know…

SHARKY. Yeah… Thanks…

RICHARD. What? Is something wrong?

SHARKY. No, I'm… I'm just…

RICHARD. Ah, buck up, will you, Sharky! I don't want the whole –
(*A mocking, unfair impression of* SHARKY.) 'Aw, life is too hard
and I can't take it!' off you today now, right? Do you hear me? We
all know you're an alcoholic and your life is in tatters and you're
an awful fucking gobshite. We all know that. But you know what?
You're alive, aren't you? (*Beat.*) Aren't you?

SHARKY. Yeah.

RICHARD. So come on! Buck up now! It's Christmas day and I feel
like going to mass, so go on and put the kettle on! Ivan!

IVAN *jumps.*

IVAN. What?

RICHARD. You better get a cup of tea into you, come on, we're
gonna go up to mass. And see if we can get one of the monks to
broker a peace deal for you. (*Going towards the stairs.*) Hey,
Shark, do I have a clean shirt?

SHARKY. I left one on your bed.

RICHARD. Good man, stick on a bit of toast, will you? Ivan, you
might come up and help me get a shave in a minute, is that alright?

IVAN. Yeah, no problem, Dick.

RICHARD (*going up*). Hey, lads, we really showed that fucker, didn't
we?

IVAN. We sure did.

RICHARD. There was funny smell off him. Get Ivan a bit of
breakfast, will you, Sharky?

SHARKY. Do you want a bit of toast, Ivan?

IVAN. Oh, I don't think so. I don't think I'm quite there yet.

SHARKY. Well, I'll put the kettle on.

RICHARD (*as he disappears*). Good man, Sharky. That's the way.

SHARKY *goes to the kitchen.* IVAN *wanders over to the stereo. He takes a CD from* SHARKY'*s gift parcel. Morning is really beginning to pour in now. The wind has died down. The sky is clear.*

IVAN. Hey, Shark! She has good taste, your one who sent you these…

SHARKY *comes out with a tray, tidying up.*

SHARKY. What's that?

IVAN. No, I said you got some good music off your friend down the country.

SHARKY. Yeah?

IVAN. Yeah. These are classics.

SHARKY. Stick one on.

IVAN. Will I?

SHARKY. Yeah, go on…

SHARKY *continues to tidy up while* IVAN *puts on a CD. John Martyn's 'Sweet Little Mystery' begins to play softly.* IVAN *stands nodding his approval in time with the music and then goes off up the stairs to help* RICHARD. SHARKY *pauses for a moment. He reaches into his pocket and takes out the card he received in Act One. He stands there reading, and as John Martyn sings the sunlight seems to stream in brighter and brighter for a moment, before it fades away with the music.*

End.

THE BIRDS

From the short story by Daphne du Maurier

*Then the Lord God placed the man in the Garden of Eden to cultivate
it and guard it. He said to him, 'You may eat the fruit of any tree in
the garden, except the tree that gives knowledge of what is good and
what is bad. You must not eat that fruit of that tree; if you do, you will
die the same day.'*

Genesis 2:16-17

*I am the eye with which the Universe
Beholds itself, and knows it is divine.*

Percy Bysshe Shelley,
Song of Apollo, 1820

The Birds was first performed at the Gate Theatre, Dublin, on 29 September 2009, with the following cast:

DIANE	Sinead Cusack
JULIA	Denise Gough
NAT	Ciarán Hinds
TIERNEY	Owen Roe

Director	Conor McPherson
Designer	Rae Smith
Lighting Designer	Paul Keogan
Sound Designer	Simon Baker

The play received its American premiere at the Guthrie Theater, Minneapolis, on 25 February 2012, with the following cast:

NAT	J.C. Cutler
JULIA	Summer Hagen
DIANE	Angela Timberman
TIERNEY	Stephen Yoakam

Director	Henry Wishcamper
Set Designer	Wilson Chin
Costume Designer	Jenny Mannis
Lighting Designer	Matthew Richards
Sound Designer	Scott W. Edwards

Characters

DIANE, *late forties/fifties*
NAT, *forties/fifties*
JULIA, *twenties*
TIERNEY, *fifties*

Setting

A house in the countryside.

Author's Note

It would be preferable if stage management remained invisible for
this play and the actors make any necessary changes to the set
between scenes themselves. This way we also get an opportunity to
watch them living together.

Scene One

In the darkness we hear DIANE*'s voice through speakers. It should
sound intimate. We hear her thoughts. Lights onstage gradually
reveal an isolated house in the countryside.*

DIANE (*voice-over*). I met the man on the road. We had both
abandoned our cars and decided to take our chances cutting
through the fields. We broke into a house beside the water and
locked ourselves in. The waves of bird attacks continued for the
next two days, punctuated by terrifying hours of inexplicable
silence. The man, who said his name was Nat, was sick. I nursed
him while he slept through a restless delirium. And that night was
the last broadcast we ever heard.

*New England in the near future. It is night. The shutters are
closed. We hear birds rustling outside the house. A fluttering of
wings here and there.* NAT *is asleep.* DIANE *is trying to tune in a
radio. All she gets is static with the odd voice trailing in and out.
She adjusts the dial and begins to pick up a signal as voices fade
in. Throughout the broadcast, random voices and sounds obscure
what's being said. There is chaos in the studio from where the
broadcast is coming.*

VOICE 1. Okay, so centres, aid centres, places where people can feel
safe, somewhere to sleep. They know there's a meal there…

VOICE 2. I never said that. I can't say that.

VOICE 1. Yes, but they can…

VOICE 2. There are people there, they seem organised, maybe it's
safer there, that's what we're…

VOICE 1. We're saying Mountstewart, St Thomas, Port Argus…

VOICE 2. Port Argus won't be able to take the strain.

VOICE 1. Well, Lowtown, Newchurch?

VOICE 2. Well… And Winford, we think, although…

VOICE 3 (*distant, off-mic*). No…

VOICE 1. Sorry, what?

VOICE 3. No, there was no... eh...

VOICE 2. From Winford...

VOICE 1. Don't go to Winford.

VOICE 2. No, what we are saying is what we can't confirm. I'm not trying to tell people where to go. I'm saying that I've been given this advice, that I have received...

VOICE 1 (*to* VOICE 3). What's the situation with Winford?

VOICE 3 (*unintelligible*).

VOICE 2. Because, I wouldn't even have said St Thomas myself.

VOICE 3 (*distant*). There are people there...

VOICE 1. There are people there. One could go to St Thomas...

VOICE 2. So it seems but...

VOICE 1. City Councillor John Little announced today that if he couldn't organise a quorum here tonight in Mountstewart that he will propose a... I can't read this...

VOICE 4. Listen, the situation is...

VOICE 1. Sorry, Dr Brodie, you want to come in there.

VOICE 4. The situation is – (*Interference.*) simply because no one could have prepared for a...

Interference...

VOICE 2. This is what I'm saying, we are all in the same situation, but there's no point in...

VOICE 3 (*distant*). They got into the gym at Cottonhills last night...

VOICE 1. Sorry, what?

VOICE 3. They got into the gym at Cottonhills last night so...

VOICE 4. You see, once they're in...

VOICE 2. We're talking about crows, sea birds, robins, sparrows! I mean, you think a man could... a grown adult can...

VOICE 4. Yes, but your average gull is big! Four or five or six pounds in weight coming straight down out of the sky, easily reaching speeds of forty miles an hour, can cause a tremendous amount of damage to a...

NAT *stirs restlessly.*

NAT. Sarah?

DIANE *switches off the radio.*

Sarah! No! Don't!

DIANE *goes to him, taking a cloth from a bowl of water to soothe his forehead.*

No! Stay away from me!

DIANE. Shh...

NAT *suddenly springs up towards the door.*

NAT. I have to get out!

DIANE *puts her hands on his shoulders.*

DIANE. No, don't do that.

NAT *grabs her roughly, forcing her back across the room.*

NAT. I'll fucking kill you! I mean it...

DIANE. You're just having a dream. It's okay, it's me, it's Diane.

NAT *looks at her, his eyes are wild.*

NAT. It's so cold.

DIANE. Why don't you lie down? Here, come on...

DIANE *goes and holds the blanket for him to get back into his 'bed'. He looks around the room.*

NAT. The baby was here.

DIANE. No. It's okay...

NAT. She was over there. She came in the door. She... (*Goes towards the stairs.*)

DIANE. No, come over here and lie down.

He obediently goes to her and goes to lie down, suddenly springing up.

NAT. I hope she didn't go back out!

DIANE (*gently*). No, no, it's alright. Shh... Just try and rest. Try and stay warm. I'm here.

NAT *quietens down and we hear birds shuffling around outside, enlivened by the voices.*

Scene Two

Dusk. DIANE *is at the stove, putting some fuel in. We can hear some wings flapping outside and scratching or pecking here and there.* NAT *is awake, watching* DIANE.

NAT. What time is it?

DIANE. Oh, hi. Are you hungry?

NAT. I'd love a drink of water.

DIANE. Yeah.

She pours him a cup of water from a plastic bottle. He gulps it down.

More?

He nods and she pours him another cup.

NAT. Thanks. How long was I asleep?

DIANE. Two days.

NAT. What?

DIANE. Your temperature broke yesterday. It must have been at least a hundred and three.

NAT. Oh... I'm sorry; did you say your name was Diana?

DIANE. Diane.

NAT. Oh yes, Diane. No sign of the owners, of this place?

DIANE. No.

NAT. Is everything...?

DIANE. Everything's... the same.

NAT. No news or…?

DIANE. Nothing for the last twenty-four hours.

NAT. Right. God… But nothing like, from the Government or…? I mean, how can all the phones all just be out?!

DIANE. I don't know. They think it's the tides.

NAT. What is?

DIANE. The birds go out with the tides. And they come back at high tide. Every six hours.

NAT. Oh.

DIANE. I mean, they don't know why.

NAT. God… I thought maybe it was all a dream.

DIANE. I know. It's high tide now.

Pause. They listen to the birds scrabbling around outside.

NAT. Do you think they know we're in here?

DIANE. Yeah. I do.

Pause.

NAT. Did you say you had a daughter?

DIANE. Yes. But, you know, grown up. Moved away. Et cetera. I was on my way to see her. It was her birthday and I was… going to…

Pause.

NAT. What about your husband?

DIANE. We're separated.

NAT. Right.

DIANE. He lives abroad.

NAT. Is this happening everywhere?

DIANE. It seems to be.

Pause.

NAT. What does he do?

DIANE. Who?

NAT. Your husband.

DIANE. He's a writer. We're both writers.

NAT. Really?

DIANE. Yeah, really.

NAT. What do you write?

DIANE. Books… you know. I haven't written one for a while but…

NAT. Well, I'd say it's tough enough to… to write a book, I mean…

DIANE. Do you have any children?

NAT. Well, I… no, they're my… the children of my ex.

DIANE. Ex-wife?

NAT. …My… ex-girlfriend – or partner, I suppose. Not wife. We were living together. But not… not recently.

DIANE. Right. (*Short pause*.) Well, you were a family.

NAT. Yeah.

A loud smash somewhere makes them spring up. NAT *grabs a hammer and wields it like a weapon.*

DIANE. How old are they?

NAT. Six and eight. But I haven't seen them in about… ten months, a year.

DIANE. Right. Well, that's hard.

NAT. Yeah. And the break-up was… you know…

DIANE. Mmm…

NAT. It was… (*Looks at the shutters where some wings are heard flapping, birds bang against the glass*.) difficult, so…

DIANE. Yeah. Well, that's…

NAT. Yeah.

Pause

DIANE. Was this Sarah?

Pause.

NAT. Yeah, how do you know?

DIANE. Because you were talking to her.

NAT. What do you mean?

DIANE. You were talking to someone called Sarah. You pushed me right across the room.

NAT. Are you serious?

DIANE *just gives a little wry smile and raises her eyebrows.*

Oh, I'm sorry. Did I hurt you?

DIANE. No – (*Beat.*) just my finger.

NAT. Oh, no. I'm sorry. Is it bad?

DIANE. No, it just got bent right back, you know when that happens.

NAT. Oh God… Listen, I'd never do anything like that. I mean…

DIANE. I know.

NAT. I'm sorry.

DIANE. No, it's okay.

Pause. A concerted effort by a bird to fly repeatedly through a window makes them fall silent. The noise passes.

NAT. I can't believe I did that. She's absolutely crazy. I mean, she had me locked up, you know?

DIANE (*looking at him standing there with a hammer in his hand*). Who?

NAT. Sarah.

DIANE. In your dream?

NAT. No, like really. In real life. She's crazy.

DIANE. What do you mean 'locked up'?

NAT. Not in prison. She signed me into a… hospital. And she's the one who's nuts! That's the… that's the sick… irony.

DIANE.…Right. Was this recently or…

NAT (*playing it down*). No… About a year ago?

DIANE....Right.

NAT. I mean, I wasn't well. I'm not saying that I wasn't. I certainly wasn't a hundred per cent. I was just suffering from a... a form of exhaustion really. But the way she decided to... to deal with it was... it was hugely disproportionate.

Pause.

DIANE. Right. (*Pause.*) What... happened, I mean, I'm...

NAT. Oh no, it's nothing to worry about.

DIANE. Right. No. (*Pause.*) You don't mind me asking. I'm just, I don't want to...

NAT. No, no, it's fine. No, just... There were just... a lot of arguments – you know how that... is...

DIANE. Mmm.

NAT. And a lot of criticism, coming my way from her family. About money, about other things... And I'd started getting these headaches and I wasn't able to sleep.

DIANE. Right. (*Pause.*) Do you... still get headaches, or...?

NAT. No. No, not for a long time. Yeah. No, I'm okay. I was always okay, really. There was just a lot of, you know *other* stuff going on there. You know. Certain agendas. But I still... I mean, you worry about people. I mean, I just... that's where I was going when all the... the birds started to happen. Probably a stupid fucking thing to do really.

DIANE. Oh, I don't know. You know what they say.

She gets up, tidying away her cup.

NAT. What?

DIANE. The first cut is the deepest.

NAT. Mmm.

He sits, looking into firelight of the stove.

Scene Three

The lights bring us to daylight. The door is open. The shutters are open, revealing boards up outside the windows. NAT comes in.

NAT. Listen, em… I think someone's been outside.

DIANE. What?

NAT. The padlock on the shed door was on the ground out there.

He shows her.

DIANE. Is anything gone?

NAT. I'm not sure. I thought I saw a can of kerosene in there a few days ago. It's not there now. And a shovel, I think, is gone.

DIANE. When do you think it…?

NAT. I think maybe just this morning when we were at the gas station. I mean, it might have even just been while we were down at the lake. I don't know.

DIANE. Just now?

NAT. I don't know!

NAT walks restlessly into the hall, looking around and comes back.

DIANE. Who would it be?

NAT. I think there's someone in that house across the lake.

DIANE. Where?

NAT. On the other side of the lake. I saw him yesterday morning when I was scavenging in the gas station. I think he had a gun, or a shotgun. He stepped back in behind the wall when he saw me.

DIANE. Why didn't you say anything?

He shrugs.

He must be watching us.

NAT. Yeah well, if it was him. If he's still there, I mean... I don't know.

DIANE. Let's go round there. We might see him. We might see smoke coming out of his chimney, I mean, if there's someone else living here we should... I mean, shouldn't we at least... be...

NAT. He's got a fucking gun though, Diane!

She is taken aback by the forcefulness of his outburst. He sees this.

I'm sorry.

DIANE. No. I know.

NAT goes. DIANE stands there.

Scene Four

Night. The room is lit by a candle or two. DIANE is tuning the radio, getting only static. The wind is howling. Occasionally a thump makes her look up as a bird tries to smash its way in. NAT comes down the stairs carrying a toolbox.

NAT. They can't get in.

DIANE. Doesn't it seem louder to you, tonight? I mean it sounds like there's a lot more of them.

NAT. Maybe they see the light. Maybe they hear us.

DIANE wonders if NAT is telling her to shut up. She switches off the radio and sits despondently, perusing a road map. NAT regards DIANE, then reaches into a hiding place and produces a bottle of cheap sherry with a screw top with about half left in it.

Listen, em, I picked this up in the office of the gas station, I don't know if it's... I mean it's a screw top. (*Reading label.*) It says it's wine... or sherry...

DIANE. Oh great...

NAT. I don't know when your birthday is, or was exactly, or was it your daughter's?

DIANE. Ah, Nat! It was Nina. It was her birthday.

NAT. Well, you said something about a birthday… and…

    NAT *gets two cups…*

    A birthday's a birthday. So happy birthday to Nina, right?

DIANE. Yeah. God, this is very swanky.

NAT. Well, I wouldn't say that.

    He opens the screw top.

    Fuck knows what this is like.

    He sniffs it and recoils…

    Oh Jesus

DIANE. Hit me.

    He pours them drinks.

    Thank you.

NAT. No cake, but…

DIANE. You can't have everything.

NAT. You can't have anything!

    They laugh mordantly.

    You could blow out a candle.

DIANE. No, I'm good.

NAT. Good luck.

DIANE. Cheers.

    They drink. They both grimace. DIANE *proffers her cup anyway.*

DIANE (*hoarsely*). That's not too bad.

NAT (*hoarsely*). No!

    He pours them another drink.

DIANE. It gives you kind of a nice warm…

NAT. Yeah, when you get it down!

    They laugh. They stand near the glow of the fire. DIANE *suddenly puts her face in her hand and cries silently.* NAT *looks at her for a moment, unsure what to say.*

DIANE (*regaining her composure*). Sorry.

NAT. No…

DIANE. Thanks, Nat.

NAT. No…

DIANE goes to get the map, bringing it to NAT.

DIANE. Listen, I've been looking at this. We could get to St Thomas and back – in six hours.

NAT. Yeah…

DIANE. I mean, there's got to be a supermarket. There's got to be something.

NAT. Diane…

DIANE. We could be there in two, two-and-a-half hours. At the very least we'd have had a good…

NAT. Yeah, but…

DIANE. And even if we… if somehow we got… that we thought it was getting too late, there has to be somewhere that we could… I mean, what do we…

NAT. Shh! (*Holds his hand up to silence her.*)

They hear shouting in the distance. Different voices. Sporadic.

Blow out those candles!

They quickly douse the lights. The voices fall silent. There is a lot of flapping and scratching as the birds become excited coming and going from the roof of the house.

They wait listening. They only hear the birds. Then they hear a church bell off in the distance. Lights fade as they listen.

Scene Five

It is a bright afternoon. All is quiet. A girl of about twenty, JULIA, comes into the room, rolling a cigarette. She has a dressing over a cut on her head. She is wearing a pair of high-heeled shoes. She finds some matches. A tape is playing in a radio/cassette player. It is someone playing a piano. She smokes, taking a saucer as an ashtray. DIANE arrives, a blanket wrapped around her. She throws a cold eye on the scene. JULIA gets up and turns down the music.

JULIA. Sorry.

DIANE. Is that the radio?

JULIA. No, I found a few tapes upstairs in a shoebox.

DIANE. Tapes will wear down the batteries.

JULIA. Okay. Sorry.

She switches it off.

And I found some shoes. They're going to kill me, but they'll have to do.

DIANE. How are you feeling?

JULIA. You have no idea what it means to me to be here, Diane. I can hardly believe it. I haven't felt safe like this for so long.

DIANE. How's your head?

JULIA. It's sore. But I want to start pitching in with all the chores now. When I stop feeling dizzy.

DIANE. Should you be smoking if you feel dizzy?

JULIA. Probably not.

JULIA stubs the fag out.

DIANE. Where did you get the cigarettes?

JULIA. I found some tobacco in a drawer upstairs. It's kind of horrible actually.

DIANE. Is it okay if you don't smoke in the house?

JULIA. Yeah, sorry, I didn't think.

DIANE (*indicating a mattress and blanket on the floor*). Are you finished with your bed?

JULIA. Yeah. Oh sorry.

She goes to help DIANE *tidy it away.*

DIANE. Show me that dressing.

DIANE *goes to* JULIA *and maternally looks at her wound.*

I didn't do a great job. Let me put another one on.

JULIA. Thanks, Diane.

DIANE. Lie up here.

JULIA *lies on the sofa.* DIANE *wipes her hands and gets the first-aid kit. She goes to* JULIA *and carefully removes the dressing.*

What did you say he hit you with?

JULIA. A bell.

DIANE. A bell?

DIANE *gently dabs at the wound with some antiseptic.*

JULIA. I know. He found it in the classroom where we were hiding. And this particular person, he'd been trying to… you know… trying to be with me for a few nights, I woke up and he was trying to, you know, get close to me.

DIANE. Where were the other girls?

JULIA. They were in a different classroom and in the office. I was in a kind of big closet off one of the rooms. I'd been asleep.

DIANE. How many were there?

JULIA. Two other older girls. But I don't think they would have helped me. I had to get out. I ran across a huge football field, he came after me, but he was drunk. The birds got him. I heard him trying to get back into the school, but I don't think he made it. I hope he didn't.

DIANE. The birds didn't come after you?

JULIA. No. I hid in the church for a few hours and then I started walking out down by the road, but because I had no shoes and my legs were really wobbly, I was like… Then when I saw the smoke from your chimney I just thought, God, this is a miracle!

Pause.

DIANE. But why did you leave Port Argus?

JULIA. It was insane there, Diane. The whole place was drunk. There was a fire in the library and everybody had to leave. We had tried to get into Mountstewart. But no one was getting in. They'd closed the whole place down. So we started fucking walking. We slept in a house out in the country like this for a night but it was too crazy. Birds got in.

She winces in pain.

DIANE. Sorry.

JULIA. No it's fine. Then we slept in a factory, but that was horrible. We were in the school then for two nights. They'd found a load of malt liquor in a truck and I was sleeping away from the others 'cause I knew that something was going to happen. Something bad.

DIANE *finishes dressing the wound and starts tidying up.*

Thanks, Diane.

DIANE. You're welcome. It really needs a stitch.

JULIA (*lightly touches the dressing*). Thanks for looking after me.

DIANE. Hey, anyone would do it.

JULIA. I don't know about that! Nat told me you have a daughter. Is that right?

DIANE (*nods*). Mm-hm.

JULIA. How old is she?

DIANE. Older than you.

JULIA. I hope you get to see her again soon.

DIANE. Well. We'll see…

DIANE *is over where they keep their food.*

Julia, there was a can of spaghetti here.

JULIA. What was it?

DIANE. There was a can of SpaghettiOs on top of that box there.

JULIA. I don't know.

DIANE. You didn't see it?

JULIA. No. I only had half a stock cube and some water all day.

DIANE. But it was right there.

JULIA. There's pasta in the other box.

DIANE. I know, but the canned stuff is… I'm always very careful with it, because we can mix it with other things. And we never…

DIANE *is searching for it.*

JULIA. Maybe Nat will bring some back from the gas station.

DIANE. Yeah, but that's not what I'm talking about.

JULIA. Diane, I swear to God… I was just looking for tobacco. Diane. I didn't eat the spaghetti. I wouldn't do that.

NAT *arrives in the doorway. He carries a few things, not much.*

NAT. What's happened?

JULIA. Some food is gone missing. I was just telling Diane I didn't take it.

DIANE. I didn't say that. It's just, there was a can right here on top of the box and now it's gone.

NAT. I ate it.

DIANE. What?

NAT. I ate it.

DIANE. When?

NAT. Before I left. I had to or I couldn't walk all the way round the lake.

DIANE. Oh. Well. I'm sorry, Julia. I didn't know.

NAT *is taking off his overcoat, hat, belt, etc.…*

JULIA. No. That's okay. I know. Do you want a glass of water, Nat?

NAT. What?

JULIA. Do you want a drink of water?

NAT. Hm?

JULIA. Do you want a drink?

NAT. Thanks.

DIANE. Here.

> DIANE *pours a drink of water for* NAT. *She hands it to* JULIA *who brings it to him.*

NAT. Listen. (*Pause.*) There's nothing left up there. Your friends cleared it out.

JULIA. I knew they would.

DIANE. What are we going to do? Try St Thomas?

JULIA. We'll have to.

DIANE. What about we just get the fuck out of here?! Try to keep going!

NAT. There's nothing organised out there! You should have seen what they did over at the gas station. We could run into any kind of... (*Indicating* JULIA*'s injuries.*) St Thomas is as far as we could make it.

DIANE. Well, let's do it.

JULIA. We found food in a place about four miles or five miles from here. It was a house with a shop.

NAT. Where exactly?

JULIA. On the way to Port Argus.

DIANE. How long would it take us?

JULIA. Three hours, four, maybe more, depending.

DIANE. We could do it.

JULIA. I could show you where it is.

DIANE. We could take the wheelbarrow. Or the other handcart. Take turns wheeling it through the traffic jams.

NAT. I don't know. I don't like the idea of no one being here.

> NAT *begins closing up the house.*

DIANE. Why? Nat. Why?

NAT. I don't know. I just... No reason, I suppose.

JULIA. You and me could go, Nat. I can show you exactly where it is.

NAT. Let me think about it.

JULIA. We'd be quick.

NAT. Yeah, I just think it's crazy not to have checked everywhere around here before we start going miles away.

Pause.

DIANE. Did you get anything?

NAT. I got some candy.

DIANE takes some rice and considers it. NAT starts shutting up the house.

JULIA. I like candy.

She shuts up immediately when she gets nothing from the others. The sound of birds gradually builds taking us into:

Scene Six

The birds are going crazy outside the house. They are whacking into the boards, scraping, fighting. DIANE, NAT and JULIA all sit huddled in blankets. They have no lights on. They are dark, frightened silhouettes, trying to wait out the onslaught.

This gradually becomes:

Scene Seven

Silence. It is late afternoon, near dusk. JULIA *is looking out the window, peeping between the boards while* NAT *shaves.*

JULIA. What's the bigger one to the left?

NAT. You don't know what that one is? Have a guess.

JULIA. A sycamore?

NAT. No, those two down there are sycamores. That one there on its own, is that the one you're talking about? That's an oak.

JULIA. Oh, an oak. Do you think it might be related to, em... broccoli.

NAT. Broccoli?

JULIA. Don't you think it looks like a big broccoli?

NAT (*laughs*). I suppose it does!

JULIA. It could be.

NAT. Whoever planted everything out there knew what they were doing. You see where the line of the old ditch meets the wall down there? That's practically prehistoric.

JULIA. Yeah, I mean, you do think that...

NAT. What.

JULIA. That we're safe here?

NAT. We're... pretty... safe here. They can never get through those boards – as long as we're alert, and even if one got in, or more, we'll go in the cellar in the kitchen. Wait for the tide to go out...

JULIA. The tide could change though.

NAT. The tide won't change!

JULIA. How they react to it might change. (*Pause.*) Where's Diane?

NAT (*checking his watch*). I don't know.

JULIA. Nat?

NAT. Yeah?

JULIA. You don't think that maybe Diane feels like… that I'm like…

NAT. Diane is a good person, Julia. She's a great person. We all have to look after each other. And if someone else came here we'd have to look after them too. Right?

JULIA *nods*.

I mean, that's… I mean, this is the new… This is the new way of living. Right? I mean, we're here.

JULIA *nods*.

DIANE *enters wearing a fencing mask. She wears a coat and gloves. She carries a bag with not much in it.*

Jesus, you're cutting it close! Where did you go?

DIANE. Down to the crossroads and into the little post office. I got some candles, oh, and some confetti.

NAT. …Great…

DIANE. I know.

NAT. Anything to eat? (*Throws a look at* JULIA.)

DIANE. Two cans of 7 Up. And a pack of yellow tomato seeds.

NAT. Oh well. We could grow them in here.

DIANE. I know. (*To* JULIA.) Here, I got you a watch.

JULIA. Oh. Thanks, Diane.

DIANE. The time is right. Don't mess with it and I'll show you how to wind it later. Right, we've about one hour, who's going to light the fire?

Pause. NAT *watches* DIANE *put her things away.*

NAT. We're okay for a couple of days, right?

DIANE. Not really. We have some rice. We have prunes.

NAT *looks at* JULIA

NAT. Turn on the light.

DIANE. What?

NAT. Turn on the light.

DIANE. Nat, I'm not in the mood!

NAT. Diane, turn it on.

DIANE. Are you serious?

She goes to a wall switch.

NAT. No, not that one. The lamp.

DIANE. Really?

She goes to a switch. A lamp comes on.

When did the power come back?

NAT. I fixed the generator. It burns a fuck-load of juice but as long as we're careful...

DIANE (*deflated*). And here I thought it was the end of the end of the world...

NAT. We could even rig up a little hotplate, if we can find one.

DIANE. All we need is the food.

JULIA. Diane. We have food.

She produces a big basket of food.

DIANE. Oh my God, where did you go?

NAT. I didn't go anywhere. I was working on the generator. It was Julia.

JULIA. You didn't tell me where you were going. I went after you. You were gone but I found a house with a big cellar in the back.

DIANE. Is it nearby?

JULIA. My arms are killing me! I thought I nearly wasn't going to make it!

NAT. Look, pound cake!

JULIA. Pound cake. Easter eggs. Cans of fruit. Pasta. Cans of soup.

DIANE. Where was it? Is there much left?

JULIA. I think there is. I couldn't look through everywhere properly 'cause I was afraid I was going to run out of time!

DIANE. Well, we can go back tomorrow.

JULIA. I hope I can remember where it is.

NAT. What are you talking about? Of course you'll remember.

JULIA. I nearly got lost coming back.

DIANE. Where did you go?

JULIA. Right, right over, over the other side of the lake. All the way over behind the trees, behind the quarry.

DIANE. What in the name of God were you doing all the way over there?

JULIA. I don't know, I just went for a quick look. And I… I just kept going and I just had this mad thought, 'I bet I can find something.' I knew I would.

DIANE. Julia…!

JULIA. I just thought… I'll have a quick look before I come home. I was so frightened!

DIANE. It's so dangerous going off on your own in a place like that!

JULIA. I knew the tide had gone out at one o'clock – Nat said.

DIANE. I know, but what if…

JULIA. You go off.

DIANE. I never go that far! I'm always…

NAT. Look. Diane's right, Julia, you shouldn't go off like that – without saying or…. What if you ran into the people you were with before – or anything could happen.

JULIA. I didn't mean to go that far! (*Throwing things back in the box*.) I just ended up over on the other side of the lake and I just thought, 'Well, I'm here, I might as well see what I can, you know, see if I can… see if I can contribute.'

NAT. Well, yeah, no, thanks this is great, I mean… (*Looks at* DIANE.) But…

DIANE. No, it's great, but, you know… If this is someone's food and they saw you or…

JULIA. I got four bottles of wine for Nat's birthday! So now we can have a little party and cheer ourselves up, because we can even play tapes now!

JULIA *storms off up the stairs. Pause.*

DIANE. I didn't know it was your birthday.

NAT. Well… it's around now.

Scene Eight

Night. The piano player's tape is playing on the stereo. Three empty wine bottles stand on the table. They have all dressed up. JULIA wears a wedding dress. NAT stands opening the last bottle. JULIA holds DIANE's hand in hers, reading her palm…

JULIA. Jesus Christ, Diane, there's an awful lot of pain here.

DIANE. Don't say that.

JULIA. No, it's all in your past.

DIANE. Good.

JULIA. All the old pain is going to melt away, Diane.

DIANE. When?

JULIA. It's all going to be gone.

DIANE. When?

JULIA. You won't believe how it can go. But it will.

NAT. Is this the only tape we have?

JULIA. Leave it on. I see so much peace in your future. You're so lucky.

DIANE. Is this all true?

JULIA. Yes.

They laugh.

Your whole life story is here, Diane, if you could read it you'd know.

DIANE. How can you read it? I want to believe you.

JULIA. You want to believe me because you know that it's real.

DIANE. Who showed you how to do it?

JULIA. My mother showed me. She could see a lot more than me though. She died when I was twelve.

DIANE (*sympathetic*). Oh…

JULIA. She had a room where she read fortunes up this old windy
staircase down a side street in Port Argus. I used to go there after
school. She used to make me sit in a big chair facing the wall to do
my homework where the people couldn't see me. She had all
kinds of people would come. Politicians, rich people, poor people,
drunks, people who'd cry.

DIANE. Wow, what a way to grow up.

NAT. Hey, I never had my birthday cake.

JULIA. Get the pound cake, Nat!

NAT. I love pound cake…

    NAT *goes to get the cake.*

JULIA. The chemicals they put in make those things last a thousand
years I heard one time.

NAT. I fucking love chemicals.

DIANE (*indicating her hand*). Tell me more.

JULIA. That's all I see, all the pain stops, Diane. It's like someone
opens a little door here and you step into paradise.

DIANE. That sounds like I'm going to die!

JULIA. No, it's your life, Diane.

DIANE. All the old pain…

JULIA. It's going to melt away.

DIANE. I wish I could believe it.

JULIA. You do believe it. Your body knows. Your mind wants to stop
your body.

    NAT *is slicing the cake.*

DIANE. Why?

JULIA. Because you're afraid. (*Pause.*) Have you ever read the
Bible, Diane?

DIANE. Oh, please…

    DIANE *is looking in the cups for her drink.*

JULIA. What do you mean, 'Oh, please…'

NAT *holds up a can with a white label and a distinctive green stripe, but no writing.*

NAT. Hey, Julia, what did you say was in these cans? Fruit?

JULIA. Yeah, it's pears.

NAT. Who wants pears with their cake?

NAT *is opening the can.*

JULIA. We should get a Bible. You should read it, Diane.

DIANE. I don't want to read the Bible, Julia.

JULIA. I know, but...

DIANE *turns way from her.*

DIANE. Where's my drink?

JULIA. Hey, Nat, you're next!

NAT. Next for what?

JULIA. I'll tell you your fortune.

NAT. No way!

JULIA. Why not?

NAT. I don't want to know.

DIANE. Good thinking.

NAT. Tell me something from the Bible. Something nice to cheer me up.

DIANE (*irritated*). Ohh... Nat, you're drunk.

JULIA. Diane's an atheist.

DIANE. I never said that.

NAT. No, but do tell me something. Not my fortune. Tell me something that'll make me feel happy.

JULIA (*spreads her arms a little*). 'Someone who is always thinking about happiness is a fool. A wise person thinks about death.'

Pause. NAT *looks at* DIANE *and back at* JULIA.

NAT. Thanks.

JULIA (*laughs*). No, that's wise words, Nat. Ecclesiastes. Ecclesiastes is so beautiful, Diane. 'Sorrow is better than laughter; it may sadden your face, but it sharpens your understanding.'

NAT. I think I'd prefer to be happy and not understand.

DIANE. Yes.

JULIA. 'When a fool laughs, it is like thorns crackling in a fire. It doesn't mean a thing.'

My mother always said she could see herself in Ecclesiastes. She said it's like a mirror.

NAT. Who wants pears with their pound cake?

JULIA. The Bible's not just about God, you know, Diane. It's about people as well. Real people like you and me.

DIANE. Stupid people like me.

JULIA. You're not a stupid person, Diane! (*Short pause.*) Does anyone else ever feel like there's someone upstairs?

DIANE *and* NAT *do not answer her.*

NAT. Right, who wants pears? I'm having pears. Oh, balls!

JULIA. What's wrong?

NAT. I've just put onions all over my cake!

JULIA. Onions?

NAT. It's not pears, it's onions!

DIANE *and* JULIA *start laughing.*

I've ruined my birthday cake!

JULIA. No, have another slice!

NAT. Whoever heard of canned onions?

DIANE. You moron…

NAT (*looking at the can*). Where does it say it's pears?

JULIA. I don't know… I… I think it must have said 'pears' on the cardboard tray they were in…

NAT. That's a pain in the balls. That's what God gives us now for laughing at him.

NAT *brings his plate to clean it off and get some more cake.*

JULIA. I'm sorry, Nat.

DIANE. Have mine, Nat.

JULIA. Have mine.

NAT. No, it's alright, there's more.

JULIA. Oh, hold on!

> JULIA *goes and gets a little box of birthday-cake candles.*

> Put one of these on!

> NAT *lets her put a candle in his slice of cake. She lights it. They all sit at the table.*

> (*Sings.*) Happy birthday to you…

NAT. Oh no…!

> DIANE *joins in…*

JULIA *and* DIANE (*singing*). Happy birthday to you, Happy birthday dear Na… at… Happy birthday to you!

> *They applaud him…*

JULIA (*sings*). For he's a jolly good fellow, for he's a jolly good fellow,

NAT. Oh God…

JULIA. For he's a jolly good fe… el… low… Which nobody can deny. Which nobody can deny…

NAT. Please…

JULIA. Make a wish. Wait! Did you make a wish?

> *Pause.* JULIA *blows out the candle… They applaud.*

DIANE. I hope you made a wish to get us out of here!

> NAT *stands up unsteadily and raises his drink.*

NAT. I just want to say…

JULIA. Speech! Speech!

NAT. I just want to say… I know that this is… I know that this is a… well, a terrible time for all of us. For everybody. But… Be that as it may, I just want to say… to both of you, to all of us. Thank you for giving me a birthday… treat.

DIANE (*claps a little*). Thanks, Julia.

NAT. It's not easy. It's not easy for any of us. But I think that the three of us have done admirably. And I don't know what the future holds. Only Julia knows that...

They laugh.

JULIA. Ah fuck off...

NAT. But while we have been here. And for the time we have left to come, whatever is going to happen, I just want to say that I'm proud of... of both of you, of all of us.

DIANE. Hear, hear...

NAT. Because it's not easy and... Well... Look, we're all different people. We all have different lives and... But you know, as long as there's... (*Pause.*) kindness... there's hope, right? (*Pause.*) Every day, I've been waking up. Wondering if this is my last day alive. So frightened that this is the end, every day. But recently, I mean, just in the past few days I've been... at the end of each day, I've been actually *thankful* for that day. (*Almost starts to cry, but recovers.*) When I was a boy I always dreamt of being in the Army. Of course, they wouldn't fucking have me. But be that as it may, I always felt... safe when I was having those dreams. Because I was ready, I suppose. Ready for any disaster. We were equipped for it. We were ready. Mmm. But I feel that the three of us... we can... We can make it. I know we can. (*Shouts at the windows.*) Fuck them! Fuck you! Fuck you!

There is a flurry of activity from the birds as they hear him shouting.

Yeah, that's it! That's it...

NAT *laughs and goes to the shutters, banging on them to* DIANE *and* JULIA's *alarm. Then he starts to open them in a mad attempt to fight them.* DIANE *and* JULIA *go to him, shouting, 'Stop! Nat, don't!', etc....* DIANE *slaps* NAT *across the face.* NAT *abruptly stops shouting and stares at* DIANE *while* JULIA *quickly closes the shutters.* NAT *goes back to the table. The others follow warily.*

Anyway. Thank you. Thanks. Thank you.

Pause.

JULIA. I always think whoever used to play that piano is still upstairs. (*Pause.*) I let someone die. About four days before I got here. We were in a factory, in the office. Suddenly there was a loud bang and there were hundreds of birds outside. We got under the desk and a tiny little one pecked its beak through one of the windows. I just went through a door and up these stairs, I turned at the top and I looked at this girl and she was holding birds in both her hands and a bird had her eyelid in his beak and he was just pulling and pulling up towards the ceiling. (*Tearfully.*) That's all I saw and I ran upstairs and hid in an oven.

Pause.

NAT. You didn't let her die.

Pause.

DIANE. That's right.

DIANE *embraces* JULIA.

NAT. There was nothing you could do.

Pause.

DIANE (*fixing* JULIA*'s hair*). The last time I saw Nina, my daughter. She had decided to go and visit her father, who lives on the other side of the world with his girlfriend and their young child. A taxi was picking her up to take her to the airport at six o'clock in the morning. I'd been up all night because I'd run out of these sleeping pills I'd been taking – and we had a huge fight. I was just so scared she'd never come back. (*Pause.*) She sent the taxi away, but I told her she was being stupid and I called her another one and she made it. She told me that she never wanted to see me again.

Pause.

JULIA. To kindness.

DIANE. To kindness.

They drink. In the distance they hear dogs howling. With the music gone off they can hear the birds scratching and banging round the house.

JULIA. What is that?

NAT. Dogs.

JULIA. How are they alive?

NAT. They're living up in the caves up there beyond the quarry. They hide in there. It's a full moon tonight.

JULIA. Won't the birds hear them?

Pause.

NAT. People all round here used to worship the moon.

JULIA turns the stereo back up. She goes to NAT and takes his hand. He dances awkwardly with her at first, in a slightly formal way. They laugh at their inability. But soon the music takes him and JULIA holds him closer and they dance slowly, enjoying the closeness. DIANE watches, a lonely figure at the table, as the lights fade.

Scene Nine

It is a hot afternoon. They are all in states of undress, the heat being almost unbearable. JULIA taps out a few desultory notes on the piano. NAT is mending a gear mechanism from a bicycle. DIANE writes in a notebook. We hear her voice as she writes.

DIANE (*voice-over*). Day after day, you know it's not a dream when you wake up into reality's heavy deadness. We've scavenged what we can out of all houses in the area – always avoiding the farmer's house on the other side of the lake. We never see him. Maybe he's dead. For three days in a row we went off to locate the house where Julia found all the goodies, but she'd forgotten which way she went! We got lost and arrived back frustrated and exhausted and barely talking to one another. Nat deals with stress by setting about practical tasks; mending the boards or tinkering with a broken lamp brings him the steady rhythm of meditation, and Julia...

DIANE watches JULIA. JULIA smiles at DIANE. DIANE smiles back and we hear her thoughts without her necessarily writing anything.

Julia. I can't decide whether she sees us as her parents or if it's something else. She seems so open, but there's something there that I can't see. That she doesn't show. Or just doesn't show me. When Nat gets down, and we all get down, you can feel her anxiousness like a physical vibration in the air. But she never comes to me to share it. I can't help feeling that they communicate something to each other in the silence. But all I get is the silence.

And the strange… hatred that consumes me isn't just for them and their proximity and the claustrophobic pain of never having any privacy – it's a hatred of myself too. Sometimes it grows so great I feel like just picking something up and…

JULIA. You have lovely legs, Diane.

DIANE. What?

JULIA. You have lovely legs. Doesn't she, Nat?

NAT (*working*). Mmm. (*Goes out to the hall.*)

DIANE. Really?

JULIA. Were you ever a dancer?

DIANE. No!

JULIA. No!

DIANE. No. (*Relenting.*) I've always done a lot of walking.

JULIA. And you have lovely feet.

DIANE. Do you think?

JULIA. Yeah, they're in nice proportion. I have fat toes.

DIANE. You have very nice feet.

JULIA. They're nothing like yours. Yours could be in a commercial. For sandals or something.

DIANE *considers her feet.*

What do you write about?

DIANE (*closing her notebook*). Oh, nothing, just… you know, thoughts.

JULIA. Like a diary?

DIANE. I suppose.

JULIA. God, it's so hot…

DIANE. I know.

JULIA. I'm so bored!

DIANE. I know.

JULIA. What time is it?

DIANE. Where's your watch?

JULIA. It's around somewhere.

DIANE. Around or lost?

JULIA. Around, Diane. It's around.

DIANE. Two more hours of high tide.

JULIA. And no birds.

Pause.

DIANE. I know.

They are looking at each other. But not wanting to get their hopes up.

JULIA. And none yesterday.

DIANE. I know. What do you think? Try for St Thomas…?

JULIA. Yeah, just go for it. Do it in the morning. Just even you and me go.

DIANE. Do you think.

JULIA. I'm going out of my fucking mind, Diane.

NAT (*coming in*). What's this? (*Pause.*) We'll find that house.

JULIA (*exasperated*). Oh!

NAT. I mean, it's got to be nearby!

JULIA. But I don't know where that is. I can't remember!

NAT. Come on, how far can it be? If it saves us going all the way to St Thomas. It's definitely worth having another good…

JULIA (*with force*). I told you, I can't remember where it is!

Pause.

DIANE. We have the bikes now, Nat.

NAT. We have two bikes and one of them the gears are jammed.

DIANE. Alright, well then we'll draw straws.

JULIA. Diane and me can go, Nat.

NAT. Aw, get real…

DIANE. We'll draw straws.

DIANE *goes and takes three long matches, snapping one in two.*

NAT. Listen, all I'm saying is why don't we wait until we get another bike and…

DIANE (*simultaneous, overlapping* NAT). Because I'm not going to wait around here starving to death while you go…

NAT. That way if we get stranded, we're not separated, and at least we all know what's happening…

DIANE (*simultaneous, overlapping* NAT)….round the countryside looking for a suitable bike! We're drawing straws, so just draw a straw, because someone's going and if you don't want to go, someone's going, so draw a straw.

NAT. No, I'm not going to draw a straw.

DIANE. Draw a straw.

NAT. No, I'm not doing this.

JULIA. Nat.

DIANE. Draw a straw.

NAT. No.

DIANE. Draw one.

NAT. No.

JULIA. We're all doing it.

DIANE. Just draw one!

NAT *reluctantly draws a straw. It looks long.* DIANE *offers the straws to* JULIA. *She draws one. It looks about the same length at* NAT'*s. They look expectantly at* DIANE, *who reveals that she has the short straw.*

NAT. Happy?

JULIA. Okay?

Pause. NAT *just goes back into the hall.*

DIANE. Right. (*Pause.*) Okay.

JULIA. You can go the next time.

DIANE. Yeah.

Scene Ten

Morning. A grey sky. The door is closed over. DIANE *is alone, doing some sit-ups. All is quiet. Then a figure passes the door.* DIANE *looks up, wondering did she see something. No one is there. A shadow appears in the doorway, a key turns in the lock and the door is gently opened.* DIANE *can only watch the door in horror. A big, heavyset man in his fifties has come in, carrying a plastic bag and a shotgun. He is filthy. He has what looks like a bamboo waste-paper basket with eye holes cut out over his head.* DIANE *stares at him, as though she can't believe this is happening. He takes his 'helmet' off.*

TIERNEY. All on your own?

DIANE. No.

TIERNEY. No, you are, that was rhetorical. I'm your neighbour.

DIANE. What do you want?

TIERNEY. I brought you a few gifts. To say hello. I was wondering why you didn't go off with the other pair this morning. Where are they gone? St Thomas? (*Pause.*) There's nothing there. I could've told you, but you're never sociable.

DIANE. They're only down at the lake. They'll be back in a few minutes.

TIERNEY. I saw them going off up the road more than two hours ago towing a wheelbarrow. They're not at the lake.

DIANE. What do you want?

TIERNEY. This is my sister's house. I grew up here.

Short pause.

DIANE. Well, I'm sure you understand that all bets are off. I mean, we don't want to be here either, but we don't have a choice. Just take whatever you want and…

TIERNEY (*gives a little laugh*). All bets are off, I like that. (*Produces a bottle of brandy from his bag.*) Have a drink with me.

DIANE. No, I'm… I'm fine, thank you.

TIERNEY. Mind if I grab a cup?

DIANE. Do I have a choice?

TIERNEY. Of course you do. Hey, welcome to reality – where anything is possible, right?

TIERNEY takes two cups and pours them both a drink.

Seen anyone else about?

DIANE. No. (*Short pause.*) Have you?

TIERNEY. Not for weeks. Nothing on the radio any more. Nothing on the TV. Nothing nowhere. (*Drinks.*) What do you think? Are we the last people left in the world?

DIANE. I don't know.

TIERNEY. They never saw this one coming, ha? No one ever thought nature was just going to eat us. (*Pause.*) Mm? (*Short pause.*) Jesus Christ, it's so *quiet*! (*Pause.*) Sometimes I wonder if I'm going insane! (*Laughs grimly.*) Probably lost it long ago. Here.

He offers her an open envelope.

DIANE. What is it?

TIERNEY (*shakes it a little*). Pills. Tablets. All the kids from Port Argus and Mountstewart used to take them. I got them out of a pharmacy. They're a controlled substance you might say. If you take them with a drink they make the time pass quicker.

DIANE. No, I'm alright.

TIERNEY. They kill pain.

DIANE. No thanks.

TIERNEY. Okay. (*Pops a pill and shudders.*) I have to stop taking them. (*Pause. Regards DIANE.*) Why do you look so familiar?

DIANE. I don't know.

Pause.

TIERNEY. Look. I got food. I got drink. I got medicine. I got the lot. I've got a whole lock-up. I can get by for years. I've seen you going around with Romeo. But the girl's with him now. Your days are numbered.

DIANE. What do you mean?

TIERNEY. You're crowding them out. The girl wants him to herself. What good are you to her?

DIANE. What are you talking about?

TIERNEY. Ah, wake up, will you? You're on the final countdown here, baby.

DIANE. No. Look, I think you've… You see, the three of us. We don't want to be trespassers but we're just trying to…

TIERNEY. Do me a favour and don't be stupid, will you? You think that girl was out there surviving by her wits and her charm? Anyone who's left out there is an animal! The people she was with ransacked the whole place over at the crossroads. They killed a woman who'd been hiding in the house up behind the gas station. I saw the body. Her mouth was wide open, like this – (*Does the dead woman's face.*) screaming into the floor.

DIANE. That wasn't Julia, she was with some bad people for a while but…

TIERNEY. Use your brain, missus, she's out for herself. I know!

DIANE. How would you know?

TIERNEY. Because… I've lived like that. I was one of the armies of the road. In the eighties, the nineties. Living on the streets over in Wolchurch – and Birhaven. Years, I lived like that before I came back. To look after my mother. You go from morning to night, morning to night, that's all you know about. That's all you know. I can see it in her. I know exactly who she is. It's not her fault, but she'll have to get rid of you.

DIANE. No, you don't know her.

TIERNEY. So you say.

DIANE. Well, I don't agree.

TIERNEY. Well… Hey, be a Christian. Watch where it gets you. (*Pause.*) Look. What I'm saying is… If you… if you want to… you can come with me. (*Short pause.*) You can be safe. (*Pause.*) It's not easy for me to come here like this. I never even meant to. I never would have… But as time goes on… (*Drinks.*) When I lie down at night and… it's so dark. For some reason I see your face and I know I could… take care of you. And we could…

DIANE. Look…

TIERNEY (*suddenly shouts*). I'm a gentleman, missus! But any plant, be it a weed or beautiful flower, needs the water and the sun!! We're all just the same! It's so cold on the other side of the lake. Don't you see what a waste it's gonna be when she gets her way? The two of them will be nice and cosy on their own here. And the wind will just blow across the water. (*Pause.*) Bluejays killed my dog. Maybe just as well.

Pause.

DIANE. I can't go with you. I'm sorry.

Short pause.

TIERNEY. Hey, I know who you are. Your photo was on those books my mother used to read. I read one. Am I right?

DIANE. I don't know.

TIERNEY. That's it. I knew I'd seen you. You wrote that book about the woman with the wart on her face, right?

DIANE. A long time ago.

TIERNEY. Well, I'll be damned. What about that? It's good to meet you.

Pause.

He takes some cans from his bag. They are white with a distinctive green stripe on them, but no writing.

No hard feelings. Here, these are pears. I'll leave them here.

DIANE. Thank you.

TIERNEY. And here. (*Leaves the envelope of pills on the table.*) I have millions.

TIERNEY *goes to the door. He stops and turns to* DIANE.

What am I gonna do?

DIANE *has no answer for him. He leaves.* DIANE *waits a moment then bolts the door. Turning, she considers the cans. She grabs the can opener and opens one of them. She sniffs it and puts it down on the table.*

Scene Eleven

Night. NAT sits drinking a glass of whiskey. A box with more whiskey bottles sits nearby. JULIA is reading a book. DIANE is staring at the fire. Outside a wind blows softly. A bird flits from a branch to the roof. The atmosphere is solemn. They are all oppressed by boredom. Nothing happens. They even seem oblivious to the sounds of birds scratching or thumping at the house outside. JULIA wanders to the radio, switches it on and spins the dial. She only gets white noise and high-frequency whining. She switches it off.

JULIA. Don't drink too much, Nat. You'll get a hangover.

NAT. Yeah…

    Pause. JULIA regards DIANE.

JULIA. Getting all that rice wasn't bad, right, Diane?

DIANE. Hm?

JULIA. Just saying, all that rice we got.

DIANE. Yes, no, that's… that's fantastic.

JULIA. And there just wasn't a huge amount of time. (*Pause.*) I
    mean, even if we don't drink all the whiskey, we could…

NAT. What?

JULIA. Well, if we ever met anyone else we could trade it.

NAT. For what?

JULIA. I don't know. If they had something we needed.

NAT. With who?

JULIA. I don't know.

DIANE. If we have any left.

NAT. Hey, I carried it back… Have a drink, Diane.

DIANE. Whiskey was never my drink.

NAT. Mix it with something.

DIANE. With what?

NAT. Tomato juice.

DIANE. I'll leave it thanks.

JULIA. I'm going to use the bucket.

She takes a bucket and goes upstairs.

NAT. Look, I'm sorry we didn't do better, Diane. Jesus Christ, it was so creepy in St Thomas. I thought we'd never get back. I was just waiting for someone to jump out of a doorway and…

DIANE goes to the stairs and looks up, listening for JULIA. She goes to NAT.

DIANE. Nat. Listen. The farmer who's over on the other side of the lake. He came here today.

NAT. What?

DIANE. The guy who we've seen on the other side of the lake. He was here. He said this is his sister's house.

NAT. You're joking.

DIANE. No, he was here.

NAT. What did he want?

DIANE. Company. He says he has food and medicine.

NAT (*loudly*). Why didn't you tell me? What did he say?!

DIANE puts her finger to her lips and gets one of the white cans with the green stripe. She brings it to NAT.

DIANE. He gave us this.

NAT. Yeah…?

DIANE. He said it was pears. But I opened one. It's onions.

NAT. Yeah, we know these are onions.

DIANE. But why did Julia think they were pears? She said they were pears too. (*Pause.*) How come she could never find that house again – where she got all the stuff?

NAT. She said she got lost.

DIANE. No. What if he gave her all that stuff?

NAT. She would have told us! (*Pause.*) Why wouldn't she have told us?

DIANE. I don't know. (*Pause.*) Listen, Nat. I know you probably don't want to tell me, and I can understand but...

JULIA comes back down the stairs. DIANE and NAT fall silent. JULIA goes to where she was sitting and picks up her book, sensing a strange vibe.

JULIA. It's gone very quiet in here.

DIANE. We've run out of things to talk about.

JULIA (*holds up her book*). It won't be long then before we have you reading the Bible, Diane. We can have a book club.

DIANE. Yeah... You didn't find any other books?

JULIA. There were other books there, there were loads of books about farming and tractors but I didn't see anything you'd like, I mean, I didn't know what kind of books you're in to.

DIANE. Oh, anything...

JULIA. Yeah but we were really looking for food, Diane. We didn't want to get stuck out after dark.

DIANE. Yeah, I know.

JULIA. We'll go back. We'll get you some books.

DIANE. It's okay.

JULIA. I'm sorry.

DIANE. No. It's okay.

The three of them sit there thoughtfully, the wind blowing. JULIA gets her bedding and starts to bed down. DIANE opens her notebook. As the lights dim to black, we hear her voice...

(*Voice-over.*) They say people who've killed someone think about it like no other event in their lives. And they say that to taste it and walk away unpunished is worse than being caught and confessing. The universe seems indifferent to your act – people die every day and the cold Earth doesn't care how they go. But you, the killer, return to it over and over in your mind. No drug can induce its giddy exhilaration. No agitation can match its tantalising meaninglessness. Once you have killed, it calls to you again and again. So they say.

Scene Twelve

Night. Darkness. The wind is howling. Lightning illuminates JULIA *and* NAT *standing in a corner, discussing something quietly and urgently. A thunderclap wakes* DIANE. *She sits up and shines her flashlight at* NAT *and* JULIA.

DIANE (*lighting a candle*). Is everything alright?

JULIA (*returning to her bed*). Just stay out of it, Diane, alright?

DIANE. What's going on?

JULIA. Why do we all have to sleep in this one fucking room?

DIANE. What?

JULIA. We've no privacy! Why can't we be alone to even talk?

DIANE. Sleep where you want! Am I in the way here?

NAT. No. We were… We were just talking…

NAT *reaches for the whiskey bottle.*

JULIA. Nat! Stop drinking.

NAT. My head is fucking killing me!

JULIA. Well, that'll only make it worse! (*Beat.*) Tell her, Nat.

Pause.

DIANE. What.

NAT. We'll talk about it in the morning.

JULIA *picks up her bedding.*

JULIA. I'm sleeping upstairs.

NAT. It's not safe – they got in up there before.

JULIA. I'll take my chances. Thanks, Diane.

DIANE. For what?

JULIA. Don't act all innocent. You needn't bother.

DIANE. What? What did I do?

JULIA (*on her way up the stairs*). Oh spare me, Diane, the lies have to stop somewhere.

> JULIA *is gone.* DIANE *looks at* NAT, *who cradles his drink, down by his mattress.*

DIANE. Will she be okay up there?

NAT. The tide's gone out.

> DIANE *gets a cup and comes to the table. She pours a drink and sips it. She grimaces.*

DIANE. Are you lovers?

NAT (*rubs his face*). She's pregnant.

DIANE. What?

NAT. She's pregnant.

DIANE. How long?

NAT. I don't know. She said a few weeks.

DIANE. A few weeks?

NAT. We were going to tell you but…

DIANE. Am I that bad?

NAT. No, of course not!

> DIANE *goes to a window and opens the shutters, looking out. The first brush of dawn is in the sky.*

DIANE. Look, don't worry.

NAT. How can I not worry? We can't bring a child into… into this.

DIANE. We'll pull together.

NAT. Jesus, the last thing I wanted to do was to cause any trouble… You have to know that, Diane, I… The first time, it was… It was the night we had my birthday.

DIANE. Yeah, okay, Nat…

NAT. I was dreaming and then, there she was beside me. I thought she was frightened. I thought I was protecting her.

DIANE. Society's gone, Nat. No one's keeping score. So you can do whatever you want…

NAT. Yeah, well, all that is fine when you're writing your novels, Diane. But this is bigger than that! This is… A child is…

DIANE. How do you know it's yours?

NAT. Because I asked her. I had to.

DIANE. Is that what you were whispering about?

NAT. I just asked her.

DIANE. What…

NAT. I asked her if she was with him for the food…

DIANE. What did she say?

NAT. She said no.

DIANE (*unconvinced*). Mmm.

NAT. She said no, Diane. I didn't even know she was pregnant. She only told me yesterday. All the way to St Thomas she kept trying to hold my hand. But God forgive me, I just wished she'd fuck off.

DIANE. Sweetie, who knows where she was before she got here? Who knows what happened out there? She could easily have been pregnant before you even met her. If she is pregnant. (*Notices that* NAT *is holding his head, wincing.*)

NAT. Oh, I haven't had a headache like this in so long.

DIANE. Come on. Sit down over here.

He goes to her and they sit on the sofa.

It'll be okay.

NAT. I'm sorry.

DIANE. I know.

From her pocket she takes the envelope TIERNEY *gave her with the pills. She considers it.*

Let me get you some water.

Scene Thirteen

Late afternoon. DIANE *is alone. She is reading* JULIA*'s Bible. It is grey and still.* JULIA *steps into the room from outside.* DIANE *closes the book.*

JULIA. It's okay, Diane, you can read it. I wouldn't stop you.

DIANE. I know.

JULIA. Where's Nat?

DIANE. He's gone for a walk.

JULIA. Is he feeling better?

DIANE. I think he just wanted to get some fresh air. While there's time.

JULIA. Right.

    JULIA *stands there awkwardly.*

    I wasn't sure if you were talking to me.

DIANE. I wasn't sure you were talking to me!

JULIA. Of course I am.

DIANE. You weren't too happy with me last night.

JULIA. I just couldn't believe that you'd say something like that to Nat. About me.

DIANE (*goes to* JULIA *and takes her hand*). I'm sorry if I offended you, that's not what I meant to do.

JULIA. Okay.

    Pause. DIANE *goes to get their dinner ready.*

DIANE. You know you could have come to me any time and told me about… what's happened.

JULIA. I just… I've always been a bit too… afraid to talk with you about… certain things, Diane.

DIANE. Why?

JULIA. I don't know. I sometimes think that you always think I came here and wrecked it for you and Nat and that's not...

DIANE. Julia, everyone in the world is dead. We've no food and we can't go anywhere because we'll all be killed. Believe me, I have bigger things to worry about.

JULIA. It's just that Nat's been really hurt.

DIANE. In what way?

JULIA. Well, you've made him question whether he's the father of our baby.

DIANE. Jesus Christ, Julia! Who knows who the father is?

JULIA. I know!

DIANE. Oh, please...

JULIA. That's the problem with you, Diane, it's always 'Oh, please... Oh, please...'

Oh, please what?

DIANE. Julia...

JULIA. I've read your diary, Diane.

Pause.

DIANE. Ohh... how could you?

JULIA. I had to! And I was right to, because now I know what's really been going on around here.

DIANE. Julia...

JULIA. If Nat knew half the things you say in there about him...

DIANE. But that's not, I mean, it's not what you think.

JULIA. I know what the word 'love' means, Diane.

DIANE. I don't mean it in that way. I'd have feelings like that for anyone I care about or worry about...

JULIA. Love is love, Diane. That's the whole problem, isn't it? That's why you're against me.

DIANE. Don't be so stupid.

JULIA. What's stupid about it?

Fishes DIANE's *diary out from under the cushion and throws it on the floor at* DIANE's *feet.*

You even say it yourself. You wrote it down – that no one has ever loved you and your daughter hates you.

DIANE (*going and grabbing a can*). Look, when some... man comes in here with those cans that you came in here with and says they're pears, but they're not, and starts offering me food for... for... whatever, I have to ask where you got it.

JULIA. What does it matter where I got it? You ate it, didn't you? It's kept you alive. What does it matter where I got it?

DIANE. It matters because Nat is upset and worried about it. And he's right to be, because you lied to us.

JULIA. I didn't lie. I got that food fair and square.

DIANE. Really...

JULIA. Yes, really... You know what your problem is, Diane, you think everyone else is like you. Sneaking around, writing in our little notebooks, scribbling down all your horrible blackness and then turning around and being all sweetness and light to everybody.

DIANE. Right...

JULIA. Yeah.

DIANE. Well, maybe you should look at your own behaviour, Julia, crawling across the floor in the middle of the night. Waiting until we're all asleep to make your sordid little advances, sticking your nose into my private thoughts where it doesn't belong.

JULIA. That's bullshit. You don't even have a clue what you're talking about. Myself and Nat have discussed this together. The human race has to continue, Diane.

DIANE. The human race!

JULIA. People can still love each other. We all need to take responsibility! You just don't see it that way because nobody loves you!

DIANE. Are you fucking nuts? What are you trying to bring a baby into the world for? You think it's all going to be a fairy tale? That there's going to be a coach and horses for the fairy princess to take you off, with your precious young ovaries in a little jewellery box on your lap? Look around you, child!!

JULIA. You're just jealous.

DIANE. Oh, please.

JULIA. 'Oh, please…'

DIANE. Yes! You know, if you like I can sort this all out in a heartbeat.

JULIA. Oh yeah, how?

DIANE. All I have to do is walk over to that farmer and ask him exactly what you did for all that chocolate. (*Beat.*) And the wine.

Pause.

JULIA. Well, do then!

DIANE. I will.

JULIA. Well, go on then!

DIANE. I'll go when I fucking well like!

JULIA. Well, do go, because when you know you're wrong, you'll know the truth.

DIANE. Fair enough, and if that's the case I'll apologise. Now are you going to sit there all day? Look at this place. It's like a fucking pigsty!

DIANE *goes to the stove and begins to put wood in.* JULIA *starts to tidy up. She looks at an axe that is nearby. She walks to it and picks it up. She looks at* DIANE *kneeling at the stove. She approaches* DIANE *from behind and stands there getting ready to hit* DIANE.

JULIA. Hey, Diane…

DIANE (*without looking round*). What.

JULIA *realises she can't do it. She turns away, stifling her tears of frustration.*

JULIA. Nothing… (*Puts the axe down and looks outside. Pause.*) It's getting dark.

DIANE. Mmm.

Pause.

JULIA. You don't think anything has happened to Nat, do you?

DIANE. I hope not.

JULIA. I mean, the tides going to turn. Where did he go?

DIANE. I don't know. To the lake I think.

JULIA. You don't think he might have fallen asleep?

DIANE. I know he hasn't been well, but surely he wouldn't fall asleep out there?

JULIA. How long do we have?

DIANE. I guess a half-hour.

Pause.

JULIA. I better go. I'll just be a minute.

DIANE. Well, don't be long.

JULIA. No, I'll be quick.

JULIA *is about to go. But she turns to* DIANE.

I never meant for any of this, Diane. I'm sorry I read your diary. But I had to.

JULIA *runs out of the house.* DIANE *goes to the door. She looks out, watching* JULIA, *then steps back inside. She shuts the door and bolts it, putting up whatever wood they use to block it, locking* JULIA *out. She closes the shutters. She comes back to the chair by the fire and sits there. The room is very dark. We hear* DIANE*'s voice…*

DIANE (*voice-over*). When you do kill someone, the first thing you think is, 'That was easy. What's all the fuss about?' The peaceful silence that descends when you've done it fills you with such relief. But it's more than that. It's the power that you get. You get that person's power. They are so completely subdued and obliterated. They have bent to your will completely and they are just… gone. You thank God for the strength and you wonder why you didn't use it long before.

The room darkens as night falls…

But then as time goes on, you realise that you not only have that person's power. Something else has happened. You have their soul inside you. And it's impossible not to feel their pain, their rage and their embarrassing frailty, which joins with your own. You get it all.

As dusk gathers outside, we hear the first flapping wings of the night.

Scene Fourteen

Morning. DIANE *is in the chair as the lights come up. It is just past dawn.* NAT *comes down the stairs. He is naked from the waist up. He has a blanket wrapped around his lower half. He gingerly makes his way down, squinting.*

NAT. What time is it?

DIANE. Just after six-thirty.

NAT. Six-thirty what? In the morning?

DIANE. You slept for twenty-four hours.

NAT. Where's Julia?

DIANE. She's gone.

NAT. Gone where?

DIANE. I don't know.

NAT. What do you mean she's 'gone'?

DIANE. She left last night.

NAT. She left?

DIANE. Before it got dark.

NAT. But where did she go?

DIANE. I don't know.

NAT. What happened, Diane?

DIANE. Nothing happened.

NAT. Well, what did she say?

DIANE (*taking up the Bible*). She told me that I was to tell you that Ecclesiastes says…

NAT. Are you fucking serious?

DIANE. She said I was to tell you that – (*Finding passage.*) 'I found something more bitter than death – the woman who is like a trap. The love she offers you will catch you like a net; and her arms round you will hold you like a chain.'

NAT. Is that it?

DIANE. That's it.

NAT. What does that mean?

DIANE. How would I know?

NAT. But she'll die out there!

He goes to the door and peeps out through the boards.

DIANE. Maybe she had somewhere she could go. I tried to stop her. I'm sorry, Nat.

NAT. There's something you're not telling me, Diane.

DIANE. I swear to God. She said I was to show you that bit from Ecclesiastes. I told her she was being crazy. I tried to make her stay.

NAT. Read it again.

DIANE. She was too strong for me, Nat.

NAT. Read it again!

DIANE. Oh, for God's sake! 'I found something more bitter than death – the woman who is like a trap. The love she offers you will catch you like a net; and her arms round you will hold you like a chain.'

NAT. I don't get it.

DIANE. Do you think she's saying she's… set you free? (*Pause.*) Go to bed, Nat.

NAT goes to walk up the stairs.

NAT. I have to look for her. I mean maybe she's…

He stops, hearing a flutter of birds outside.

How long have the birds been out?

DIANE. Only an hour.

NAT *comes back, unsure what to do.*

NAT. Gimme that.

DIANE *hands him the Bible. He looks at* DIANE. *He takes it upstairs.*

Scene Fifteen

Night. The wind is howling outside. NAT *sits at the table.* DIANE *brings two bowls to the table. They both sit, despondently.*

NAT. What is this?

DIANE. Onions. (*As* NAT *pushes it away.*) Do you want some ketchup? There's rice.

NAT *puts his fork down.*

Try and eat, Nat. Do you want some curry powder?

NAT. No.

DIANE (*gets up*). I'll get us some food. Look, if nothing else, I'll go over to the farmer. Maybe Julia's there.

NAT. Julia's not there.

DIANE. Maybe I can talk to him.

NAT. He's dead. I saw his body in the rushes two days ago.

DIANE. We can get his food.

NAT. There's nothing there. (*Gets up and moves away.*) Listen. When I was up under the eaves fixing the boards, I could see that the birds have been laying eggs.

DIANE. Are there birds up there?

NAT. No birds. Just their eggs. I can get in with a stick and smash some of them up, but to get them all – they're in between the floor, the insulation and the ceiling, if I get in to get them all, then the whole roof is exposed up there, it won't be safe.

DIANE. Nat, if the birds aren't sitting on the eggs, they can't hatch, they'll be too cold.

NAT. Well, I don't know! I don't like it! I mean, what if they do hatch? What if hundreds of birds suddenly get their way down through the plaster and down and in here?

DIANE. Surely we could… Couldn't we board it up?

NAT. Look, I just don't feel good about it. I think we should just go. I can't sleep.

DIANE. Do you want to take a painkiller?

NAT. I don't want to take anything.

Pause.

DIANE. Where will we go?

NAT. I don't know. Find somewhere else. Start again?

Pause.

DIANE. Okay.

NAT *gets up and goes to the fire.* DIANE *stays near the table alone.*

Scene Sixteen

Dark grey daylight. Forbidding black clouds. The wind howls.
DIANE *and* NAT *are packing up, making some final arrangements.*

DIANE (*voice-over*). Today we leave and wander into the wilderness.
I lay awake all night. Nat's right. Anything would be better than
the cold ghost of the girl – and her child – blowing round here in
the evenings. We're finally going to St Thomas. Together, if we're
careful, maybe we can we make it for another year or two, or
longer, who knows?

She picks up her notebook and reads to herself. NAT *goes to the
door and looks out up into the treetops and the sky.*

And then what? If only I could give him a child. My genes will
never make it past me now. We'll all be extinct soon. All my life
I've always thought, 'What's so precious about the human race
anyway?' When there were loads of us all clogging up the planet I
always thought, 'How disgusting.' But now that there's so few of us
left, I think – (*Looks up – out at us.*) 'Wait a minute, in all the cold
eternal expanse of the cosmos, what if we are the only life anywhere
in the vastness of time that can actually think, and knows that it
exists, and that knows that it will die? And I realise that God is real.
Because I am God. But I never realised before how helpless God is
– in the face of reality and eternity. And how alone God is.

NAT *approaches* DIANE. *He is ready for the road. An old coat is
tied by a piece of string across his belly. He holds a stick like a
pilgrim.*

NAT. Are you ready?

*DIANE nods and puts her book down, leaving it on the table. She
takes her bag and puts it on her back.*

Do you not want your book?

DIANE. No.

Pause.

NAT. Okay?

DIANE *nods*.

DIANE. Let's go.

They leave, closing the door firmly behind them as they walk out into the wind.

Lights down.

End.

THE VEIL

For Fionnuala and Sumati

The Veil was first performed in the Lyttelton auditorium of the National Theatre, London, on 4 October 2011 (previews from 27 September), with the following cast:

MRS GOULDING	Bríd Brennan
CLARE WALLACE	Caoilfhionn Dunne
MARIA LAMBROKE	Ursula Jones
MR FINGAL	Peter McDonald
REVEREND BERKELEY	Jim Norton
CHARLES AUDELLE	Adrian Schiller
HANNAH LAMBROKE	Emily Taaffe
MADELEINE LAMBROKE	Fenella Woolgar

Director	Conor McPherson
Designer	Rae Smith
Lighting Designer	Neil Austin
Sound Designer	Paul Arditti
Music	Stephen Warbeck

Characters

LADY MADELEINE LAMBROKE, *a widow*
HANNAH LAMBROKE, *her daughter*
MARIA LAMBROKE, *known as 'Grandie', Madeleine's
    grandmother*
THE REVEREND BERKELEY, *a defrocked Anglican minister*
MR CHARLES AUDELLE, *a philosopher*
MRS GOULDING, *a housekeeper and nurse*
MR FINGAL, *an estate manager*
CLARE WALLACE, *a housemaid*

Setting

A fine old house in the Irish Countryside. Early summer, 1822.

ACT ONE

Evening of Wednesday May 15th, 1822. Late in the evening – after 11 p.m.

The spacious drawing room of a big house in the countryside in Ireland. The room is gloomily lit by one or two candles. There are large windows, beyond which are mature trees with rich foliage, but for now they are unseen in the darkness. Heavy raindrops are heard falling out in the night.

There is a mantelpiece, stage right, with a large mirror above it. Some dark old portraits and landscapes grace the walls. The effect should be that the house has seen better days and needs some care. This room was once a versatile social space for receptions and dancing, now it looks bare. What chairs are here are lined against the walls, the only exceptions being one near the fireplace and one near a piano.

Among the entrances are a main door to the hallway, stage left, and high double doors in the back wall, leading to a conservatory with steps to the garden.

A man, MR FINGAL, *stands in the room, perhaps peering out the window, lost in thought. He wears dirty boots and a shabby-looking coat which is wet and torn. An old horse blanket is draped round his shoulders. While he may be younger, he looks at least forty. He is broad-shouldered and strong but looks tired. He hears a door slam out in the hallway and looks up. Light spills in as* MRS GOULDING *approaches, carrying a lamp and a bucket. She stops in the doorway. She is about sixty, small and wiry with a lined, intelligent face.*

MRS GOULDING. Mr Fingal!

FINGAL. Mrs Goulding.

MRS GOULDING. I might have known it was your muddy boots!

FINGAL. What?

MRS GOULDING. You have dirt and mud and whatever else all across the floor out here.

FINGAL. Oh, I'm sorry.

MRS GOULDING. What way did you come up?

FINGAL. I came up through the scullery.

MRS GOULDING. The scullery!

FINGAL. Clare let me in…

MRS GOULDING. I don't believe this! Could you not look at what you were doing?

FINGAL. I couldn't see! Sure there's hardly a candle lit in the place!

MRS GOULDING. Do not dare rebuke me, sir! Where have you been?

FINGAL. I was abroad – almost up as far as Queensfort! – looking for Miss Hannah.

MRS GOULDING. Yes, well, her ladyship found her herself.

    MRS GOULDING *crosses to the coal scuttle near the fireplace and, using a rag, takes some pieces of coal, which she puts in her bucket.*

FINGAL. Where was she?

MRS GOULDING. Down in the glen. We're heating water for her bath.

FINGAL. What happened?

MRS GOULDING. I don't know. They had an argument.

FINGAL. Were you not here?

MRS GOULDING. No. I had the evening off.

FINGAL. Well, that's nice…

MRS GOULDING. I had the evening off to go to my niece's house. Nearly every child in the parish has scarlet fever, and her baby got it.

FINGAL (*chastened*). Oh, well…

MRS GOULDING. Yah. We were waiting for a woman from Clonturk who was supposed to have the cure. She arrived full of poitín and nearly fell into the fire, the bloody tinker.

FINGAL. How is the child?

MRS GOULDING. My niece's child?

FINGAL. Yes.

MRS GOULDING. She won't last the night. (*Wipes her hands.*) Where's the boy? We need turf brought in.

FINGAL. I sent him home. I'll bring turf in.

MRS GOULDING. No, I'll get it. We were heating some stew for Miss Hannah. It'll be nearly warm if you want.

FINGAL. I'm alright. I'm just waiting for her ladyship.

MRS GOULDING. You can give me those boots now.

She pulls the horse blanket from his shoulders and throws it on the floor.

FINGAL. Hah?

MRS GOULDING. Stand on that. Here.

She moves a chair for him to sit on. He starts to unlace his boots.

I'll kill that young one for letting you walk all up here like that.

FINGAL. It wasn't her fault.

MRS GOULDING. Not a brain between yous.

FINGAL. It was dark, she didn't see.

MRS GOULDING. I'll rip her bloody ear off for her. (*Tugs at his torn sleeve.*) Where's your good coat?

FINGAL. It got wet in the rain.

MRS GOULDING. You didn't lose it playing cards down in Jamestown, no?

FINGAL. No.

MRS GOULDING. No?

FINGAL. No!

MRS GOULDING. You were always a bad liar, Mr Fingal. Which is why you shouldn't play cards.

FINGAL. Yes, well, I don't.

MRS GOULDING. Yah, right you don't. Down in that kip. With them animals. Sure look at you! You're not able for them, man. The dark rings under your eyes. What are we going to do with you? And no good coat to present yourself tomorrow.

FINGAL. What's tomorrow?

MRS GOULDING. Thursday.

FINGAL. I know what day it is. I mean why do I have to present myself?

MRS GOULDING. Has no one told you?

FINGAL. No.

MRS GOULDING. Her ladyship's cousin, the Reverend Berkeley, is arriving from London.

FINGAL. What!

MRS GOULDING. He's bringing a companion and they'll want to go grousing, I've no doubt, so you better see about them horses. Madam is fit to be tied – both horses lame and she going out to look for Miss Hannah earlier.

FINGAL. The both of them?

MRS GOULDING. They're both lame. Mike Wallace had to hitch up his old grey mare to the buggy and she could hardly pull it! Madam is not the least bit happy, I can tell you. And listen, we'll need to stir a churn of milk out of somewhere for tomorrow.

She takes up his boots.

FINGAL. Why?

MRS GOULDING. Because the cows are all huddled up the far end of the field under the trees and won't be shifted. (*Indicates the rifle.*) What's that rifle doing in here?

FINGAL. Some young lads were throwing stones at us earlier.

MADELEINE LAMBROKE, *the lady of the house, appears at the door to the hallway. She is in her early forties. She is attractive and sombrely dressed. She looks worn out from worry.* MRS GOULDING *looks at her.*

MRS GOULDING. I'll have your boots down at the door. I'll give you a can of stew for the boy's supper on the way out.

FINGAL. Thank you.

MRS GOULDING. Madam.

MADELEINE. Thank you, Mrs Goulding.

MRS GOULDING. Yes, madam.

MRS GOULDING *leaves, taking the boots and bucket with her.*
MADELEINE *and* FINGAL *stand there for a moment.*

FINGAL. I trust Miss Hannah is alright.

MADELEINE. Yes, thank you.

FINGAL. We went looking for her up towards Queensfort. There are
some new foals up there. I thought she might have gone for a look.

MADELEINE. No. She was sitting down by the brook in the glen. A
place her father used to take her.

FINGAL. I see.

MADELEINE. Well, thank you for looking.

FINGAL. Of course.

Pause.

MADELEINE. Well?

FINGAL (*producing some coins*). Of the householders I could find
and speak to, four holdings have paid quarterlies. Thirty-seven
have withheld all payment.

MADELEINE. Thirty-seven?

FINGAL. They have organised themselves into one body formally
requesting they might delay payment until their crops are renewed
in the autumn.

MADELEINE. And you have accepted these terms?

FINGAL. I have accepted nothing. If you agree, I will go to the
magistrate in the morning. Perhaps he could have a constable
down here by the end of the week.

MADELEINE. Huh! That's exactly what happened before and here
we are again.

FINGAL. They have not the means, madam.

MADELEINE. Yes, well, neither do I! Think how different it would
be if there was a man in charge here.

FINGAL *looks down.*

Water is pouring in the gable end of the upstairs landing.

FINGAL. I will take a look at first light.

MADELEINE. It needs a roofer, Mr Fingal.

FINGAL. Yes, madam.

MADELEINE. Did you call on Colonel Bennett?

FINGAL. Yes, madam. He is happy to extend further credit if and when your estate should require. And he has also reiterated his offer to buy the houses you own in Jamestown. And he has suggested again he is willing to make an offer for the entire estate if…

MADELEINE (*impatiently*). Yes, I am well aware of the Colonel's addiction to acquiring property. Look, the reason I wanted to see you, Mr Fingal…

FINGAL. You received my letter…

MADELEINE. Yes, I received your letter, but that is not the reason I wanted to see you.

She holds an unopened letter to him.

FINGAL. You have not opened it.

MADELEINE. No I have not. Is it of a personal nature? (*Pause.*) Is it of a personal nature?

Pause. He takes it.

FINGAL. Yes.

MADELEINE. Then I will not read it. I want no more of these letters, Mr Fingal. While I appreciate your offers of… friendship, understand that such is impossible. I cannot reciprocate on any level. My status as a widow is one I bear without regret. Entirely.

FINGAL. Yes, madam.

MADELEINE. So kindly desist. While matters remain cordial.

FINGAL. Yes, madam.

MADELEINE. But thank you.

FINGAL. Yes, madam.

MADELEINE. The reason I wanted to see you is that my cousin, the Reverend Berkeley, arrives here from London tomorrow. He will accompany Hannah to Northamptonshire where she will be married in six weeks' time.

FINGAL. Married?

MADELEINE. Yes. (*Short pause.*) Her fiancé is the Marquis of Newbury, the eldest son of Lord Ashby, whose seat is outside Northampton.

FINGAL. I see.

MADELEINE. My cousin being a trusted spiritual advisor to Lord Ashby, has kindly agreed to chaperone Hannah to Northampton while I settle my affairs here. These matters have been undertaken with great delicacy and as such I have not been at liberty to disclose anything to you or the household before now.

FINGAL. I understand.

MADELEINE. It is my intention to travel to England for the wedding.

FINGAL. Of course.

MADELEINE. And I will remain there.

Short pause.

FINGAL. For how long?

MADELEINE. Indefinitely.

FINGAL. I see.

MADELEINE. I am mindful you have not received your salary for…?

FINGAL. Thirteen months, madam.

MADELEINE. Yes. Well, Hannah's forthcoming union will release a good deal of revenue towards this estate and all outstanding debts will be satisfied.

FINGAL. Thank you, madam.

MADELEINE. Despite the problems we have been beset with here, Mr Fingal, I hope you will remain as estate manager in my absence. Things have been run tolerably well and I expect may be maintained to a satisfactory degree under your charge.

FINGAL. Yes, madam.

MADELEINE. While I have been advised to sell the estate, and indeed I may have to, I am disinclined at present. This is our home. I regard those we know here as our friends.

FINGAL. Of course.

MADELEINE. I know how all of this must appear disruptive,
Mr Fingal…

FINGAL. No…

MADELEINE. But one must act in the interests of the estate.

FINGAL. Naturally.

MADELEINE. And Hannah's best interests obviously.

FINGAL. Obviously. You will forgive me for seeming forward… but
I had heard…

MADELEINE (*softens towards him*). Heard what?

FINGAL. That Miss Hannah was… That an old complaint had…
returned.

MADELEINE. Who told you?

FINGAL. Only those that are within the house.

MADELEINE. Who? Clare? (*Pause.*) Yes well, I'm sure half of
Jamestown knows so you may as well tell me. What have you
heard?

FINGAL. I have heard that Miss Hannah says she has been hearing
voices here again.

Pause.

MADELEINE. Yes, well, so she says.

FINGAL. Do you think this is an appropriate time for her to be
married?

MADELEINE. You are too forward, Mr Fingal.

FINGAL. Yes, madam.

MADELEINE (*dismissively*). She used to always claim that while she
played the piano, she could hear someone… singing. Or crying. I
forget which. She always said that.

FINGAL. Yes, I remember.

MADELEINE (*playing it down*). So… (*Pause. Considers him,
unable to stop herself from opening up.*) Now she says she heard
some man shouting in here on Sunday evening. She ran down to
the kitchen and sat with Clare until I came back from the
Colonel's dinner. You weren't calling out to the boy outside or…?

FINGAL. On Sunday we had our dinner in Jamestown. There was no noise or shouting here to my knowledge. I mean, it might have been...

MADELEINE (*interrupting him*). Yes, well, I am sure there is some explanation. In any case, a change of environment will do her the world of good.

FINGAL. As you say.

MADELEINE. Now, when I went to fetch her today I wanted to take the buggy but both our horses were lame, Mr Fingal.

FINGAL. I only just found out myself...

MADELEINE. Mike Wallace had to loan me his senile old mare. Only with great good fortune did I guess where Hannah had gone and luckily I found her before the cold and the rain had quite chilled her. You will see to the horses, Mr Fingal. How can such a thing have happened?

FINGAL. I don't know.

MADELEINE. Are the horses not your responsibility?

FINGAL. They are the boy's responsibility.

MADELEINE. Well, you will have to put him before his responsibilities.

FINGAL. Yes, madam.

MADELEINE. Our guests will no doubt want to ride abroad in the days they are here, so please see to it.

FINGAL. Yes, madam.

MADELEINE. This is not good enough.

FINGAL. I know.

MADELEINE *goes towards the door, but pauses near him before she leaves.*

MADELEINE. I want you to know that the gate lodge will continue to be at your disposal, for you and the boy, Mr Fingal, no matter what happens.

FINGAL. Thank you, madam.

MADELEINE. I believe Mrs Goulding has some warm stew. You will take some home for your supper.

FINGAL. Yes, madam.

> MADELEINE *leaves.* FINGAL *stands there for a moment, then takes up his rifle and the horse blanket and exits. The lights change to a bright fresh morning. Birdsong is heard outside.* CLARE, *a young housemaid of about twenty or so, comes into the room carrying a tray with a silver teapot and cups and saucers which she places on the table. She is a local girl. She is quick-witted and understands the nuances of everything that goes on about her, but has the intelligence never to let on. The* REVEREND BERKELEY *follows her in, absent-mindedly reading a newspaper. He is about sixty and wears the black garb of a vicar. While he is jovial and likable for the most part, he is very serious when it comes to things he cares about. In these matters he brooks no contention and displays the confidence of a man who entirely believes in the uniqueness of his vocation. It is two days later, 10.20 a.m. Friday May 17th.*

BERKELEY. Thank you, Clare, for a delicious breakfast.

CLARE. You're welcome, sir.

BERKELEY. Oh, Clare, here…

> CLARE *stands waiting awkwardly while* BERKELEY *roots in his waistcoat and trouser pockets for a coin he can't find.*

I'm sorry, Clare, I seem to have…

CLARE. No, sir.

BERKELEY. Will you remind me later to give you a coin?

CLARE. I'm sure I won't, sir!

> *She goes about her work setting the room up.*

BERKELEY. Then I'll just have to remember myself. And I will!

CLARE. There is no need, sir, honestly.

BERKELEY. Little Clare Wallace! I scarcely believe the last time I saw you, you were this high. Do you remember me?

CLARE. Of course I do, sir.

BERKELEY. I have changed terribly, no doubt.

CLARE. No, sir.

BERKELEY. Whilst lying is always a sin, 'In certain lies there is but kindness.' Do you know who said that?

CLARE. No, sir.

BERKELEY. That's one of mine.

CLARE. Oh, very good, sir…

CHARLES AUDELLE enters. He is in his mid-forties. He is striking-looking, somewhat intense, his eyes always searching for hidden depths.

BERKELEY. Ah, Mr Audelle, you rise. And you have missed a delicious breakfast.

CLARE. Would you like me to bring you some up, sir?

AUDELLE. Please, don't go to any trouble. Is that tea?

CLARE. Yes, sir.

AUDELLE. Tea is fine.

BERKELEY. Slice of soda bread, Audelle?

CLARE. A slice of toast, sir?

AUDELLE (*without enthusiasm*). Em…

BERKELEY. Bring him some toast and some butter, Clare, should you be so kind.

CLARE. Yes, sir.

BERKELEY. Thank you, dear.

She exits.

(*Ominously.*) Well, sir, how did you sleep?

AUDELLE. Not well. And when I did drop away it was only to play host to some terrific nightmares.

BERKELEY. I thought as much.

AUDELLE. And you?

BERKELEY. I must confess, this place being something of a childhood home for me allied to the considerable relief to have arrived after such a turbulent journey, I had a passably comfortable night – but tell me, of what did you dream?

AUDELLE. I dreamt of a presence.

> BERKELEY *pours some tea, watching* AUDELLE *take in the room.*

> This is the room.

BERKELEY. This is the room. He hung the rope from a brace above the mirror, stepped off the mantelpiece and hung there until young Hannah had found him.

AUDELLE. The heart of the house. How old was she?

BERKELEY. Eight or nine. Yes. However, having heard the stories that have seeped under the door down the years, it is my belief that rather than stepping into oblivion he has found himself trapped here in an endless bad dream. Somehow caught between this world and the next. One of time's own prisoners.

AUDELLE. And Hannah has heard him…

BERKELEY. She has heard something.

AUDELLE. It is quite uncomfortable here, Berkeley.

BERKELEY. Is it bearable?

AUDELLE (*brusquely, advancing on the tea things*). Yes, it's bearable, but I suggest here is where we begin. When you begin.

BERKELEY. These occasions require a subtlety you might best leave to me, Charles.

AUDELLE. Oh, I intend to!

BERKELEY. For now, we are merely here to escort Hannah to Northamptonshire…

AUDELLE. Of course…

BERKELEY. However, when the household is more relaxed and we have gained a certain confidence, we may encourage such shadows that dwell here to make themselves manifest, which once apprehended… Ah!

> *He breaks off seeing that* MRS GOULDING *has appeared in the doorway. Beside her is a little elderly lady known as* GRANDIE. *She has Alzheimer's disease; while she makes eye contact and smiles from time to time, she rarely speaks.*

MRS GOULDING. Reverend!

BERKELEY. Mrs Goulding! Why, you have not changed one bit! And Grandie!

BERKELEY *gives* MRS GOULDING *a kiss.*

MRS GOULDING. Oh, you say so…

BERKELEY. But it's true. It is true. You are radiant. And Grandie, how are you, my dear?

He offers her his hand.

MRS GOULDING. You remember the Reverend, Grandie. Will you shake hands?

GRANDIE *smiles vaguely, but does not shake hands.*

She'll be alright. Sometimes new people confuse her a bit. Sit down, Grandie, and we'll get you a slice of cake in a minute. That's right.

GRANDIE *does not sit, but places herself with her hand on the back of a chair, watching them.*

BERKELEY. Mrs Goulding, may I present my travelling companion, Mr Audelle?

MRS GOULDING (*shaking hands with* AUDELLE). You are welcome, sir. And anything we can do to make your stay more comfortable, you will tell us.

AUDELLE. I cannot see how that could be necessary.

BERKELEY. And this is Grandie, grandmother to the lady of the house. Quite a beauty in her day, Mrs Goulding.

MRS GOULDING. Oh, they all got their looks from her! Didn't they, Grandie? We'll get you a slice of cake now in a minute. You are looking hale and hearty, Reverend. And but I had no idea of the nature of your trip, sir! Is it true you will accompany Miss Hannah to England!

BERKELEY. For her wedding!

MRS GOULDING. Well, I am overcome. With joy, of course, but with sorrow too.

BERKELEY. Mrs Goulding has been almost a second mother to Hannah, Audelle.

MRS GOULDING. To both Hannah and her mother. I am like another grandmother to this house, I have been here so long.

BERKELEY. We used to call Mrs Goulding our 'maid mother'. And you are keeping well yourself, Mrs Goulding?

MRS GOULDING. I am middling well, thank God. What more can we ask? I'm sorry, your grace, and I'm sorry to you, sir. It's just… to suddenly see yourself again after so long, Reverend. Suddenly all the time that seems to have just…

She wipes her eyes.

BERKELEY (*puts an arm round her*). No, no, come now, we are all happy. These feelings are as natural as a leaf falling to the earth. To know a little sadness on account of past joys is surely a cause for gratitude.

MRS GOULDING. You are right, sir.

MADELEINE enters, holding the door for CLARE, who carries a tray in with more tea, cups and some slices of toast under a napkin. MRS GOULDING supervises CLARE at the table, and they pour tea for all during the following.

BERKELEY. Madeleine!

MADELEINE. Berkeley.

BERKELEY. I have longed for this embrace.

He comes to her and embraces her. She allows him to kiss her cheek.

You cannot be eating well, Madeleine. Where have you gone? Ha ha ha! Oh, but you make me feel old. Finally I may introduce you. Lady Madeleine Lambroke, eternal succour to all in her protectorate; Mr Charles Audelle, gentleman of letters, philosophy and higher learning.

AUDELLE (*takes her hand*). Madam, such pleasure at last.

MADELEINE. We did not want to disturb you, Mr Audelle.

AUDELLE. With embarrassment, I must assure you I do not normally sleep on past seven o'clock, but we have not had comfort such as your wholesome dwelling provides for some nights now, and I am afraid I could not stir myself.

MADELEINE. I would have preferred to greet you last night, but the hour had grown so late, I had assumed you would not arrive until today.

BERKELEY. The bridge was half destroyed by so-called revolutionaries.

MRS GOULDING. Oh no!

BERKELEY. Yes! So we had to wait for the ferry, but the waters had risen so in the deluge, the pilot wouldn't go! We were loath to turn back and face our depressing lodgings at Jamestown so it was our good luck that a fisherman, who was determined to get home, took us across for two shillings. And thank you again, Clare, for admitting us so late. It was almost gone two o'clock!

MRS GOULDING. She is a well-mannered girl, is she not?

BERKELEY. Most decidedly!

MRS GOULDING. Say thank you, Clare.

CLARE. Thank you, sir.

MRS GOULDING. And Mr Audelle.

CLARE. Thank you, sir.

AUDELLE. No, thank you, Clare.

CLARE. Thank you, sir.

BERKELEY. Thank you, Clare.

MADELEINE. Yes… You will have noticed the deterioration of Jamestown, Berkeley.

BERKELEY. To an extent I had scarcely suspected, Madeleine. Our coach stopped near what we now realise was the workhouse.

MRS GOULDING. Oh, yes.

BERKELEY. Desperate men and women suddenly descended upon our coach. So numerous were the pale hands outstretched towards us, it was only later I understood that an insensible infant thrust before me by a cadaverous wild-eyed woman must surely have been deceased…

MADELEINE. Oh, Berkeley…

BERKELEY. Yes.

AUDELLE. I'm afraid it was so.

MRS GOULDING. Clare, why don't you run along and tell Miss Hannah there is tea in the drawing room.

CLARE. Yes, Mrs Goulding.

She goes.

MADELEINE. Times are hard here, Berkeley, there is no doubt. The meagre crop has failed again. But we have sought to assist those we can, have we not, Mrs Goulding?

MRS GOULDING. We have indeed, madam. Those as we can, God help us.

BERKELEY. Well, of course.

Pause.

MADELEINE. And you reside with the Reverend at present, Mr Audelle?

AUDELLE. I do, which is perhaps another reason I slept so late – I am not accustomed to the silent pleasures of a room of one's own. I am sorry to say the poor Reverend's snoring vibrates the slim walls of our modest apartment in Highgate at the best of times, but to share a room with him as I have these past few nights on our way down here, is to have one's very teeth shaken out of one's head!

They laugh.

BERKELEY. And I am blissfully unaware of it! More's the irritation! But we make good company, do we not?

AUDELLE. Oh, yes!

MRS GOULDING. Madam has always cried out in her sleep.

MADELEINE. Oh, not for a long time.

MRS GOULDING. And loud enough to wake me and I on the floor below.

BERKELEY. Oh dear! There is little so disturbing as the cry that reefs you to the surface!

MRS GOULDING. Now you said it!

MADELEINE. I haven't done that for a long, long time, Mrs Goulding.

MRS GOULDING. I wouldn't know – my hearing is not what it was.

Pause.

BERKELEY. You know, it occurs to me that each of us here in this room has been widowed.

MADELEINE. Oh, well, my sympathies, Mr Audelle.

AUDELLE. And mine to you, all.

MADELEINE. I have always envied Berkeley's faith in trying times. I must admit, I was never overly concerned for your welfare when Alice passed away – I knew your belief would hold strong. Certainly stronger than mine!

BERKELEY. My faith didn't protect me, Madeleine. It was my congregation who protected me. But only because Alice was beloved by all. Only when the Bishop took my lodgings away did I feel a loneliness that came and gutted me like a knife. That first winter I moved to London alone was... well, it was wretched.

MADELEINE. Your letters never betrayed that, Berkeley.

BERKELEY. Well. (*Short pause.*) But happily, on my travels – (*Touches* AUDELLE'S *shoulder.*) I met Mr Audelle, whose intellect and curiosity have given me great joy in our evenings together at home in Highgate. And in return he bears the burden of my company. Snoring and all!

CLARE *enters and holds the door open.* HANNAH *enters. She is seventeen and slender, alert with a keen perceptiveness of her situation and that of others. She wears spectacles and has a bandage on her right hand. She regards the room somewhat coolly.*

Can this be Hannah?

MADELEINE. This is Hannah.

BERKELEY. My word, the ten years that have passed since I was here had seemed but ten hours until now. Time itself has conjured a beautiful young lady where moments ago was a child. Do you recall me, cousin?

HANNAH. The last time I saw you we carved our names in the fairy tree near the gallops. Your initials are still there.

BERKELEY. That's right!

HANNAH. And you told me of a hanging you witnessed at Leitrim Gaol where the man called out to the Virgin Mary over and over after they put the sack on his head.

Short pause.

BERKELEY. Ha ha ha… And now we have come to take you away to be wedded to your love. Can it be so?

HANNAH. It certainly appears to be so.

BERKELEY. And I see, Madeleine, that my old sparring partner, the Bishop of Solsbury himself has been engaged to perform the ceremony. He may be a notoriously insufferable old bore, but one cannot fault him in matters of canon law. When you are married by him, it will be like an iron lock closing for ever in the eyes of God! (*Laughs.*) Permit me to introduce Mr Charles Audelle, Hannah, who has been so kind as to accompany me on my pleasant task. I trust you will find his company most instructive. Here… (*Produces a slim volume.*) is a copy of his book!

MRS GOULDING. His book!

HANNAH. Thank you.

HANNAH *takes it.* AUDELLE *offers her his hand. She presents him with her left, unbandaged, hand.*

AUDELLE. Pray, what has happened to your hand? Nothing serious, I hope.

HANNAH. I pierced it grabbing hold of some brambles the day before yesterday.

AUDELLE. I see.

BERKELEY. Mr Audelle is considered to be – especially by many young people, Hannah – one of the finest writers of the age in London. His mind is as delicate as any in his generation.

AUDELLE. Now please, Reverend.

HANNAH. I have heard of this book, sir. Weren't you recently accused of plagiarism?

AUDELLE. Well…

MADELEINE. Hannah…

BERKELEY. That was a misunderstanding…

MADELEINE. That's not a nice thing to say, Hannah.

AUDELLE. No, it's true, there was an... accusation...

HANNAH. I merely wanted to ask whom he was *accused* of plagiarising, Mother.

MRS GOULDING. What's plagiarise?

HANNAH. When you steal someone else's ideas and pass them off as your own.

MADELEINE. Hannah, that is not a kind thing to say.

AUDELLE. No, no, I'm afraid it has already been said, madam. Hannah is merely asking about something many already believe.

HANNAH. Who did you plagiarise?

MADELEINE. Hannah, you mean, who do they... say... he plagiarised...

HANNAH. Yes.

AUDELLE. Oh, some Germanic philosopher who was merely thinking along the same lines as myself. And while I allow he had already published some ideas similar to my own – they remained untranslated... and I was to all intents and purposes, unaware of them in their most recent form.

HANNAH. What was his name?

AUDELLE. Oh, I can barely pronounce it. Or bring myself to utter it.

HANNAH. You don't speak German?

AUDELLE. Certainly not well enough to dissect the latest in up-to-the-minute Prussian transcendental philosophy. No.

MADELEINE. Well, what a misfortune...

BERKELEY. The greater misfortune is that the bear pit of critical appraisal in London tends to be a hundred times more savage than the most animalistic assault in the wild.

MRS GOULDING. Dear God.

HANNAH. They had no case against you?

AUDELLE. Well, you see, some years ago I had the pleasure of visiting the universities of Tübingen and Jena. While my grasp of the language was rudimentary, like many, I was intoxicated by the potency of the lectures there. Certain ideas were... hung in the ether, like unplucked fruit upon an overripened vine, and while I had mistakenly assumed I was the first to give their utterance…

HANNAH. You were in fact not.

Pause.

AUDELLE. No.

BERKELEY. Such a thing can easily happen.

HANNAH. And you do not tire of philosophers inventing worlds where nobody lives?

AUDELLE. I, personally, have no need to invent a world to argue about – since the one I find myself in already confounds me quite enough.

HANNAH. But isn't every world an invention?

MADELEINE (*interrupts*). Oh, it is surely far too early in the day for such discussion, is it not? The sun is finally peeping out to beckon us to the garden.

BERKELEY. Precisely, Madeleine, the magic gardens call me here yet. We arrived in darkness and Mr Audelle has no idea of the beauty and wildness that surround us.

MADELEINE. There are plenty of old boots down by the kitchen door. You must spare your shoes after the rain. Mrs Goulding, will you show the gentlemen?

MRS GOULDING. Certainly, madam.

MADELEINE. Perhaps Grandie would like some air. Clare, you may leave the tea tray. Hannah and I will take a cup before we join you.

BERKELEY. Capital.

CLARE. Would you like some freshly brewed, madam?

MADELEINE. No thank you, I'm sure it's fine. We will join you presently.

AUDELLE. Thank you, Lady Lambroke. May I say what a pleasure it is to have finally met you, Miss Lambroke.

MADELEINE. You are welcome, sir.

MRS GOULDING *offers her arm to* GRANDIE *who takes it.*

MRS GOULDING. Now, Grandie.

GRANDIE *suddenly goes and kisses* HANNAH *on the cheek.*

Now, there's a lovely kiss. Let's go and get some nice cake.

BERKELEY *leaves, followed by* AUDELLE, CLARE *and* MRS GOULDING, *who helps* GRANDIE *out. From the hall we hear* BERKELEY.

BERKELEY (*off*). Now, you see that painting above the fireplace?

AUDELLE (*off*). Oh yes, I saw that.

BERKELEY (*off*). That's the very view one is furnished with as we approach the gazebo.

MRS GOULDING (*off*). Come down this way, Mr Audelle.

AUDELLE (*off*). Yes, thank you, I'm coming.

MADELEINE. I see your temper has yet to abate.

HANNAH. Yes, well, I'm sorry, Mother. But to actually walk in and meet the men who are to take me away filled me with such anxiety I had spoken before I knew it.

MADELEINE. And must you articulate your anxiety with such bad manners? Do you know what Lady Fitz-Morris said.

HANNAH. What.

MADELEINE. She said a marriage such as you have before you would be the envy of any English girl, let alone an Irish girl who lives where the prospect of a decent match is remote.

HANNAH. Really?

MADELEINE. Oh, so what would you prefer? One of the Colonel's cockeyed twits, with not an idea in his head that doesn't pertain to beagles or billiards? In England you may reside three or four months of each year in London. Can you imagine I had but a month there in my whole life? I was presented to women and men of such nobility my limbs were positively liquid in uncontrollable acknowledgement of their position. And you will meet them as an equal!

HANNAH. With a husband who bears me no love.

MADELEINE. Of course he will love you.

HANNAH. It is his father who is attached to me. Surely you have seen that.

MADELEINE. Oh, nonsense. He admires you.

HANNAH. All the time we were there the old man's eyes followed me like black holes of insensible longing, while the Marquis spoke to me only of dogs and guns. When he deigned to actually ask me anything my answers were greeted with a decidedly unenthusiastic silence.

MADELEINE. So what, you will you remain here at Mount Prospect with its endless debts, enduring the hatred of those who rent your holdings, until you too are finally turfed out? You will be alone for ever – stigmatised as a bumpkin from the colonies whose only dowry is the odour of our failure!

HANNAH. Yes, I know about dowries. You have bought your way out of this place with whatever you could get for me!

MADELEINE (*slaps* HANNAH). How dare you! You are not too old to be spanked, my girl.

HANNAH. Hit me then! If you must! Your marriage was arranged for you and look how that ended!

HANNAH *goes to the door.*

MADELEINE. Hannah, come back here!

MADELEINE *gets there first and blocks her way.*

HANNAH. Get off me!

MADELEINE. Yes, my marriage was arranged. What could I know at nineteen years of age about husbands and how the world works? What happened to your father was due to… what he bore within him, before we ever even met. As such it was unavoidable yet impossible to foresee. (*Pause.*) Please understand how worried I have become. I undertake none of this lightly. I know how you like the solitude of your room and your books and your fire and your walks. But now you will always have those things! And have them where you are safe and well – within yourself. Where these sudden… voices cannot distress you.

HANNAH. Yes, well, I wish I had never said anything about that now.

MADELEINE. What would you have me do? Take Dr Henry's advice and put you in a hospital in Dublin?

HANNAH. What if they are trying to tell me something?

MADELEINE. Who?

HANNAH. The voices.

MADELEINE. Oh, Hannah! I cannot imagine they have anything
good to say.

HANNAH. Perhaps they are warning me against the very plans you
have made.

MADELEINE. Oh, come now.

HANNAH. Well, why not?

MADELEINE. Because the voices cannot love you like I do. I will
help you in your new life, with your new family.

HANNAH. You would come also?

MADELEINE. Well, of course.

HANNAH. No.

MADELEINE. What do you mean, no?

HANNAH. I would forbid it, is what I mean.

MADELEINE. And go alone?

HANNAH. Why not? You have already arranged my chaperones.

MADELEINE. Hannah, I know you don't mean it.

HANNAH. No – I will endure Hell there with him or Hell here with
you, but I will not endure both.

MADELEINE. Hannah!

HANNAH. And if I must be sold, I will sell myself into personal
sovereignty. And you, madam, may do as you wish.

MADELEINE. And you would leave me here? Where will I go?

HANNAH. Why, Mother, but you are putting me out!

BERKELEY *appears in the doorway holding a stick.*

BERKELEY. Ladies! The sky is burst through with sunlight behind
the blackest clouds you have ever seen. Mr Audelle has described
it as an aspect of the sublime! Please say you will join us as we
walk down to the old pond.

MADELEINE. Of course.

BERKELEY. And I almost forgot to mention it! I have a letter from
Hannah's prospective father-in-law.

MADELEINE. A letter?

BERKELEY *puts his stick down, takes an envelope from his inside pocket.*

BERKELEY. A letter he has asked me to read aloud before our assembled company after dinner one of these evenings. I must say I have rarely seen him so satisfied, Hannah. You will be a queen among his household.

MADELEINE. Let us walk then. Hannah. You will take my hand?

BERKELEY *examines the envelope as he goes out into the hallway. HANNAH regards MADELEINE for a moment, then steps forward and takes her hand. MADELEINE holds it tightly, grateful for the affection. HANNAH looks down. MADELEINE kisses HANNAH's hair. They regard each other in a moment of reconciliation, and leave.*

(*Off.*) You may lead the way, Berkeley.

BERKELEY (*off*). Yes, oh, just let me find my stick. The damp air gets me in my hip, I'm afraid.

BERKELEY *returns for his stick. He stands for a moment looking up at the brace above the mirror by the mantelpiece then follows them out. The lights change, bringing us to evening, two nights later, Sunday May 19th. It is about 9 p.m. There is still a trace of dusk in the sky. FINGAL helps CLARE light one or two oil lamps in the room. FINGAL then stands looking at a chessboard. CLARE stands as though waiting for his attention, but leaves when AUDELLE comes in, carrying a candle and a glass of red wine.*

AUDELLE. Ah, Fingal… You see what I've done there.

FINGAL. You certainly know how to use those rooks.

AUDELLE (*seeing some decanters with liquor*). Brandy! Thank God… (*Knocks back his wine and advances on the spirits.*) Care for a drop?

FINGAL. Em… Maybe later.

AUDELLE. I don't think you can escape.

FINGAL. I think you may be right. (*Knocks over his king on the board.*) You win, sir.

AUDELLE. A good game. Set them up again and you can be white. Good God, did you see those poor wretches who came into the yard for soup earlier on?

FINGAL (*setting up the pieces*). I did.

AUDELLE. I had no idea things were so bad.

FINGAL. Yes, they're bad from time to time.

AUDELLE. To my shame I had not the confidence to approach them. Would they have spoken to me?

FINGAL. Ah, yes. They are a curious people; they would show you great interest and courtesy, no doubt.

AUDELLE. I will greet them the next time.

FINGAL. Oh yes, they are always keen to learn English, sir.

AUDELLE (*savouring a large gulp of brandy*). Well, I have no doubt, in the future, the Irishman will be beholden to no one and walk amid the spirit of his age with pride.

FINGAL (*uncertainly*). Mm.

AUDELLE. No doubt. You were born near here, Mr Fingal?

FINGAL. I was.

AUDELLE. How do you all get on?

FINGAL. Who?

AUDELLE. You and the locals.

FINGAL. Ah, I'm neither one thing nor the other any more. Each side rejects you and everyone is suspicious.

AUDELLE. How unpleasant.

FINGAL. My father always said it suits the nature of a contrarian, Mr Audelle.

AUDELLE (*laughs*). Yes, it must rather. But this house is generous, is it not?

FINGAL. As generous as it may afford to be. Against the advice of many, her ladyship took in an orphan a few years ago. A boy who resides with me down at the gate lodge. He was given the name James Furay.

AUDELLE. Oh yes, I have seen him. I attempted to exchange greetings with him out on the steps this morning but he just looked at the earth.

FINGAL. He means no discourtesy. He's often silent in himself, but he's conscious of his great debt to the house in ways others I may mention are not. Here, sir.

FINGAL *holds out a coin to* AUDELLE.

AUDELLE. What's this?

FINGAL. Our wager, for the chess game.

AUDELLE. Oh no, sir, I will not accept your money.

FINGAL. A wager is a wager.

AUDELLE. No, no, come now.

FINGAL. I insist or we cannot play again.

AUDELLE. I was warned about you Irish. I'll tell you what, keep your money, but perhaps you might do me a small favour. (*Taking a piece of paper from his pocket.*) I have a doctor's script for some pain-relieving tincture which I was accustomed to buying in London. You see, I have a permanent jabbing in my lower back, sustained in a fall from a window some years ago. I had a small bottle with me, but unfortunately it cracked when we took our bags down from the coach in some haste in Jamestown the other evening. I asked the girl. Is her name Clare?

FINGAL. Yes.

AUDELLE. Yes, I asked her if she might take this and procure me some during her errands in town, but she returned it to me this morning saying Mrs Goulding forbade her to make the purchase! Can you believe that!

FINGAL. What's in it, sir?

AUDELLE. Nothing harmful!

FINGAL *takes the script, reading it…*

Medicinal herbs…

FINGAL. I see. Mrs Goulding has some firm ideas, I'm afraid.

AUDELLE. And you, sir?

FINGAL. Less so.

AUDELLE. You're a good man, Fingal.

FINGAL. I always pay my debts.

AUDELLE. Debts! Why, it's a little wager over a game of chess, not a bank loan, man. Only as long as it's no trouble.

FINGAL. It's no trouble, sir.

AUDELLE. I knew I could count on you. Goodness, this brandy evaporates so swiftly! Can I pour you one?

FINGAL. A... very small one only then, sir, to be social. Please allow me.

AUDELLE. Not at all. (*Pours them both quite large drinks.*) Have you eaten? We had some excellent trout earlier, at table with the curious young Hannah. Does she ever eat?

FINGAL. I assume she must.

AUDELLE. Our conversation ventured to an old tomb nearby which her mother seemed uneasy talking about. Do you know of it?

FINGAL. Up at Knocknashee?

AUDELLE. That's it.

FINGAL. It's just an old hole in the ground.

AUDELLE. What do they call it? The Queen's Tomb?

FINGAL. Some do. Others will not speak of it.

AUDELLE. What do you think it is?

FINGAL. I couldn't say. A doctor came over from Oxford when I was a boy. He said there's a passage underneath that's maybe been there for thousands of years.

AUDELLE. I'd love to see it.

FINGAL. Don't go up there on your own, sir.

AUDELLE. Is it frightening?

FINGAL. No, it's not frightening, but there are gangs of boys, and men, in that locality who would have certain perceived grievances with anyone they see wandering up from out of here. Up around the cottages at Knockmullen.

AUDELLE. I see.

FINGAL. If there's time I'll bring you up in the buggy maybe some morning, but please do not wander up there on your own, or at night.

AUDELLE. Understood.

FINGAL. The Reverend would know more about it than me.

AUDELLE. He knew much that he has forgotten.

FINGAL. He has indeed aged since I saw him.

AUDELLE. Well, that's what the Church of England has done.

FINGAL. Can I ask why he was he expelled, if that's not an impertinent question?

AUDELLE. Not at all. Perhaps you might ask him yourself if you have a spare hour or two to withstand his account.

FINGAL. You are not religious then, I take it.

AUDELLE. My religion is philosophy, sir. Do you pray?

FINGAL. No.

AUDELLE. Never?

FINGAL. Maybe in the night. I don't know.

AUDELLE. In the night.

FINGAL. Mmm.

Pause. FINGAL looks down. AUDELLE regards him. The door opens and HANNAH enters. The men stand. She shuts the door.

HANNAH. Am I disturbing you?

AUDELLE. Not at all. We were just talking about you. Please, sit by the fire. I was just sipping some brandy for my cold whereas Fingal is just drinking. I'm joking. Come. Join us.

HANNAH comes into the room and stands looking into the fire, her hand on the back of a chair.

FINGAL. I meant to tell you, miss; Liam O'Leary's mare had two beautiful foals. I thought you'd probably want to go and have a look before you leave.

HANNAH. Twins?

FINGAL. Yes.

HANNAH. Oh, I will.

Pause.

AUDELLE. How nice it is to sit here at your fire. Three nights ago
we were at a ghastly inn at Jamestown. You must know it. We
dined in the front parlour with a fire which, no matter how much
coal the old pot boy shuffled on, never seemed to penetrate the
damp chill of the room. The handful of diners as were present ate
with their coats on. Nothing stirred in the street outside. The only
sound was the hollow ticking of a clock in the hallway. Dear Lord.
After a few restless, frozen hours in a narrow bed beside your
kicking cousin, the Reverend, I went for a dawn walk that burnt
my skin raw. Where the street ended and became countryside was
the brick wall of the workhouse and a crowd of haggard-looking
men and women turned to look at me with such alien ferocity I
thought that should I ever find myself stranded here, I'd blow my
brains out. Now, there's a thought.

FINGAL. So why come at all?

AUDELLE. Well, besides accompanying the Reverend... I came in
search of ghosts, Mr Fingal.

FINGAL. Ghosts?

AUDELLE. Ghosts, Mr Fingal.

HANNAH. Why here?

AUDELLE. Well, Hannah, while the city of London will present the
ghoulish at every corner, a true doorway to the eternal seems to
demand the spiritual quietude and awesomeness as only desolate
places such as Ireland may possess.

HANNAH. The vicar at Ballycliff says the eternal resides in the
everyday things we see.

AUDELLE. Yet few ever seem to hear its song until it's too late!

HANNAH. Perhaps they are deaf.

AUDELLE. But you have heard, have you not? Here in this house?

HANNAH. Not just in the house, here in this very room, sir.

FINGAL. Miss Hannah...

HANNAH. Well, it's true, Fingal.

AUDELLE. Do tell us.

FINGAL. Mr Audelle, I think it would be better were we to take our dram and…

The door opens. MADELEINE *and* GRANDIE *come in with* CLARE, *who lights some candles.* MADELEINE *looks on the company disapprovingly.* FINGAL *and* AUDELLE *rise to their feet guiltily.* BERKELEY *comes in behind her waving a letter.*

BERKELEY. Gather ye! Gather ye! I bring news from beyond the realm.

HANNAH. Oh, Berkeley, please, must you read it?

BERKELEY. Of course I must! I am under strict instructions. It will be read 'before the host who inhabit the child's home,' to quote Lord Ashby directly.

HANNAH. This is outrageous.

MADELEINE. Hannah, we will all watch our manners.

BERKELEY. He assures me it is not long and I have no doubt it is perfectly innocuous. Now, where are my spectacles?

HANNAH. Oh God…

MRS GOULDING *puts her head round the door. She wears her best evening dress. It may be quite old but has a striking amount of gold brocade and ornamentation.*

MRS GOULDING. Have I missed the letter?

MADELEINE. No, you are just in time.

HANNAH. Of course! Come in! Come in! Clare, do take a seat.

MRS GOULDING (*lampooning* HANNAH's *concerns. She is drunk and consequently emotional and energised*). Oh, the drama of it all! You would swear it was your funeral you were heading off to rather than a wedding that would be the envy of any young girl in the world. Will Grandie take a sherry? She will, won't you, Grandie?

BERKELEY. Is that Irish whiskey I spy?

MRS GOULDING. It is. Only freshly bought – and sampled, personally – this morning.

BERKELEY. My throat is… (*Waves his hand in front of his throat.*)

MRS GOULDING. Clare, pour a drop for the Reverend. I will have a drop also, begging your ladyship's grace. Clare, you may have a small sherry, and one for Grandie.

CLARE. Madam?

MADELEINE. Not for me, Clare, pour yourself a sherry.

MRS GOULDING. A small sherry. But pour me a fitting measure of our Lord's tears.

AUDELLE. And I will join you if I may. Fingal?

FINGAL *hands* AUDELLE *his glass.*

REVEREND. Easy, my friend. Mr Audelle has been sipping spirits for that terrible cold he has had this past year and a half.

There is some laughter at this.

MRS GOULDING. Well, as Mr O'Connell said in his speech at Loughferry – 'It will take a strong draught to blow back the veil of confusion!'

Laughter.

AUDELLE. Well said.

BERKELEY. Now, if we are settled… (*Unfolds the letter.*) He has such a fine hand. (*Sniffs the paper.*) And always the best Corinthian ink.

MRS GOULDING. But of course. Clare, settle!

CLARE *looks for a seat.*

FINGAL (*offering* CLARE *a seat*). Clare, please.

MRS GOULDING. Leave her where she is. She is at work.

FINGAL. As are we, Mrs Goulding. Clare, take a seat here.

MADELEINE. Yes, sit here, Clare.

CLARE *goes to* FINGAL*'s seat.*

HANNAH. This is agony.

AUDELLE. There is seldom sport without it.

MRS GOULDING. Just sit somewhere, child, you will spill your drink. Do you think you could have fit any more in that glass? Look at it!

MADELEINE. Hannah! Berkeley, please begin.

BERKELEY. Ahem… 'My dear Miss Hannah, Tonight the wind rages about the eaves and far across our lands the animals huddle for warmth. The house creaks about me, and yet as I sit here long after all have retired and the last embers colden…' Is that a word? (*Squints at it.*) Colden?

MADELEINE. I don't think so.

HANNAH. Oh God…

MRS GOULDING. The word is 'encolden'.

BERKELEY. Is it?

FINGAL. I have never heard that word.

MRS GOULDING. To encolden – to grow cold, or lose warmth.

MADELEINE. You are having us all on now, Mrs Goulding.

MRS GOULDING. Doesn't his lordship use it himself in his letter?

AUDELLE. Perhaps he has partaken of the early dew. (*Helping himself to a drink.*) Fingal?

FINGAL. No, thank you.

BERKELEY. Audelle, may I continue?

AUDELLE. Forgive me. A smallish dram as I have grown just a tad encoldened.

Laughter.

MRS GOULDING. I am also a tad encoldened. (*Brings* AUDELLE *her glass.*)

BERKELEY. Alright, settle down. 'The house creaks about me, and yet as I sit here long after all have retired and the last embers colden, somehow the memory of your visit to our house last Easter is alive in the mind, as though I am staring through the glass wall of time and observing those happy days when you and your beautiful mother dwelt amongst us and lit our house like a tiny sun. I hear you playing the piano. It still echoes through our hallways; a joyous yet saddening music which only reminds us of your absence and your longed-for presence.

That my eldest, and may I say most time-consuming, son should have you as his prospective bride brings a secret joy to my heart and I sing its mysterious melody tonight. I do admit I may have burdened him with the unrealistic expectations of an inexperienced father – burdens I have perhaps never placed on my subsequent sons – and thus he may have struggled in the past to accept his place in the world satisfactorily. But I am filled with confidence now, because I know your companionship will be, for him, both the steady ballast of his moral bearing and a guiding hand on his tiller.' (*Clears his throat.*) Ahem.

'Until you are with us I send you thanks and warm wishes in recognition of the gifts you have already granted us; your grace and your temperate solemnity. I hear the birds calling far away in the forest and I know that dawn is approaching. I will pass this letter to my rock and spiritual advisor, Reverend Berkeley, and should all befall as one may dare to hope, he stands before you reading it now while I languish hundreds of miles away on my own fair isle of England, but my words are now among you and blessed to be so. My friends, I remain yours, George, 16th Earl of Loughborough and Northampton, humble servant of the King and our Lord God Almighty.'

He lowers the letter.

MRS GOULDING. Well, now, that's what I call a letter!

BERKELEY. I am not in the least surprised. His lordship is a thoughtful creature. He has worried so about his boys since the departure of their dear mother, and he longs to see them settled. He is an especially intuitive soul and I believe he has spotted in Hannah a unique aspect I myself have often wondered about.

GRANDIE. The dog is at the door.

MRS GOULDING. Shush now, Grandie, and drink your sherry.

BERKELEY. Those of a spiritual bent can see that someone of Hannah's beauty must be in touch with something *elemental*. In my numerous and varied travels on the British Isles, I have encountered a great many people in a great many places and please hear me without prejudice when I say that certain persons have a strange energetic effect on the very nature of time itself. His lordship has apprehended this. Hear the passion with which he addresses Hannah as though she is still in his house, one can almost sense his terror he will not be close to her unique atunement again.

MADELEINE. Berkeley, you will frighten the girl…

BERKELEY. Oh, come. (*With sudden unexpected seriousness*.) We all know that Hannah hears echoes of a past none else can hear.

MADELEINE (*straining to be jovial*). I must forbid this conversation. Such seriousness! That letter has quite unsettled me. Clare, tidy up.

MRS GOULDING. Madam, the Reverend is correct. Do not be unsettled by that letter and under no circumstances reconsider your plans. The girl must go to England. Look at the creatures who inhabit this place around us. If she stays here, what will she inherit? The ingratitude of the wretches who skulk about this island? Who are these people? The wildness in them. And the badness in them. They are only filthy tinkers the half of them. I grew up in Jamestown, Reverend. My people had a decent shop. We were schooled until we were eleven years of age. The women out here would thieve anything. And when we serve them soup all out in the back there. All in the yard, the tables lined up, eight gallons of water, onions, turnips, the four legs of a lamb, mind you...

FINGAL. Now, Mrs Goulding, you are too exercised...

MRS GOULDING. Bags of rice in the stew, bags of meal. All out there this year and in 1821 as well. The thieving red-haired look they'd give you, as they hunch over carrying it all out in under the trees out there so as not to share it with each other. The suspicion! They are in league with the devil the half of them. Clare, replenish me.

She holds her glass out to CLARE, *who takes it to get her a drink of whiskey.*

MADELEINE. You can scarcely believe such a thing, Mrs Goulding.

MRS GOULDING. I don't have to believe it, madam! It's just true! Take Mistress Hannah to England, and if you must go yourself, then go. Grandie will be happy with me here. There is less magic in England, and more good sense. The glow that comes off Hannah will bring her good luck there. Here it will only darken all her evenings. The fairies are jealous of her.

FINGAL. Mrs Goulding... For Jaysus' sake!

MRS GOULDING. Do not dare presume to lecture me, sir! You are lost in your own squalor. Sure wasn't my own son nearly taken from us by a fairy woman?

MADELEINE. Mrs Goulding...

MRS GOULDING. He was only sixteen and came back down from working on the boats out at McKenna Island, Reverend. On Christmas Eve he was dressing up in a new shirt and collar. I hardly saw him he was gone so much over the holiday – to meet with a woman he'd met on the road, no less, standing in a hedge! I knew it was no good. Night after night he left to meet her, hurling abuse at me when I tried to stop him. The colour in his face was like the ashes in the fire. He was sick in his heart. He near faded away before my eyes over the days. Till I got the priest to come and bless him while he lay asleep one morning, stretched out in front of the hearth. When he came to he cried his eyes out. He saw that I had saved him. And I had. Yes.

Pause.

MADELEINE. Yes, well…

AUDELLE. I believe you, Mrs Goulding. Your son was lucky to have you to dispel this sapping spirit. I myself had no such good luck until I met our esteemed Reverend. Once, in Spitalfields, I went into a tent to see an exhibit – a monster so they claimed. Of course, the pitiful creature was no more than a misshapen dwarf who was clearly a halfwit. But I saw a monster there all the same. It lurked behind the pain in his eyes. Such a look will always haunt me. And for tuppence I was implicit in heaping further grief upon his soul. The glance he darted at me held such a longing for release and understanding while his keeper barked and hit him. Yes, a monster surely followed among the dirty hoard I kept company with that night as we crawled up the dock wall looking for any dim lantern in a laneway. An elemental darkness is already inside each of us, how we explain it to ourselves is for each of us to bear. Anyone with a gift such as Hannah's is like a beacon in the dark.

BERKELEY. That's right.

MADELEINE. Oh, give me a drink, someone.

MRS GOULDING. Clare…

CLARE *gets a drink for* MADELEINE.

HANNAH. Mother…?

MADELEINE. A small sherry.

MRS GOULDING. A small sherry for Miss Hannah, Clare.

CLARE. Yes, ma'am.

GRANDIE. The old man wipes his feet and says, 'We're home from the fields!'

MRS GOULDING. And for Grandie. Yes, Grandie.

HANNAH. Mama saw a ghost when she was a girl.

MADELEINE. Hannah...

HANNAH. You did.

MADELEINE. I didn't. I have never seen a ghost.

HANNAH. You told us you saw one when you were sixteen in a hotel in London.

MADELEINE. It wasn't in a hotel and I told you it was just a dream.

BERKELEY. Where was it, Madeleine?

MADELEINE. This is ridiculous. I didn't see a ghost, Berkeley. I had a nightmare while I was staying at Great-Uncle Cyril's house in Holborn.

AUDELLE. Oh, do tell us.

MADELEINE. There is nothing to tell. I had eaten too many Belgian sausages before retiring. And not being used to it, I'd had two or even three glasses of white wine. When I went to bed, it being a strange house, I had trouble sleeping. I woke up, wrapped in a knot of blankets and I... I... dreamt I saw a young man standing just inside the door.

AUDELLE. Oh my word.

BERKELEY. They all have the gift.

MADELEINE. It was a dream, Berkeley. And Hannah knows she is making mischief to bring it up.

AUDELLE. Did he say anything?

MADELEINE. Who?

AUDELLE. The young man in your bedroom.

MADELEINE. Oh, I, you know how it is, for a moment I presumed he was real and I said, 'What do you want?' And he told me that...

HANNAH. That he had been murdered...

MADELEINE. Thank you, Hannah. He said he had been murdered in this room many years before. He raised his arm and pointed across the floor. I followed his gaze and... there was his body, lying on the mat under the window, as though it had been severely beaten. With that I let out a scream which brought my aunt and cousin running to my aid. You may imagine my embarrassment as I tried to explain I had merely been experiencing a heavy bout of indigestion.

BERKELEY. Or a visit from the beyond...

MADELEINE. I don't think so, Berkeley. A child will dream.

BEREKELY (*agreeing with her as though she has made his point for him*). Yes. A child will dream. There has always been something here, Madeleine. I have always felt it. In the earth, in the trees, and in the very wind that we hear tonight.

MADELEINE. That's just your memories and a decidedly childhood association with this place, Berkeley. You are a romantic.

BERKELEY. But Hannah has heard it. (*Short pause.*) I believe people get trapped here, Madeleine. Even those we love...

Pause.

MRS GOULDING. Clare, you are excused.

BERKELEY. Let her stay.

MRS GOULDING. She's terrified, look at her.

FINGAL. Are you?

CLARE *shakes her head.*

AUDELLE. She's more terrified of walking all the way down to the scullery on her own in the dark.

FINGAL. Let her be, Mrs Goulding.

BERKELEY. There is something here, Madeleine, Hannah has heard it.

Pause.

MADELEINE. No.

BERKELEY (*to* HANNAH). Have you not?

MRS GOULDING. Holy Mary, Mother of God, pray for us sinners, now and at the hour of death, amen.

BERKELEY. There is no cause for alarm. I have prayed for souls who were trapped in Nottingham, Gateshead...

AUDELLE. Isle of Man.

BERKELEY. Isle of Man.

MADELEINE. Berkeley, I forbid this.

BERKELEY. While the light of so many living souls are gathered together here, we should not lose our opportunity to pray. Will you not pray with us, Madeleine? A prayer before bed, nothing more. I assure you…

MADELEINE. Hannah is a young girl, Berkeley.

BERKELEY. She is a woman who is to be married.

MADELEINE. She was always a dreamer.

MRS GOULDING. Do not stick a blade in the hornet's nest, Reverend.

MADELEINE. Hannah has always loved stories. Her head is always in a book. She didn't hear anything.

HANNAH. But I did.

MADELEINE. Berkeley…

HANNAH. I did hear it. Someone shouted at me here in this room. They screamed right in my ear and if there's no one who believes me I still don't care.

BERKELEY. Shh… shhh… my child…

FINGAL. You are scaring the women, sir.

BERKELEY. No, no. There is no reason for fear. We are modern people now. And as such, we know that the spirit realm resides outside of time. As human animals with material bodies we are unfortunately trapped always in this moment and we don't know how to escape it. We cannot measure the past because it is gone. We cannot measure the future because it has yet to occur and we cannot measure the present because it slips away the instant we try to grasp it. Yet a spirit, a spirit exists in God's time where all moments are one eternal moment and all time is now. Yet man is, consider ye, both spirit and matter. Our spirit longs to commune with the eternal yet is all the while trapped within the prison of time itself, longing to be free. Those who have seen a ghost will say it is shadowy and transparent, often only glimpsed on the edge of sleep – why? Because we have not seen it with our physical eye, rather it is an imprint upon the imagination where our spirit apprehends the infinite. A spirit has spoken with Hannah. No more, no less. (*Gives a little laugh*.) There is nothing to fear! Now, before we retire for the evening, let us pray…

MADELEINE. Berkeley.

BERKELEY. No, no, just a bedtime prayer before we retire. That's all. (*Joins his hands and closes his eyes*.) Dear Lord, we beseech thee, deliver the lost and restless wanderer from the nightmare of darkness that engulfs us. Tell us, traveller, what do you want here? What is the nature of your plight? Tell us, in the name of Almighty God, what time are you lost in? (*Pause*.) Who is here? (*Pause*.) Who is here?

Pause.

MADELEINE. Berkeley…

BERKELEY. Who is here? (*Louder*.) WHO IS HERE? (*Louder again*.) WHO IS HERE??!

Pause. There is a sudden deafening bang like a gunshot over their heads. It seems to blow the room apart with its sonic impact. Their drinks go flying, cups are dropped. Each instinctively cries out and cowers…

MRS GOULDING. Dear God, dear God…

FINGAL (*getting up and looking around the room*). What was that? (*Opens the door to look out into the hallway*.)

MADELEINE (*to* BERKELEY). What did you do? (*Pause*.) What did you do?

BERKELEY. I… I don't know… I…

MADELEINE. How dare you? I asked you! In my house!

FINGAL *wanders back in.*

AUDELLE. There is a spirit here.

MADELEINE. You will be quiet, sir! You are a guest here, Mr Audelle, and I will kindly ask you to mind your manners. Berkeley, you will have nothing more to drink. Mrs Goulding, take Clare down and put the kettle on. Hannah, you will retire.

HANNAH. Mama, I…

MADEINE. You will retire!

HANNAH. Yes, Mama.

MRS GOULDING. Come, Clare... Help me with Grandie.

GRANDIE pulls away from MRS GOULDING.

MADELEINE. Leave her be, Mrs Goulding. Go and warm some water.

MRS GOULDING. Yes, madam.

MRS GOULDING signals furiously to CLARE *to help her and they start tidying up.*

BERKELEY. Madeleine. I am only trying to help.

MADELEINE. Well, you are lost in the clouds, Berkeley, you always were. We will discuss this in the morning.

There is a loud knocking at the front door. They all fall silent.

MRS GOULDING. Oh my Lord...

FINGAL goes.

MADELEINE. It is probably James Furay come to see what commotion we have made. What kind of example can we be setting for the boy?

AUDELLE. But what was it? What was that report?

MADELEINE. Well, it was... it was...

Silence. FINGAL *steps into the room.*

FINGAL. Madam, there is a constable outside.

MADELEINE. A constable?

FINGAL. Yes there has been a...

MADELEINE. Yes? (*Pause.*) What is it, Mr Fingal?

FINGAL. A terrace of houses in Jamestown that belong to this estate has collapsed.

MRS GOULDING. Oh, madam.

FINGAL. A number of families were trapped inside...

MADELEINE. I see.

MRS GOULDING. Oh no...

FINGAL. The constable has ridden out to inform you.

Pause.

MADELEINE. Yes, well, bring him in and see if he wants some soup. Mrs Goulding.

MRS GOULDING. Take him downstairs, Clare.

CLARE. Yes, madam.

CLARE *goes. Pause.*

MADELEINE. Where is he?

FINGAL. He is in the parlour.

MADELEINE *looks at* BERKELEY.

BERKELEY. Come, we will go to him.

BERKELEY *and* MADELEINE *leave. The others stand or sit in a state of numb distress.*

MRS GOULDING. What have we done?

The light changes to afternoon. Sunlight falls in through the foliage outside. It is two days later, Tuesday May 21st, around 3 p.m. HANNAH *sits near the window, writing.* GRANDIE *sits near the fireplace on a stool.* AUDELLE *comes in.*

AUDELLE. Where is everybody?

HANNAH. They are gone to Jamestown with Colonel Bennett to see the ruins of the terrace.

AUDELLE. Oh.

HANNAH. Were you asleep?

AUDELLE. I must have been. Is that tea?

HANNAH. Yes, Clare just brought it. For the first time I am glad that the Reverend was here.

AUDELLE *gets himself some tea.*

AUDELLE. I am gratified to hear that.

HANNAH. Everyone hates us, Mr Audelle.

AUDELLE *takes some tea.*

Mr Audelle.

Pause.

AUDELLE. Yes.

HANNAH. What happened in here the night before last.

AUDELLE. Yes.

HANNAH. Do you think it had something to do with what has happened in Jamestown?

AUDELLE. Absolutely.

HANNAH. Does it not bother you?

AUDELLE. Why would it bother me?

HANNAH. Because people have died, Mr Audelle, children have died, in property we owned and we heard something like a thunderclap here while we were… we were… Well… whatever we were doing, I haven't slept since. Are you only outwardly calm, or are you truly calm because you have no investment in this place and couldn't care less who lives or dies?

AUDELLE. Quite the reverse.

HANNAH. Your hands are remarkably steady then, sir. I can barely raise a cup.

AUDELLE. I administered ten drops of laudanum to myself at noon.

HANNAH. Does it work?

AUDELLE. Oh yes, it works – and I might say the local brew is thankfully intense. You see, I have always been susceptible to a kind of spiritual… distress, in certain places. Though I have never actually apprehended a spirit. Unlike you.

Short pause.

HANNAH *thinks about this and returns to her letter.*

HANNAH. You will excuse me, I hope, I am trying to finish a letter I promised to send by today.

AUDELLE *drinks some tea and looks at* GRANDIE.

GRANDIE. And may I ask you, sir; I don't know did you ever see a king around these parts that has mirrors where his eyes should be?

AUDELLE. A… king?

GRANDIE. Yes, he seems to be a kind of a king, with regal bearing, you understand, but he has mirrors instead of eyes. You see yourself when he looks at you! He's out under the trees there sometimes. Did you know about St Patrick?

AUDELLE. St Patrick?

GRANDIE. Yes, St Patrick.

AUDELLE. I… think I know about him.

GRANDIE. Well, he told me who St Patrick really was. St Patrick was a gold prospector! Did you know that? I didn't. They found gold all up in the hills around Cavan and Monaghan. St Patrick came with the good book all about Jesus Christ. That's how they always come, you see, and he said to everyone, 'These gods you have are no good,' apparently. He said he'd tell them all about this better God he knew all about – a very meek God you see, and while they were all busy praying to this terribly meek God, called Jesus Christ who was dreadfully meek, St Patrick took all the gold away! Yes, he told me all about St Patrick.

AUDELLE. I see. Well, thank you for telling me that.

GRANDIE. Yes.

Pause.

AUDELLE (*turning away from* GRANDIE). Do you have any friends who live nearby, Hannah?

HANNAH. When we were younger I used to play with James Furay, a boy my mother took in. But he lives down in the gate lodge with Mr Fingal now. I sense he has been encouraged not to speak with me.

AUDELLE. I am sorry.

HANNAH (*writing*). I had another friend, Elizabeth Argyle who lived at Drumsna. We used to share a tutor here but she got married last year and now lives in County Cavan.

AUDELLE. Is she happy?

HANNAH. She has a baby who has made her happy.

AUDELLE. You will be loved when you are married, Hannah.

HANNAH (*finishes her letter, lifting the paper to dry the ink*). We do not all pine for the love of a protector, Mr Audelle. Lord Ashby's estate is vast. We will have our own house. Clean linen at breakfast, as much hot water as a person may want. I am to receive an allowance and have a carriage at my personal disposal along with weekly French lessons.

AUDELLE. I'm sure your material circumstances will improve, Miss Lambroke, indeed I believe you will rule your domain just as you do here.

HANNAH. You think so?

AUDELLE. I know so. But I do not believe you expect such things will make you happy.

HANNAH. You are very frank, Mr Audelle.

AUDELLE *shrugs and goes to pour himself some tea.* HANNAH *watches him.*

Do you know anything of my fiancé?

AUDELLE. I know. That he made the Duke of Wellborough's widow pregnant and that both she and the child perished before she could bring it forth, thus freeing him conveniently of his obligations? (*Beat.*) Thus freeing him to marry?

HANNAH. He was under her spell.

AUDELLE. Well, of course he was. And now he isn't.

Pause.

HANNAH. You know, Elizabeth Argyle heard a great deal about you when we learned you were lodging with my cousin.

AUDELLE. Really?

HANNAH. Yes. And none of it encouraging. (*Pause.*) Is it true you abandoned your wife?

AUDELLE. It is.

HANNAH. And your child?

Pause.

AUDELLE. When I met my wife I was not much older than you.

HANNAH. What's that supposed to mean?

AUDELLE. Just that you... You might think me naive, but when I looked into her face – her grey eyes were so disarming I had always felt as though I was looking *through* her eyes into something so meaningful that I swore that somehow I could behold God there. And thus every moment was a moment of adoration.

HANNAH. How nice for her.

AUDELLE. Her father had lent us a remote cottage while I tried to write. The weather had been particularly bad. We hid inside from the continuous deluge. The child was sick and crying. My wife was sick. And then I was sick. Very sick. And one morning I looked into my wife's face at breakfast and I realised I could no longer see into the eternal. It was as though a shutter had come down and God had absented himself. And I… accepted that and I tried to… I tried to… but then, while attending Sunday service one morning in March, I thought I spied God again, peering at me from the eyes of another – two others – sisters.

HANNAH. I had scarcely believed it could be true.

AUDELLE. Yes, emboldened by fortifying my brandy with laudanum, I embarked on what I can only describe as sordid interior escapades at their cottage for days on end.

HANNAH. Is it true you turned your wife away with your dead child in her arms?

AUDELLE. No, that's not true. She had walked several miles in the rain with the child to find me one night and… (*Short pause.*) But you must understand how insensible I was. I thought I had heard her voice below the window while I lay deep beneath the blankets. But I… I was… The facts are that the child passed some days afterward – not that night. (*Short pause.*) I endeavoured to take my own life some several times afterwards and I ended up living in London's parks. If not for your cousin, the Reverend – I would have probably died in the madhouse.

HANNAH. Perhaps I can never understand your actions concerning your family, Mr Audelle, and I know they are unforgivable, but I do know what it is to feel… Last week I sliced an apple knife into my hand.

AUDELLE. Why?

HANNAH. So I might experience a pain I actually understand. You see, I know now there is something real, something waiting for me, calling for me to do what my father did. And I know that belief cannot save me and I suspect that even death cannot save me, because when you are in hell you know only one thing – that only nothingness is holy. (*Pause. Composes herself.*) Will you give me some laudanum?

Pause.

AUDELLE. If you like.

HANNAH. Where is it?

AUDELLE. In my pocket.

HANNAH. How do you take it?

AUDELLE. It is best poured in a little drop of brandy.

HANNAH. Will you pour me some?

> AUDELLE *goes to the drinks and pours her a brandy. He hands her the glass, then takes a small bottle from his inside jacket pocket. She holds out her glass.*

AUDELLE. The old stones up at the top of the hill…

HANNAH. The Queen's Tomb?

AUDELLE. Yes. Will you take me up there for a look?

HANNAH. What for?

AUDELLE. To just behold their magic.

> HANNAH *shrugs.*

HANNAH. If you like.

AUDELLE. Thank you.

> *He takes the top from the bottle of laudanum and goes to pour some into* HANNAH's *glass.*

> *The lights fade.*

> *End of Act One.*

ACT TWO

Night, around midnight on Thursday May 23rd. GRANDIE *is sitting quietly near the fireplace as the fire dies. A wind is picking up outside.* HANNAH *slowly plays a single note over and over on the piano. There is a knock. The door to the hallway opens and* BERKELEY *and* AUDELLE *enter. They stand near the door, wrapped up in their coats.*

BERKELEY. Ah, some nighthawks! We didn't expect anyone to still be up.

HANNAH (*rises*). Sometimes Grandie gets up. She never knows when it's night-time.

BERKELEY. Well, we had a lovely moonlight stroll. To walk off our dinner. Are we alone?

HANNAH. Everyone was in bed.

BERKELEY. Of course. Will we join you for a moment?

BERKELEY *and* AUDELLE *come further into the room.*

HANNAH. What time is it?

BERKELEY. It's after midnight! Goodnight, Grandie. How fares the world? You know, I was only saying to Mr Audelle, Thursday was always my favourite day of the week when I was a little boy. It was the one day I was permitted out of the nursery and could sit all afternoon with my mother while my father wrote his lectures. I keenly remember the fascination and privilege I felt in their company. Every Thursday.

AUDELLE. I used to watch my father writing his sermons.

BERKELEY. I saw him preach. He was a great believer in the corrective terror of hell and damnation which lent his oratory an extra impassioned forcefulness, I remember! (*Laughs. Pause.*) You look tired, Hannah.

GRANDIE *looks at him blankly then gives a slight smile of acknowledgement, turning her face back to the fire.*

HANNAH. Well, yes I am, rather.

BERKELEY. Mr Audelle tells me you were kind enough to bring him up to the Queen's Tomb yesterday.

HANNAH. Yes.

BERKELEY. But you didn't stay long.

Short pause.

HANNAH. Yes, well, the weather was inclement.

AUDELLE. I was just telling the Reverend, for myself, laying my hand upon those prehistoric stones induced a sense of connectedness to the mysterious ancestors of this place, the sheer... force of which I had never experienced before.

BERKELEY. Oh, yes. I have always found it to be a place of dark enchantment. And you, Hannah? Did you experience a... sense of connectedness?

HANNAH. Well, I... I did not remain there for long, so...

Pause.

BERKELEY. You know, I often think of your poor father on nights such as this, Hannah.

HANNAH. I think of him regardless of the day or night.

BERKELEY. He is in your prayers.

HANNAH. With all of my family.

BERKELEY. With all of us. My dear Alice is still alive – in my mind, her fragile bones still shining beneath her transparent skin, just as poor old Edward still lives in yours. He is so strong there. So... real. In which case, how can anyone say he doesn't exist? Of course he still exists! These recent times weigh hard on you, I suspect, Hannah.

HANNAH. Well. I have many blessings. I shouldn't complain.

BERKELEY. Yes, but even good news can bring its difficulties, especially when set against a tragedy so terrible as the one we have witnessed in Jamestown.

HANNAH. Especially when it occurred on the very evening you sought to summon the spirits of the dead.

BERKELEY (*laughs, almost delighted she has risen to the bait*). 'The dead'! We didn't cause those buildings to fall down. Hasn't the Colonel himself said as much. Now, I hope you don't mind, but you will be aware I have learned something of your recent experiences, Hannah.

HANNAH. Yes, well, I don't want to discuss that.

BERKELEY. And I will come straight out with it and say it's a pity you consider the specialness of your gift a burden – when rightly it should be something you ought to cherish. And be grateful for.

HANNAH. I just want to stop it now, so...

BERKELEY. Stop it?! Well, it's my belief that would be a dreadful shame. What you really need is to *understand* it. Yes. You can take the sting of its unknowability away, and we would like to help you.

Pause.

HANNAH. How can you help me?

BERKELEY. Do you know what a... seance is, Hannah?

HANNAH. I have heard of it.

BERKELEY. Yes, on the Continent one hears a lot of rubbish about these matters, I'm afraid. The facts are quite simple. I can explain precisely why you are in your predicament, Audelle?

AUDELLE. It's really quite straightforward.

BERKELEY. Dear me, that's quite a draught. Is that door closed, Audelle?

AUDELLE *goes and shuts the door quietly.*

You see, Hannah, there is only God. (*Pause.*) Nature comes from God. It is a part of God. And man is part of nature. But we are a very special part, because only the human being can know itself and think for itself. Consider a fish or a dog. They are prisoners of their instinct, slaves to nature, where man is free.

HANNAH. No. A dog is freer than a man, if you ask me.

AUDELLE. But a dog cannot choose. No animal can. When it's hungry it will eat, when it's tired it must sleep. Thus it has no choice, correct? But man – a man may *deny* his instinct, *suppress* his appetite and decide for himself what is right or wrong. He is even free to destroy himself!

BERKELEY. Can a dog do that?

AUDELLE. Being conscious means man is both part of nature and yet free of it – all at once.

BERKELEY. You see, it has recently been proven, Hannah, beyond logical denial –

HANNAH *goes to interrupt.*

Beyond logical denial, that with the emergence of the human subject there is finally a part of nature which *knows* itself! Do you understand? All of this, everything around us, and you and I and Audelle –

AUDELLE. And Grandie –

BERKELEY. And Grandie and everything else – this is all… the mind of God awakening and coming to know itself. And when we look at each other, just as I am looking at you now, it is as though God is looking at Himself in a mirror. And each eye, the beholder and the beheld, reflect the other back and forth as mirrors do, into a kind of genuine infinity. The infinity of God. You see? We *are* God… Isn't that wonderful? Now, knowing that we are God is of course a great responsibility but it's not something we want to bandy about!

AUDELLE. Of course not.

BERKELEY. For so long we have all felt cut away from God, somehow seeking 'forgiveness' in order to be reunited. But we were never separate from Him! So you need not feel any guilt, Hannah. Your feelings are holy! And just as in any walk of life we meet people with great gifts, this one a great carpenter, that one a great musician, so you have a great talent, Hannah.

HANNAH. You call it a gift.

AUDELLE. Hannah, your gift is simply consciousness itself. That's right. And so profound is your talent in this case, so acute its perceptiveness, you are capable of beholding not just what is here in this moment, but what is beyond and before time.

BERKELEY. That's all it is! Nothing more! (*Laughs.*) And certainly nothing to fear. So in order to dispel the terror visited upon you by the voices you have perceived here in this house, I want to invite you now, through the medium of a seance, to reconsider them in this light: and thereby uncover the divine within yourself. Here. With us. Now. Tonight. We are here to support you and to help you. Why, even Grandie can take part! All humankind is welcome here! (*Laughs.*)

AUDELLE. A seance is merely a mindful contemplation, Hannah. We… sit together and reflect. That is all.

HANNAH. Will it stop me hearing things?

BERKELEY. I cannot say it will. Indeed I hope it will not! But I will stake my life on it that it will take the fear away. My life!

Pause.

HANNAH. What happens?

BERKELEY. What happens? Why nothing more than were we to open a book and read a story. The book we open is the book of time. The story is the unfolding revelation of God's presence in all things. No more. Thus we may understand who or what has been drawn to this place to seek you out. And armed with this knowledge, it is my firm belief you will progress into your new life with a hitherto unforeseen freedom, for ever.

Pause. HANNAH *is thinking about it.*

AUDELLE. Do not waste your youth as I have, hemmed in on either side by an abyss of fear.

BERKELEY. Release yourself. Permit yourself.

AUDELLE. Forgive yourself.

BERKERLEY. And trust me. Won't you trust me?

HANNAH *coughs.*

Yes, we are all getting that cold!

AUDELLE. Allow me. (*Approaches the drinks.*) Berkeley?

BERKELEY. Water for me, Audelle. Thank you. Look at you, Grandie. So well I remember your charms when you sang before the assembled throng here at Mount Prospect. Your wit. Your gameful eyes so animated with shy promise. Then, as now. Yes, I remember you, Grandie.

AUDELLE *brings a drink of brandy to* HANNAH.

AUDELLE. Sip this, Miss Hannah.

BERKELEY. Yes, a sip to clear the lungs. Well done, Audelle.

HANNAH *drinks while* AUDELLE *takes his bottle of laudanum from his pocket. He thumps his chest.*

AUDELLE. I think I need to loosen my...

Coughs lightly and indicates the bottle to HANNAH. *She holds out her glass, he pours some laudanum into her brandy and she drinks it.*

BERKELEY. Yes, Grandie. (*Holds out his hand to her.*) How you would dance the young men to a defeated collapse!

GRANDIE *reaches towards* BERKELEY *uncertainly, but then withdraws her hand.*

Yes, long ago… (*Takes a cord with a crucifix, some feathers and stones strung along it, placing it round his neck like a necklace.*) How silent is the darkness tonight. You may take my hand, Grandie. Take her hand, Hannah. She is your anchor. There is great love there still. (*Pause.*) Do not be afraid. Who else has ever offered to help you as we do? Take her hand, she loves you.

HANNAH *takes* GRANDIE'*s hand.* GRANDIE *gives her other hand to* BERKELEY. AUDELLE *takes* BERKELEY'*s hand.*

Let us pray. (*With pained concentration.*) Lord God, unknowable father, while we struggle oftbetimes to comprehend thy wishes, forgive us – sinners as we are – as we fulsomely seek to know thy bidding. Bless us here tonight. Protect us as darkness falls through the world and we gather in Your name to wish our daughter Hannah a peaceful existence, replete with spiritual calm. We are beset at every turn with temptations, with dire puzzles which would draw us from Your path and hide the light that might show us to Your dwelling where our true home awaits. Lord, shield us with the blanket of Your forgiveness, Lord…

Sound of a window rattling in the house somewhere.

GRANDIE *takes her hand from* BERKELEY'*s.*

(*Firmly.*) Grandie… (*More gently.*) Grandie. Let us say our bedtime prayers, come on now. That's it…

HANNAH. Perhaps we have done enough for now, Berkeley.

BERKELEY. We are merely saying a prayer, Hannah. Let us pray. Let us pray.

GRANDIE *looks at* HANNAH. HANNAH *returns her gaze.* BERKELEY *takes* GRANDIE'*s hand.*

Lord, as you peer into the rags of our pitiful souls, grant us safety here, to cleanse our house. To liberate the daughter of our house.

(*Pause.*) To all else who lurk here, I say unto you now – in the name of God – reveal yourselves and submit to our instruction to quit this place. No longer disturb this girl. She may hear you while all else fall deaf to your pleas, but we shall not brook that you harass her with your infernal concerns!

They hear something move, like furniture being dragged across a room above them.

Ignore it! (*Bellows.*) In the name of Our Lord, Jesus Christ…

AUDELLE. Quieter, Berkeley…

BERKELEY. I'm sorry. (*Lowers his volume.*) In the name of Our Lord, Jesus Christ, our saviour, the one true God who became man to know death as man knows it, for love of His children, I command thee – come forward and go. (*Pause.*) Come forward and show yourself!

Again something moves somewhere, a dull thud.

Ignore it. I command thee, cold spirit. Show thyself. Submit thyself. *Credo. Credo. Credo. Credo in Unum Deum, Patrem omnipotentem, factorem caeli et terrae, visibilium omnium et invisibilium.*

HANNAH *coughs.*

Deus meus ex toto corde paenitet me morum peccatorum…

HANNAH*'s body shudders.*

Credo… Credo… Credo…

HANNAH (*suddenly starts singing in a strident voice while her eyes are closed*). Oh, the green moss grows upon the heather where the briar grows upon the wood…

BERKELEY *falls silent.* AUDELLE *and* BERKELEY *look at each other.*

BERKELEY. *Non solum poenas a te juste statutes promeritus sum…*

HANNAH (*sings*). My love is sleeping in the bower where a lonely graveyard stood. She sings of an ancient flower… She sings of an ancient flower…

BERKELEY.…*Adiuvante gratia tua, de cetero me no peccaridique occasiones proximas fugiturum…*

HANNAH (*sings*). She sings… (*Her song peters out.*)

GRANDIE (*casually*). He knew my name.

BERKELEY. Shh… Grandie.

> HANNAH *looks at* BERKELEY. *She speaks gently and calmly, her eyes seeing beyond him into somewhere else.*

HANNAH. Have you seen it?

> *Pause.*

BERKELEY. Have we seen what?

HANNAH (*gently*). The infant.

BERKELEY. What infant?

HANNAH. The baby… that was here.

> *Pause.*

AUDELLE. Berkeley…

BERKELEY. Yes, yes… (*To* HANNAH.) Who speaks? (*Pause.*) Who speaks?

HANNAH.…Shh! Listen… (*Pause.*) Where is it!?

BERKELEY. Where is what? (*Short pause.*) We hear nothing.

HANNAH. Sh… (*Pause.*) Listen…

> HANNAH *suddenly stands up. She looks at the others.*

BERKELEY. Who are you that speaks through this girl?

HANNAH. You can't hear it.

BERKELEY. Are you Edward come to us?

HANNAH. I can hear her.

> *She looks round the room.*

BERKELEY. Do you hear your daughter, Edward? (*Pause.*) Are you Edward? (*Pause.*) You know you must leave here. You must quit this place. You can no longer remain.

HANNAH. But how can I leave?

BERKELEY. You are called to join your Creator. You died here, Edward. You cannot stay.

HANNAH. I cannot go. I will see my child.

BERKELEY. You can no longer see your child, Edward, because you died here. (*Pause*.) You died here.

HANNAH. It was a girl, wasn't it?

She walks round the room, as though looking for something.

BERKELEY. Who was a girl? (*Pause*.) Speak!

HANNAH. I can hear her crying!

Pause.

BERKELEY. Are you Edward Lambroke? Are you he that took his life in this room?

HANNAH. They've locked me in! They've locked me in!

BERKELEY. Well, you must leave in the name of God.

HANNAH. This is a dream. This must be a dream.

She looks desperately round the room. BERKELEY *follows her.*

BERKELEY. We abide only in the dream of our great Creator, in whose name I command you now to go.

HANNAH. No! They must show me my child.

BERKELEY. You must leave this house in the name of Jesus Christ.

HANNAH. Can you not hear it? Are you made of stone? (*Shouts*.) Can you not hear her?!

AUDELLE. Berkeley…!

BERKELEY (*holding her*). Listen no, no, no, listen, Edward. Are you Edward? You are Edward.

HANNAH. I am Hannah.

BERKELEY. No, you are not. Not Hannah.

GRANDIE. She is Hannah.

HANNAH. I am Hannah Lambroke, and I will not be told I cannot see my child!!

BERKELEY. Shhh…

AUDELLE. She will wake the house!

HANNAH *goes towards the conservatory door and tries the handle.* BERKELEY *blocks her way, she pushes against him.*

BERKELEY. I command whoever torments this girl to leave.

HANNAH. Unlock this door. I demand to see my child.

BERKELEY. Shh… Shh… Hannah, it's alright. Some help please here, Audelle.

AUDELLE goes to assist BERKELEY, *restraining* HANNAH.

HANNAH. I will see my child! I will hold my child!

GRANDIE is agitated by the disruption. She lets out a cry and moves towards the hallway door.

AUDELLE. Get her out of it, Berkeley! Get her out of it!

HANNAH. Are you mad?! Are you people mad!?

She turns and thumps AUDELLE *around the head and chest until he releases her. He tumbles backwards into the furniture and on to the floor.*

What kind of people are you that you would do such a thing?

She stands glaring at them.

BERKELEY. Hannah. Hannah. It's me. It's Berkeley. Why, we were just praying… ha ha ha… Let's have a little prayer.

HANNAH. I will not pray with you.

BERKELEY. Well, that's alright. That's alright. You just got a fright, that's all. No need for alarm. That's it. We were just…

HANNAH. Don't touch me.

BERKELEY. No, no. I won't… Here, take a drink of water, now shush…

AUDELLE has backed away towards the hall door near GRANDIE. HANNAH goes to the fireplace, her head on her hands on the mantel. BERKELEY tries to cajole her with a glass of water. He has his back to AUDELLE as the door opens. AUDELLE turns to face the music, expecting to see MADELEINE, but a very small CHILD with a pale face and dark eyes stands looking at AUDELLE for a moment before turning and leaving in the gloom. AUDELLE stands frozen, looking at the empty doorway. GRANDIE is watching AUDELLE. BERKELEY, preoccupied with HANNAH, sees nothing.

That's it. That's alright. Sit down…

HANNAH *sits down, her head in her hands.*

AUDELLE *looks at* GRANDIE *who is staring at* AUDELLE. *She suddenly opens her mouth wide and starts screaming at* AUDELLE. AUDELLE *flinches.* GRANDIE *laughs at him, opening her mouth and screaming at him, terrifying him, as though she knows he has just seen a ghost and is mocking him. She hits him with a stick.*

Grandie, shush! Grandie… now… Grandie! What did you do to her?

AUDELLE. What? I… I…

GRANDIE *screams at* AUDELLE *as* MADELEINE *rushes in carrying a candle.*

Pause.

MADELEINE. What in the name of God is happening in here?

BERKELEY. Grandie has… become a little overwrought.

Pause.

MADELEINE. Grandie. That's enough. Hannah. What happened?

BERKELEY (*quickly removing his necklace*). She's just exhausted. We all are. This last week has taken such a considerable toll on all of us.

MADELEINE. What are you talking about?

MRS GOULDING *appears in her nightdress.*

MRS GOULDING. Was someone at the door?

MADELEINE. No, Mrs Goulding. Kindly take Grandie to bed. It's time everyone retired.

MRS GOULDING. Come, Grandie.

GRANDIE *goes to* AUDELLE *and pinches his cheek.*

AUDELLE. Get off me!

MADELEINE. Grandie! Go to bed!

GRANDIE *leaves, followed by* MRS GOULDING.

MRS GOULDING. Grandie, wait for the candle!

Pause.

MADELEINE. What happened?

BERKELEY. Why, nothing! (*Short pause*.) Ha, ha, ha…

MADELEINE. What were you doing?

BERKELEY. Nothing! We were all just discussing the… horrific events of the past few days. And how upsetting it's been… and Grandie just…

MADELEINE. Hannah?

HANNAH. I need to lie down.

MADELEINE. Well, get yourself to bed.

HANNAH. Yes, Mama.

MADELEINE. You're shaking.

BERKELEY. That's a dreadful cold that's been going round.

> HANNAH *readies herself to leave. She looks at* BERKELEY *and* AUDELLE. *Behind* MADELEINE's *back,* BERKELEY *puts his finger to his lips, begging* HANNAH's *silence.*

We will all talk in the morning.

Pause.

MADELEINE. You will pack your bags tomorrow. There will be too little time on Saturday.

BERKELEY. Yes. We will all pack tomorrow. (*Pause*.) Yes.

> HANNAH *leaves.*

> MADELEINE *looks at* BERKELEY. *He gives her a little smile.*

What can I say? Goodnight, Madeleine.

She looks at AUDELLE.

MADELEINE. And what's the matter with you now, Mr Audelle? Too much or too little brandy?

She leaves. Pause.

BERKELEY. Well! Intriguing! (*Wipes his brow with a handkerchief*.) What did you make of that?! Are you alright, Audelle? You look ghastly.

AUDELLE. Yes, I'm… I'm fine.

BERKELEY. She was… I mean, we were really in the presence of something, weren't we?

AUDELLE. Yes.

BERKELEY. My word. The very air crackles. What did we unleash?

AUDELLE *doesn't answer.*

Come, we must abed. I would not anger our hostess a moment more.

AUDELLE. I will follow you.

BERKELEY *pauses.*

Please, Berkeley. I need a moment.

BERKELEY. Alright, well… Do not stay too late.

AUDELLE. No.

BERKELEY. And no more brandy. Or medicine. Come now. Directly.

BERKELEY *takes a candle and leaves.* AUDELLE *sits on the arm of a chair looking at the spot where he saw the* CHILD.

The lights darken and he leaves as the room brightens again, bringing us to the next day, Friday May 24th. It is late afternoon, between 5 and 6 p.m. The first bare fade of dusk is in the sky. CLARE *is changing candles and lighting new ones. She throws the old stubs in a cloth bag to be reused downstairs.* FINGAL *comes in through the conservatory. He opens the tall double doors and trips, almost falling into the room, dropping the rifle he carries and startling* CLARE. *He has a swollen black eye.*

CLARE. Mr Fingal!

FINGAL (*drunkenly putting a finger to his lips*). Aye aye aye… (*Looking at where he lost his footing.*) Someone needs to fix those floorboards.

CLARE (*resuming her work*). There's nothing wrong with the floorboards.

FINGAL *props his rifle against a wall and stands in the room seemingly devoid of purpose, drink having reduced his worries to an unreachable drone within his head.*

FINGAL. Miss me?

CLARE. Why would I miss you?

FINGAL. Because… I've been gone.

CLARE. You always turn up. Where were you? Down in Jamestown, I suppose?

FINGAL. And if I was?

CLARE. Look at you. What happened to your eye?

FINGAL. A bat flew into it.

CLARE. A bat?

FINGAL. I was… coming up, down the road, up out of Jamestown and – kablammo! Right in the kisser.

CLARE. Yes, well wait until the others see you.

FINGAL. Nobody can see me, Clare. I'm like a ghost now.

CLARE. You will be a ghost the way you're going.

Pause. He watches her work.

FINGAL. They found another little one this morning. In the rubble. An infant.

CLARE. Yes, I heard.

FINGAL. That's seven little ones.

CLARE. Yes, I heard already, Mr Fingal.

FINGAL. Alright, Jesus Christ! I'm only telling you. Pss.

He goes to pour himself a drink.

A bloody death hole is all it was. Still, roof over your head. (*Gloomily.*) All warm in together. (*Drinks.*) So, look, I'll have my money soon. When the dowry comes in. Thirteen months' wages, I'm owed. What do you think of that? That's when the pressure comes off. (*Pause.*) And given time, perhaps even I will be forgiven.

CLARE. Forgiven what?

FINGAL. Even you'll forgive me.

CLARE. What's to forgive? Except how you would kill your own kindness.

FINGAL. Kindness? What kindness?

CLARE. Don't act the criminal, Mr Fingal. I have seen it.

FINGAL. Where? In those whispers I stuck in your ear, so full of grog and poitín you had to hold me up in the darkness of the laneway?

CLARE. I have seen it.

Pause.

FINGAL. So anyway… Clare… Em… Can you loan me some money?

CLARE. Pardon?

FINGAL. Can you loan me some money, just until… I am in debt.

CLARE. For how much?

FINGAL. Fifty-five guineas.

CLARE. Fifty-five guineas! From playing cards!?

FINGAL. I will sign a promissory letter this very day and endeavour to have you reimbursed within the month, or when the dowry for Miss Hannah arrives, whichever is sooner.

CLARE. I have but two guineas in the world.

FINGAL. Two guineas will suffice for today.

CLARE. I can't.

FINGAL. Why not?

CLARE. It is for my passage to Ontario.

FINGAL (*disparaging*). You're not going to Ontario, Clare…

CLARE. When her ladyship and Hannah move to Northampton I will be left with no employment. What will I do without my passage?

FINGAL. But you will get your money back!

CLARE. No. My father would kill me.

FINGAL. He'll never know!

CLARE. He holds my money for me!

FINGAL. You can get it. Tell him something. What? Would you betray me to him?

CLARE. Of course not, but…

FINGAL. Then it's settled! I will bring you a letter tonight that will ease your mind. It's as good as money, I promise you. When Miss Hannah's dowry arrives, madam will settle her debts, you will have your two guineas, I'll pay the balance of what I owe in Jamestown, and we'll all…

He raises his hands in conclusion. Pause.

CLARE. Would you not… consider going away?

FINGAL. Where? (*Disparaging.*) To Canada? Come on…

CLARE. Or anywhere. Away. Away from the trouble in your nature that drags you down again and again to Jamestown. Away. Imagine a clean country. Your own little place with a fire dying in the hearth and a good meal inside you and the peacefulness maybe of knowing that your… wife or your… your child is soundly asleep nearby.

FINGAL. How can you hold out hope like that? Ha? Even for me?

CLARE. I don't know. I just see it.

FINGAL. You see a dream.

CLARE. If you like.

FINGAL. Yeah, well I don't believe in dreams.

He takes a drink.

CLARE (*sharply*). Well, ask her ladyship to loan you the money then! She likes you personally, isn't that what you're always saying?

FINGAL (*moving to quieten her voice*). Don't be ridiculous!

CLARE. Yeah? Well, I saw her here one morning talking to a soldier just out there on the stairs.

FINGAL. What soldier?

CLARE. Some soldier. At the top of the stairs just before it got bright. She never saw me.

FINGAL. From the garrison?

CLARE. No, he wasn't a rough-looking one at all. He had a fancy uniform.

FINGAL. Well, that's… What are you talking about? Can you see in the dark now?

CLARE. Why? Are you jealous? It's so clear how you think of her.

FINGAL. Don't talk nonsense, girl…

CLARE. You do. And you say you don't believe in dreams! Huh! You dream the most of any of us, Mr Fingal.

FINGAL (*loudly*). Will you shut the hell up, I said! (*Pause*.) I'll give you a dream. Before any of you were awake, the other morning, I beat the boy out in the yard. You didn't see that, did you?

CLARE. Little James Furay?

FINGAL. Yes, little James. You didn't see it because I did it before anybody was up. I woke him in the dark and I said, 'Get down here with me to the stables.' He rose without a question, rubbing his eyes, and I got him in there and I made him wash with cold water from the pail and then I said, 'What do you mean, sir, having two lame horses in your charge?' 'What?' he says. 'Take off your shirt,' says I, 'I'm to whip you for what's happened to her ladyship's horse.'

CLARE. When was this?

FINGAL. The morning after we went to Jamestown to see the ruins. Out there by the stable. And do you know what he did? He just went over to the corner and took off his jacket and his shirt and he stood there before me. This boy who's lived with me in the lodge since he was seven years old. His skinny white body, so small for his age, and his eyes so trusting and innocent and I took a whip and I turned him round and belted him so hard I stripped half the skin off his back and he couldn't get his shirt back on. His hands were too shaky anyway, so I threw his jacket round his shoulders and told him to piss off back down to the lodge.

Pause.

CLARE. Why would you do such a thing?

FINGAL. Because her ladyship told me to.

CLARE. She told you to do that to him?

FINGAL. She told me to get to the bottom of what happened to the horses.

CLARE. But, Mr Fingal…

FINGAL. I know. I know! Do you think I don't know?! (*Pause*.) I went down to Jamestown and played cards for three days and nights. I ended up in a fight over my debts and curled up in a ditch and prayed for God to punish me. But He knew, you see. He knew it would be worse to leave me alone.

CLARE. Where is the boy?

FINGAL (*shrugs*). In the gate lodge.

CLARE. On his own?

FINGAL. We must make… that assumption. Can you let me have some money tonight, Clare? Anything that I could just bring down to…

The door opens. MADELEINE *comes in with* GRANDIE. CLARE *resumes her work and* FINGAL *puts down his drink.*

MADELEINE. Clare, will you please go and see if Hannah is still in the chapel? She has a cold and I want her to come in.

CLARE. Yes, madam.

MADELEINE. And come straight back as Mrs Goulding will need you.

CLARE. Yes, madam.

CLARE goes.

MADELEINE. Mr Fingal.

FINGAL. Madam.

MADELEINE. What happened to your face?

FINGAL. An altercation regarding a personal matter which has not nor will not interfere with my professional duties.

MADELEINE. You have been in Jamestown, I take it?

FINGAL. Yes.

Pause.

MADELEINE. What say folk?

FINGAL. Regarding…?

MADELEINE. Regarding the collapse of my properties.

FINGAL. They say such is the lot of the poor.

MADELEINE. To suffer the rich.

FINGAL. They suffer themselves. They should better themselves.

MADELEINE. As you have bettered yourself.

FINGAL. As you see.

There is a short pause, and he starts to leave, forgetting his rifle.

Well, good evening.

MADELEINE. We are gathering to say farewell to the Reverend and Mr Audelle. And to wish Hannah a good journey. You may join us, Mr Fingal, should you feel up to it.

FINGAL. Thank you, madam.

MADELEINE. But may I suggest you go to the kitchen and tidy yourself up.

FINGAL. Yes, madam.

MADELEINE. And drink some tea.

FINGAL. Yes, madam.

MADELEINE. Oh, and Mr Fingal.

He halts.

Where is the boy? (*Pause.*) Where is James Furay?

BERKELEY *comes in.*

BERKELEY. Ah, Fingal! The very man. Oh dear me, that is a shiner! What happened? Are you alright?

FINGAL. A hunting accident, sir.

BERKELEY. Oh dear, well, actually, I was going to ask you. We leave tomorrow around noon, but say if I were up at five or so, could I get a pony to go down in the glen to see if I can bag a wood pigeon or two?

FINGAL. Yes, sir.

BERKELEY. I heard there were a few about.

FINGAL. Yes, sir, I'll see about a pony.

BERKELEY. Only if it's no trouble.

FINGAL. No, sir, I'll see to it personally.

BERKELEY. Thanks, Fingal.

FINGAL. Yes, sir.

BERKELEY. And don't let me go without giving you a little… eh… (*Signals a monetary tip*.)

FINGAL *nods uncomfortably and leaves*.

Poor old Fingal. Fond of the drop, I take it.

MADELEINE. No more so than the rest of his family.

BERKELEY. Mmm. Well, Grandie! We gather to say farewell – until Northampton.

GRANDIE *just returns his gaze steadily, giving him the slightest of smiles*.

MADELEINE. Yes.

BERKELEY. Madeleine. I am sorry if I disturbed you when I entered your chamber this morning. I could never have forgiven myself had I awoken to hear sobbing and had done nothing to at least to investigate.

MADELEINE. I was quite alright, thank you. It was just a bad dream.

BERKELEY. Well, it must have been very bad. May I?

He goes to the drinks.

MADELEINE. Not for me

GRANDIE. Good morning, McMickins.

MADELEINE. But a small drop for Grandie if you don't mind.

BERKELEY. Grandie, of course… I know these have been such trying days, Madeleine. Do not think I could possibly be unaware of that. My affection for you is unassailable, for you see, to me – perhaps unfortunately for you – you will always be the little child who would follow me about on my summer visits here as a young man.

MADELEINE. Oh, come, I never followed you about.

BERKELEY. No, no, you did. You were probably too young to remember. You showed such delight when we fished for trout in the lake. She was like my little sister, wasn't she, Grandie? And you still are. So when I heard you sobbing down the corridor in the darkness before dawn this morning, how could I not at least venture forth to offer you my comfort in the gloom? However, if you don't mind me saying, that you would refuse my presence with such vehemence and unexpected bad language quite unnerved me. I hardly slept after I crept back to my bed.

MADELEINE. I regret that your feelings were not spared, Berkeley, but I simply have no time for your perceived hardships at present, I'm sorry.

BERKELEY. You are growing old, Madeleine. I am already old. Mark you, even at fifty, one is very old. These years, between now and fifty – settle your affairs, dear.

MADELEINE. I am settling my affairs.

BERKELEY. Yes, your earthly affairs.

MADELEINE. Oh, Berkeley, please, I'm too tired.

BERKELEY. I mean to speak plainly with you, Madeleine, because I love you and I only want what is for the best. A sickness of denial and illusion pervades here in this room, in this very room you so boldly use. But you will not let me help you.

MADELEINE. But I don't want your help!

BERKELEY. Madeleine, I know you can see the things Hannah has experienced here. You deny your gift in order to embrace your delusion that Edward actually departed the night he ended his life here. It is my firm belief he did not depart.

MADELEINE. Berkeley, I swear I will brain you with this poker if you keep on at me, do you hear me? What were you doing in here with Hannah last night?

BERKELEY. I was assisting her, Madeleine! I was helping a girl who has endured the unimaginable strain of being the sole recipient of a communication from the beyond, with no one to believe her or help her to interpret it.

MADELEINE. Oh!

BERKELEY. The spirit realm flows through this place like a river! It always has! This is the very place that piqued my interest in everything that ever led to my downfall and my disgrace, but I don't regret it. Not for a second. Audelle is sensate. And he can feel it. I know him. And I know he can barely keep his mind together, so strong is its current!

MADELEINE. I would contend that Mr Audelle struggles to keep his mind together under the calmest of circumstances! Are you not ashamed to consort with someone with a reputation such as his? Let alone invite him into my house to instruct my daughter?

BERKELEY (*sadly*). Oh, my child…

MADELEINE. I'm not your child, Berkeley. You *are* old, I don't deny it. Age has racked your body, but it is your brain that has suffered most! I hear you speak and I believe you are like a man with an infant's toy box in his head.

GRANDIE. Woah!

BERKELEY (*shocked and angry*). Madeleine!

MADELEINE. Yes! You may say you have always regarded me as your sister, but in truth when I was a child I always thought you were an embarrassing buffoon and I was never anything less than utterly fatigued by your boring theories. I had assumed life's experience might mould you into a more agreeable person; however, I am confounded by your undeniable mental degeneration. In my opinion, mere vanity has convinced you of your holy vocation and I was not in the least part surprised you managed to get yourself defrocked! To say nothing of the unspeakable strain it must have caused your poor Alice! And while we are speaking plainly, may I say I find the fact that you are still one of Lord Ashby's spiritual advisors only makes me wonder should I worry more for his soul or his sanity!

BERKELEY. I see.

MADELEINE. None of this means I don't love you, Berkeley. And I am grateful for your introduction to Lord Ashby, but the sooner we deliver Hannah from your orbit and into the shelter of her new life in Northampton, the happier I will be.

BERKELEY. We will all be in the same orbit in Northampton, Madeleine, supping from the same well.

MADELEINE. You will not get past me again, Berkeley. And I will outlast you.

BERKELEY. Yes, perhaps I stand on the threshold of forever's mysterious twilight while you still reside in life's bright room of vitality where all appears commodious, but you cannot fool a fool. I have heard you – crying in the night, while you push away the hand that would help you.

MADELEINE. I cried while I slept! I was dreaming about those poor souls who lost their lives crowded into a dreadful terrace in Jamestown I had scarcely ever thought about! I cried at my own powerlessness and selfishness seeing how they had lived and died! What do you want me to say?

BERKELEY. Madeleine, we all heard it.

MADELEINE. Heard what?

BERKELEY. The great clap of thunder here – in this room – the night those wretches perished. Their pain was manifest here in that moment, surely to God, and yet you deny it. You see it all, Madeleine, I know you do. You, Grandie, your poor mother, Hannah, all of you have a shared capacity to apprehend the beyond. And you perhaps more than any of them have the darkest instinct for second sight.

MADELEINE. No, Berkeley.

BERKELEY. Do not lie! What is it about this place that it is such a conduit for desperate souls? Don't you care to know!?

MADELEINE. No I don't! Because there was always pain here at Mount Prospect! It was here before us and will be here after we are gone!

BERKELEY. But Hannah cannot endure it, can she? Nor could Edward. Yet while he sought the sweet embrace of the final escape, he never got out, did he!

MADELEINE. Oh, he got out. And yet he lives. And he will live wherever I live as long as I am alive. But not because he is trapped. What lives is my knowledge that what happened to him was all a stupid mistake. It was a mistake, but every single I day I believe I might somehow reach out and correct it – but I can't! Don't you see that? I can't!

There is a knock at the door.

Yes?

CLARE *appears at the door.*

CLARE. Excuse me, madam, Mrs Goulding has asked may we bring up the hot punch and scones?

BERKELEY. Thank you, Clare.

CLARE *leaves.* MADELEINE *crumples, taking a moment to compose herself.* BERKELEY *looks on uncertainly.*

Madeleine, I… I had no idea that you – (*Short pause.*) Well, I… Don't cry.

MRS GOULDING *rings a bell in the hallway.*

MADELEINE. Mrs Goulding is bringing the refreshments. I insist Hannah's last evening here be an easy and gay affair. It's the least she deserves.

BERKELEY. Well, of course.

MADELEINE. I'm warning you, Berkeley.

BERKELEY. I am the soul of joviality.

The door is opened by MRS GOULDING. CLARE *carries a large tray and* FINGAL *carries a bowl of hot punch, using napkins to protect his hands from the heat. Dusk is gathering and this scene gradually darkens.* FINGAL *is unsteady and spills some punch.* CLARE *goes to wipe it.*

Mrs Goulding's hot punch.

MRS GOULDING. Most certainly. Mr Fingal! I have it, I have it. (*Wipes up the drops.*) Scones on the mat, hot punch on the trivet, Mr Fingal.

BERKELEY. I trust you have been as moderate as ever with the rum?

MRS GOULDING. I would say I have been judicious.

BERKELEY. In that case, a measure for our generous hostess, quickly, Clare.

MADELEINE. Please, tend to yourselves first.

BERKELEY. No, no, a dram, Madeleine. Let us dispel the evening gloom. Thank you, Clare. That's right.

CLARE *helps* MRS GOULDING *fetch drinks for* MADELEINE *and* GRANDIE.

MADELEINE. Clare. Did you find Hannah?

CLARE. Yes, madam. She is changing in her room.

MADELEINE. Will you tell her we are waiting for her to come down, please?

CLARE. Yes, madam.

MADELEINE. Thank you, Clare.

As CLARE *goes,* AUDELLE *enters.*

BERKELEY. Ah, Mr Audelle's nose for impending hospitality remains impeccable.

AUDELLE. Yes, well, good evening. It's a lucky thing you rang that bell, Mrs Goulding. I was positively pole-axed up there in my room. Is that tea.

BERKELEY. Well, this will wake you up.

FINGAL *brings a drink for* AUDELLE.

AUDELLE. Oh, thank you.

MRS GOULDING. This hot rum punch was a recipe given me by my grandmother and has been the requisite post-hunting libation here at Mount Prospect for at least fifty years or more.

BERKELEY. You get a sniff of that, Audelle? It's not the gut-rot that you quaff by the pint in Chapelgate.

MRS GOULDING. On one famous occasion in 1797, a shout went up while sixty waited to dine: 'Forgo the meal,' they cried, having downed a barrel of this grog, 'Our thirst has eclipsed our appetite!' And nothing would do only except for me to go back down in the scullery – somewhat unsteadily myself – to mount a fresh barrel upon the fire.

BERKELEY. In the golden days here at Mount Prospect. The Earl in all his splendour yet. Grandie in gracious repose. The stories the Earl would regale us with – how his great-grandfather survived to see his one hundred and six living descendants, borne of four wives…

MRS GOULDING. 'And each uglier than the last.'

BERKELEY (*simultaneously*). 'And each more ugly than the last!'

HANNAH *enters with* CLARE.

MRS GOULDING. Miss Hannah may be glad her mother's line is in a straight descent from the early batch!

BERKELEY. The fresh flowers!

MADELEINE. You speak of my family, Mrs Goulding.

MRS GOULDING. Psh! They are practically my family too, madam, may I be so bold.

BERKELEY. Yes, where would Mount Prospect be without good old Mrs Goulding?

MRS GOULDING. I wonder!

BERKELEY. And Mr Fingal, of course. Remember, Fingal, those endless afternoons on the lawn, you were but a garsoon – and two or three summers in a row, if I'm not mistaken. When you were only ten or eleven. You followed that girl round and round.

MRS GOULDING. Oh yes!

BERKELEY. We talked of it so much and laughed so often! Your little moon-face behind her – her nut-brown hair always tied up in a white ribbon. Remember? She was perhaps a year or two older than you – who was she?

MRS GOULDING. She was the daughter of old Mr McElligot who used run the stables back then.

BERKELEY. Oh yes! Kate McElligot! And Fingal would follow behind her, follow her, follow her, while we all dined on blankets on the lawn. A hundred guests or more – until one day she finally turned round, in front of all of us and said, 'Will you leave me be, Fingal, or I'll break your feet to halt you!'

MRS GOULDING (*simultaneously*). '…I'll break your feet to halt you!' Yes…

They laugh.

BERKELEY. Do you remember? We were all in earshot and everybody laughed! Whatever happened to her?

Short pause.

FINGAL. She married my brother.

BERKELEY. Oh, yes. (*Beat.*) Yes… Yes. A lovely girl. (*Pause.*) Who will give us a song? Hannah?

HANNAH. I have a cold, Berkeley.

BERKELEY. A quiet song?

HANNAH *shakes her head.*

Oh, who will sing? Mrs Goulding?

MRS GOULDING. Oh dear me, no – it's far too early for me. Clare will sing.

BERKELEY. Do you sing, Clare?

MADELEINE. She has a sweet voice.

CLARE. Oh, I don't know!

BERKELEY. Oh, please do!

MRS GOULDING. Here, get yourself another dram of punch and Miss Hannah might play the piano for you?

BERKELEY. Oh, say you will. She will! I will pour you a dram. (*He takes* CLARE*'s glass*.) Hannah, please play for her.

CLARE. I have not sang for so long.

BERKELEY. No matter! No matter! What better reason not to refuse? Here, drink this. Hannah, what will you play?

MRS GOULDING. 'As I Roved Out'?

BERKELEY. Oh yes, so beautiful. Come listen to this, Audelle.

CLARE and HANNAH *look at each other in silent agreement.* CLARE *takes a drink and* HANNAH *goes to the piano and starts to play a simple accompaniment. She looks round at* CLARE.

CLARE. Oh my God...!

She laughs nervously and presently begins singing a plaintive rendition of an old ballad.

(*Sings.*)
> I dreamed I roamed on a bright May morning
> To view the meadows and flowers gay
> Whom should I spy but my own true lover
> As she sat under yon willow tree
> I took off my hat and I did salute her
> I did salute her most courageously
> When she turned around, well the tears fell from her
> Saying 'False young man you have deluded me...'
> At night I wake in my bed of slumber
> Thoughts of my love running in my mind
> As I turn around to embrace my darling
> Only darkness and grief do I find
> And I wish the Queen would call home her army
> From the West Indies, Amerikay and Spain
> And every man to his wedded woman
> In hope that you and I will meet again.

As the song ends, she is crying, as is MRS GOULDING.

HANNAH *sits quietly at the piano*. FINGAL *looks at the floor*. GRANDIE *leads the applause*.

MRS GOULDING. Isn't that lovely?

BERKELEY. Dear me. I am quite overcome now! Well done, Clare.

CLARE. I'm sorry, I... (*Dabs at her eyes*.)

BERKELEY. No, no. Such depth of emotion is only appropriate.

MADELEINE. That was beautiful, Clare.

CLARE. I'm sorry, madam.

MADELEINE *smiles reassuringly*.

BERKELEY. Has anyone lighter fare? Hannah?

HANNAH *shakes her head*.

One more song in your parlour?

HANNAH. I can't, no, I'm sorry.

GRANDIE (*suddenly sings with confidence*).
While the green moss grows upon the heather,
The briar grows upon the wood,
My love lies sleeping in a bower,
Where a lonely graveyard stood...

She applauds herself. The others clap.

BERKELEY. Thank you, Grandie.

MRS GOULDING. Very nice, Grandie.

HANNAH. Em... I just wanted to... em...

BERKELEY. Hannah...

HANNAH. Firstly, I wanted to thank everyone for all your efforts in the last few days. And thank Berkeley and Mr Audelle for travelling all this way to chaperone me and Mrs Goulding for making so many arrangements for my departure. And thank you, Mother, for putting my future so firmly at the centre of your concerns. However, something has happened to convince me that... I... I have decided... that I cannot go.

Pause.

BERKELEY (*with a slightly sickened laugh*). Hannah...

HANNAH. I am sorry and I want to apologise to everyone, but my mind has been made up and I feel unable to fulfil my commitment. I'm sorry.

She looks at MADELEINE. MADELEINE *looks down. All is silent.*

FINGAL. But she has to.

MRS GOULDING. Mr Fingal…

Pause.

FINGAL. She has to!

BERKELEY. Alright, Fingal…

FINGAL. Everything is arranged! This is… I mean… (*Laughs as though this just can't be happening.*) What are we going to do?

MADELEINE. Mr Fingal, we can discuss this later.

FINGAL (*points at* AUDELLE). No. No, hold on a minute. This is him. Isn't it? Yes, you.

AUDELLE. I beg your pardon?

FINGAL. They were supposed to escort her to her new home and settle the advancement of the estate, but they brought the undoing of the whole venture within them.

MADELEINE. Not now, Mr Fingal…

FINGAL. What?

MADELEINE. Not now!

CLARE. Willie…

FINGAL. Don't you 'not now' me, madam, now, not now, not now! (*To* AUDELLE.) Yous were seen. They were seen! You think we know nothing of your reputation, Mr Audelle? You come here with the Reverend, your heads bowed and your hands clasped together, but nothing is holy. I've heard all about you down in Jamestown, ha? Ha? What were they doing up at the Queen's Tomb?

MADELEINE. What?

FINGAL. Ask them that!

MADELEINE. When?

FINGAL. The other evening. When they were abroad on one of their nature walks.

AUDELLE. I may assure you, sir...!

FINGAL. No. You can't assure me. You were seen, sir. You were seen.

BERKELEY. What was seen? What are you talking about?

FINGAL. Miss Hannah was seen, running, and tears streaming down her face, all down the hill from the Queen's Tomb and your man here chasing after her and pursuing her down into the trees! Yes!

AUDELLE. No!

FINGAL. Where God knows what happened.

AUDELLE. No!

FINGAL. You were seen!

AUDELLE. I swear to you. I swear before you all...

FINGAL *grabs his rifle and points it at* AUDELLE.

FINGAL. What? Ha? What?

BERKELEY. Fingal!

MRS GOULDING. Mr Fingal, how dare you?

FINGAL. Ah, ah. Now, nobody leaves till we get some answers.

MADELEINE. Mr Fingal...

FINGAL (*attaining a semblance of responsibility through his drunken fog*). You have nothing to fear, madam. I know this type. We will have an answer.

MADELEINE. Put the gun down, Mr Fingal, this instant.

FINGAL. No, do not presume to order me about! I haven't been paid in over a year, so I may as well take his brains with me on my way out. What have I got left anyhow? I don't care. You deflowered her, sir, didn't you?

AUDELLE. I did not.

FINGAL. You defiled her!

AUDELLE. I did not.

FINGAL. You have rendered her worthless.

AUDELLE. No, sir.

FINGAL. Well, I will shoot you dead, sir.

He points the barrel at AUDELLE*'s head.*

MRS GOULDING (*shouts*). Mr Fingal!

FINGAL. What?

Short pause.

MRS GOULDING. You are not well!

FINGAL. I am well enough.

BERKELEY *puts himself between* FINGAL *and* AUDELLE.

BERKELEY. Surely to God this is a misunderstanding!

Hannah…

HANNAH. That's not what happened, Mr Fingal.

FINGAL. Do not be afraid, Miss Hannah. There is no need for any lies now. This man does not deserve your protection.

AUDELLE. Hannah, please… Tell him…

HANNAH. Mr Fingal, I don't know who saw us, but they have misinterpreted what they saw.

FINGAL. You say I am a liar?

HANNAH. No!

FINGAL. But you say none of it happened?

HANNAH. Not in that way.

FINGAL. Then in what way? What way?

HANNAH. Mr Audelle asked if I might show him the Queen's Tomb. There was still just enough light so we walked up the path, up out of the glen and on up the side of Knockmullen…

Short pause.

FINGAL. Go on.

HANNAH. Mr Audelle went on ahead of me as I was fatigued. When I reached the tomb I sat alone. After he had been out of sight for some minutes I realised there was someone sheltering within the mouth of the tomb, a man and a woman who were watching me. I called out for Mr Audelle to show them I wasn't alone. On hearing my voice, the figures in the tomb stumbled out. And as they lurched towards me I realised I was somehow seeing… myself and Mr Audelle! It was us but… our corpses… walking. And I… I turned and ran. I slipped and slid all the way back down to the road at Knockmullen, until Mr Audelle caught up to me. I was unable to tell him what had happened, as I scarcely know myself, but that is the truth, Mr Fingal, and that is the event which must have been witnessed and of which you have heard. For myself, I said nothing.

MADELEINE. Oh, Hannah…

HANNAH. What could I say? I am so tired of all the trouble I keep bringing on this house!

MADELEINE. You don't. You never do.

BERKELEY. The child saw some hungry souls sheltering in the hollow. The gloaming and her imagination did the rest. Indeed we are maybe thankful Mr Audelle was on hand, we should thank him.

Pause.

FINGAL. You gave her that laudanum to drink, didn't you?

AUDELLE. No, I… I… (*Laughs.*)

MADELEINE. Laudanum?

FINGAL. Laudanum. And it has unbalanced the child.

MRS GOULDING. No, sir!

AUDELLE. No, no… It's merely a tincture I use as a cough suppressant.

MRS GOULDING. I know what laudanum is, Mr Audelle. You were trying to get Clare to procure it for you in Jamestown and I forbade it!

FINGAL. And me, like a bloody fool getting it for you.

MRS GOULDING. You got it for him?!

FINGAL. I didn't know the devil was going to give it to a child! A child!

AUDELLE. No! I meant no harm…

FINGAL. No harm? Look at her! Look at her!

BERKELEY. I'm sure Mr Audelle only wanted to help Hannah suppress her cough.

FINGAL (*disparaging*). Ah! Rather he wanted to render her senseless and have his way. I know that game!

HANNAH. No. I asked him for it. Yes, I took it, but I asked him for it!

MADELEINE. Oh, Hannah! Why?

HANNAH. Because I needed to see the future. And I did. I saw it. We performed a rite and I saw it!

MADELEINE. You performed a what?

BERKELEY. No, no… Not a rite.

HANNAH. We performed a rite in here. And I saw it.

MADELEINE. What do you mean, 'a rite'?

BERKELEY. No, no, no, no, no, no, no, not a rite. Some prayers merely, a few words in order to…

FINGAL. Why don't you shut up, Reverend? I'm tired of hearing your interminable voice, and I don't want to hear another damn word out of you. I am in charge here tonight so you can just shut up. And you too, Mrs Goulding.

MRS GOULDING. I never said a word!

FINGAL. Yes, well, don't.

MRS GOULDING. Yes, well, I didn't.

FINGAL. Yes, well, don't.

MRS GOULDING. Well, you have said enough. You gobaloon.

GRANDIE. Let her sing!

MRS GOULDING. Yes, shush, Grandie, shush now.

MADELEINE. Berkeley, you better tell me what you did or I'll take this gun and shoot you myself.

HANNAH. No. I needed to understand what was happening to me, Mama. But I know now I was seeing and hearing what is yet to be! Not the past! I have never seen the past. I saw that the child I have heard crying here is my child, the child I will never know because I will perish bringing it into the world.

MADELEINE. No!

HANNAH. After I go to Northampton. Yes.

MADELEINE. Hannah, no…

HANNAH. Yes! And I saw that I would forever wander looking for my baby. I have seen what eternity holds for me.

MADELEINE. No! This is preposterous!

HANNAH. I will be locked in a room. And that room is death and there is no door from which to leave. I saw it all!

MADELEINE. No!

FINGAL. Right. (*To* AUDELLE.) You see what yous have done? You see it? You put the girl in a state like that, and you drive her insane? What possible purpose can you have? You have no purpose. No purpose but to defile and destroy and degrade. (*Aims the rifle to shoot* AUDELLE.) What conceivable good can your presence bring in the world?

BERKELEY. Wait, Fingal…

MADELEINE. Mr Fingal…

AUDELLE. No purpose.

Pause.

FINGAL. You brought this on yourself, Mr Audelle, for none can make sense of your actions.

HANNAH. Or your actions, Mr Fingal!

FINGAL. Ha?

HANNAH. I say what of your actions?

FINGAL. My actions?

HANNAH. You skulk in here and sit in judgement on all of us like the coward who can only hold his head up when he has a weapon. What do you know about fairness or rightness, you ignorant lout?

FINGAL. You dare to speak to me like that? You were always mad. All of yous always were. Look at your Grandie. She's never had a bloody clue what in the name of Jaysus is going on! Or your father? Who brought this whole place to its knees before hanging himself in front of his own child practically! Your cold-hearted mother there, hardly even of this earth so remote and incomprehensible are her secret wishes!

MADELEINE. You are drunk, Mr Fingal.

FINGAL. I'm not drunk. Nor was I drunk all those nights I was fetched up here to lock that mad bastard in a room upstairs while you and I sat here with the long hours ticking by.

MADELEINE. You are drunk, sir, and you will put that gun down this instant.

She goes to grab him. He pushes her away roughly.

BERKELEY. Fingal!

FINGAL. I don't care, do you hear me?! I've had it up to here with all of you. No longer will I walk out of this bloody house, ignorant of the forces that keep me perpetually on my knees! No longer!

MADELEINE. No, sir! You are drunk, sir! What ever will you think when you have come to your senses?

FINGAL. I am in my senses.

MADELEINE. Well, what do you want? What are you asking of us?

FINGAL (*drunkenly*). What?

HANNAH. Mr Fingal cannot bear to come to his senses for then he must face what he has done.

FINGAL. I'm in my senses, don't you worry about that.

HANNAH. Oh yes, and were you in your senses when you did what you did and went and beat James Furay? Have you seen him? (*Pause.*) Have you?!

MRS GOULDING. What happened to James Furay?

HANNAH. Tell them what you did.

Pause.

MADELEINE. What did he do?

FINGAL. No... I...

MRS GOULDING. Is he alright?

HANNAH. I have seen him, Mr Fingal. I went to say goodbye to him today. And I found him in the gate lodge. Yes. With no fire lit. No candle burning. I found him curled up in the cold of the loft, Mr Fingal, lying in his own mess of congealed blood and pus.

Pause.

FINGAL. Yes… well…

MRS GOULDING. What happened to him?

Pause.

What happened to him?

FINGAL (*quietly*). I beat him.

MRS GOULDING. What?

FINGAL. I beat him! I beat him!

MRS GOULDING. What did you beat him for?

FINGAL. I had to.

HANNAH. You had to? He couldn't get down the ladder from his bed by himself. He couldn't even look at me. He forbade me to fetch the doctor. He begged me not to tell anyone. I bathed his wounds which are so deep and vicious he will surely be marked for the rest of his life. I couldn't even bandage him for fear the cloth would only stick into his wounds causing him greater agony – and I knew I was supposed to be leaving here tomorrow!? We both wept there, Mr Fingal, each of us hiding their tears from the other. I, for the misery I was about to leave him in. But do you know why he wept? Out of shame, sir! For shame! That boy who was brought up as my brother, and was almost as much as your son! But you are not worthy of him, Mr Fingal. How can I go and marry a man I hardly know when I am unable to provide affection for those I truly love?! You have caused me to stay, Mr Fingal. Not Mr Audelle, not Berkeley or my mother, but you, sir! So do what you will and go home.

FINGAL *looks at them all.*

MADELEINE. Mr Fingal. Why would you do such a thing?

Pause.

FINGAL. For you.

MADELEINE. For me?

FINGAL. I wanted to show you I can be strong. I wanted to show you I can bring discipline to this place, and I'm not just some… joke.

MADELEINE. But, Mr Fingal…

FINGAL. You were so angry about the horses! You told me to put the boy before his responsibilities!

MADELEINE. But I would never have wanted you to beat him, Mr Fingal!

FINGAL. It was the morning after all the buildings collapsed! I'd been up the whole night, sitting up on my own, knowing how bad things were going to get now. You never think how hard it is for me. To have to show my face in Jamestown! Even my own family are ashamed of me! They hate me all round the country all around here because of my loyalty to you. No one respects me. But I stay. I stay. And I stay because I am faithful to you – (*Short pause, he looks at the floor.*) and because I've always loved you! I can't help it! You don't know how hard I've tried to ignore it. To banish it! But then once again your eyes fall on me and my heart submits. It's never stopped. It's beyond my abilities. I walk around with no money in my pockets, it doesn't matter, the locals and their keepers laugh at me, it doesn't matter. I see your face in my mind and it just doesn't matter because I know I would live in a moment forever if you might just deign to put out your hand to me. Even if it were my last moment on this earth. Don't you see that? Of course you do. You have seen it. You know it. But what do you do? You use it. You use it to keep me, and use me. And you know what? I don't care, do you see? I don't care because I still love you! (*Pause. Looks at them all.*) It's all just a big trick though, really, I suppose, isn't it? It's just a big joke that keeps us all running around in God's playground for his amusement. And we all think it's so real…

Pause. FINGAL is drowning in his own confusion. He has ended up on the floor near MADELEINE. She reaches out, touches his face tenderly then brings her lips to his. They kiss for a moment and then lay their heads together, their foreheads touching.

BERKELEY. Well… There now, my good man. That's alright.

BERKELEY goes to FINGAL and takes the gun from him gently.

We are all overwrought. Yes. That's alright. A little drink of water.

He hands the gun to CLARE behind FINGAL's back. She takes it out to the hall quietly and comes back to stand in the doorway.

Mrs Goulding.

MRS GOULDING. Yes, of course.

She pours some water to bring to BEREKLEY.

BERKELEY. There's a good man. Let us walk out to the steps and get us some fresh air, shall we? Yes…

BERKELEY *signals for* MRS GOULDING *to open the doors to the conservatory, which she does.* BERKELEY *leads* FINGAL *towards the conservatory.* FINGAL *turns to the room.*

FINGAL. I'm… I'm sorry.

BERKELEY. That's alright. Come on now, there's a good man.

BERKELEY *brings* FINGAL *out through the conservatory.*

MADELEINE. Are you alright, Mr Audelle?

AUDELLE. Yes.

MRS GOULDING. I don't know what has come over him. He has lost his mind completely. Here, Mr Audelle, sit down, take a drink.

AUDELLE. Thank you.

MRS GOULDING. And Grandie. Poor Grandie.

AUDELLE. Is she alright?

MADELEINE. She'll be fine.

MRS GOULDING *gets them some drinks.*

Are you alright, Clare?

CLARE. Yes, ma'am.

MADELEINE. You are gone quite pale. Will you sit by the fire?

CLARE. No thank you, ma'am.

MADELEINE. Are you sure?

CLARE. Yes, ma'am.

Pause.

MRS GOULDING. Yes, well. I will make a bread poultice to bring down to James Furay.

MADELEINE. But bring him up to stay here tonight, please, Mrs Goulding.

MRS GOULDING. Yes, madam.

MADELEINE. Can we light some more candles please?

MRS GOULDING. We will, of course. Clare, come and help me light the house.

CLARE. Yes, ma'am.

MRS GOULDING *and* CLARE *leave. Pause.*

HANNAH. I'm sorry, Mama.

MADELEINE. No.

AUDELLE. Do not fear your future, Miss Hannah. A child you cannot save, being locked in a room from which you cannot escape. That is not your future, I can assure you.

HANNAH. How so?

AUDELLE. Because you saw my present, not your future. The locked room is this moment I may never escape from. The child you hear crying is the ever waking dream child whose sobs I dose myself to quiet. She is the child I abandoned. Such is your gift, you saw Hell, Miss Hannah. But it was my hell. The nightmare unto which each morning delivers me and each evening awakens me to contemplate. Do not fear your future. It is as open as the sky. I must ask you ladies to forgive me. I must administer my medicine.

AUDELLE *bows to them and goes out.*

GRANDIE (*listening*). The old dog.

MADELEINE. Are you alright, Grandie?

GRANDIE. The blind old dog used live here long ago.

MADELEINE. What of him?

GRANDIE. Can you hear him? Barking?

Pause. There is a sudden deafening bang in the hallway which shakes the whole house. They are startled into silence.

MADELEINE. What is it?

HANNAH *steps towards the hallway door.* BERKELEY *comes in through the conservatory doors holding a candle, as smoke drifts in from the hallway.*

BERKELEY. Did you hear it? Did you hear it again?

Offstage, we hear CLARE *scream and run down the stairs.* HANNAH *stands looking into the hallway, her hands up to her face.* CLARE *comes in.*

CLARE. It's Mr Audelle! (*Short pause.*) He got the rifle!

BERKELEY. Where is he?

CLARE. He's in the hallway! (*Turns and goes out*.) Oh, Mrs Goulding! Mrs Goulding!

The lights change as everyone but GRANDIE *drifts out to the hallway. An afternoon materialises around* GRANDIE *as she sits there. It is two weeks later, Friday June 7th.* FINGAL *comes in, puts some hardbacked ledgers on the table and stands waiting, much as he did in the first scene of the play. He wears a new dark coat with brass buttons. His hair is brushed across his head and his black eye is healed.* MRS GOULDING *comes into the room with a shawl round her shoulders.*

MRS GOULDING. Well, Mr Fingal.

FINGAL. Mrs Goulding.

MRS GOULDING. Your arrangements are all made?

FINGAL. Yes. We leave tonight.

MRS GOULDING. Yes?

FINGAL. We'll be married in Swords in County Dublin and sail for Liverpool next Tuesday morning.

MRS GOULDING. When do you leave for Canada?

FINGAL. In the following week. Clare's sister will house us.

MRS GOULDING. Very good. Clare is a clever girl.

FINGAL. I know.

MRS GOULDING. Well, look after her. (*Pause*.) She is your salvation, Mr Fingal.

FINGAL. I have left a copy of the accounts here for madam.

MRS GOULDING. Yes, she will be into you herself in a moment. The Colonel is delayed. You heard he shot at some intruders last night.

FINGAL. Yes, I heard. (*Short pause*.) Is it true you will be kept on?

MRS GOULDING. Yes, the Colonel has asked me personally to keep the house for his daughter. James Furay will remain in the gate lodge and act as groundsman to the estate.

FINGAL. Well, that's... He'll make an excellent groundsman.

Pause.

MRS GOULDING. Yes, well, I wish you luck, sir.

FINGAL. Thank you.

She shakes his hand. MADELEINE *comes in.*

MRS GOULDING. Would Grandie like some tea? I think she would. Are you warm enough there, Grandie?

She goes and settles some cushions around GRANDIE.

I'll bring us up some nice soup, will I?

MADELEINE. Thank you, Mrs Goulding.

MRS GOULDING. Yes, not at all.

She leaves.

MADELEINE. Are these the accounts?

FINGAL. Yes, madam, in order of year, most recent on top.

MADELEINE. Grim reading no doubt. Have you received your money?

FINGAL. Yes. Thank you. (*Hands her a small bag with some coins in it.*) I wondered if I might give you this to pass on to James Furay for me. I haven't had a chance to… to see him.

MADELEINE. That's very generous. I'm sure he will be most grateful. You have enough for your passage?

FINGAL. Yes, we'll be fine.

MADELEINE. Well, congratulations.

FINGAL. Thank you.

MADELEINE. When is the wedding?

FINGAL. Next Monday. In Swords, in County Dublin. A relative of Clare's knows the curate there. We sail for Liverpool on Tuesday.

MADELEINE. I'm very pleased for you both.

Pause.

FINGAL. I trust Miss Hannah is in good health.

MADELEINE. Yes, I had a letter from her just this morning. She is arrived in Northampton. All is well. As soon as I have settled my affairs here with Colonel Bennett, myself and Grandie shall join her.

FINGAL. Well, please send her my congratulations and I wish you all the very best.

MADELEINE. Thank you.

FINGAL. Right, well. (*Gathers himself to leave but halts near the door.*) Madeleine.

   MRS GOULDING *returns*.

MRS GOULDING. Madam, a boy came to the door and says the Colonel will be here in thirty minutes. They are inspecting the back gate.

MADAM. Thank you, Mrs Goulding.

MRS GOULDING. Is it chilly? Will I light the fire?

   MRS GOULDING *goes to the fireplace and rakes it with the poker*.

MADELEINE. Light it for Grandie. I don't particularly want to encourage the Colonel to stay. Bring some tea for him in the small parlour and we may conduct our business in there.

MRS GOULDING. Very good. I haven't forgotten you, Grandie. Wrap up there, we'll light this for you in a minute and I'll be back with hot soup in the flea's time.

FINGAL. Right. Well, I'll… Goodbye.

MADELEINE. Goodbye, Mr Fingal. Thank you.

FINGAL. Goodbye.

MRS GOULDING. Goodbye, Mr Fingal.

FINGAL. Goodbye.

   He leaves. Pause.

MRS GOULDING. Right.

MADELEINE. Thank you, Mrs Goulding.

MRS GOULDING (*tone of 'That's that…'*). Now…

   She leaves.

   MADELEINE *looks out the window then starts to peruse the ledgers*.

GRANDIE. A boy once proposed to me who was from Northampton, but Daddy wouldn't brook it. He had a kind face. He wasn't good-looking but he was kind. Yes. He said he thought his feelings might kill him.

MADELIENE. Who did?

GRANDIE. He said he hadn't slept for three weeks.

MADELEINE. Oh dear.

GRANDIE. He was very tired.

MADELEINE. Yes, well, he must have been.

GRANDIE. Well. He married in the end. And I married.

MADELEINE. Yes.

GRANDIE. He wasn't good-looking but... he was... You always look after me so well, Madeleine. Don't think I don't know.

MADELEINE. What's that?

GRANDIE. I say even when I don't know who is here or how old I am, I always feel safe when I see you. And you know that love is a gift from God.

MADELEINE. Well, that's good, isn't it?

GRANDIE. Yes. You are a good mother, Madeleine.

MADELEINE. Am I?

GRANDIE. You don't mind?

MADELEINE (*smiles*). How could I mind?

GRANDIE *shrugs*.

Of course I don't mind!

BERKELEY *comes in. He looks a bit sleepy. He wears a woollen cardigan.*

Oh, hello, did you have a good sleep?

BERKELEY. Yes. Too good. Have I missed the Colonel?

MADELEINE. No, he was delayed. Did you hear he shot at some intruders on his estate last night?

BERKELEY. No!

MADELEINE. Yes, well, he's on his way.

BERKELEY. Intruders!

MADELEINE. Yes.

BERKELEY. Right. Oh dear, well… I thought I should say hello.

MADELEINE. We received a letter from Northampton this morning. Hannah has arrived.

BERKELEY. Oh, that is good news. And… she is well?

MADELEINE. She slept soundly, remarking on the peculiar silence of the estate.

BERKELEY (*concurring*). Yes.

MADELEINE *brings him the letter*.

MADELEINE. Lord Ashby sends you his personal condolences about Mr Audelle.

MADELEINE *goes back to her work*.

BERKELEY. How kind. (*Glancing over the letter.*) I had the strangest dreams. I woke up feeling quite anxious, I must say. You do think we are doing the right thing, Madeleine? Leaving Audelle here? When we go to Northampton?

MADELEINE. Oh yes. I should think he likes it here, Berkeley. The graveyard is so quiet and such a peaceful place to rest. And I know the Colonel would never mind you paying your respects when we return on a visit. Leave him here, Berkeley.

BERKELEY. Yes, I know. You are right. I just… I mean, I was his family.

MADELEINE. Of course. And you were very good to him, Berkeley. (*Short pause.*) Now, Mrs Goulding is bringing some soup up for Grandie. Will you have some? You will.

BERKELEY. Yes, Madeleine. Thank you.

MADELEINE. Good. (*Looks out the window.*) Oh. Will you sit with Grandie for a few minutes, Berkeley?

BERKELEY. Of course I will.

MADELEINE *picks up the ledgers and makes to leave*.

Good luck.

MADELEINE. Thanks.

BERKELEY. I know you will charm a price way over the odds from him.

MADELEINE. Oh, stop it now.

BERKELEY. Will you tell the Colonel I must say hello before he goes?

MADELEINE. I will.

BERKELEY. Madeleine?

She halts at the door.

I… appreciate your… understanding.

MADELEINE. What's to understand?

She leaves. BERKELEY *opens the letter and brings it to the window for better light.*

BERKELEY. Well, Grandie, we'll all be going soon now, won't we?

GRANDIE. Yes.

BERKELEY. We'll all ride a cock horse to Banbury Cross. And delicious soup on the way. We are such lucky souls are we not?

GRANDIE. We are, yes!

GRANDIE sings softly, almost silently, to herself while she goes to the mantelpiece. She gently touches some of the ornaments there, glancing at herself in the mirror. MRS GOULDING *brings in a tray with some bowls, and lays the table for their lunch, then leaves to fetch the food.* BERKELEY *stands in the window, absorbed in the letter with his hand to his face.* GRANDIE's *singing fades to silence while she stands looking high into the mirror.* BERKELEY's *attention is drawn from his letter. He observes* GRANDIE *as the lights gradually fade.*

End.

THE DANCE OF DEATH

After August Strindberg

This version of *The Dance of Death* was first performed at the Trafalgar Studios, London, as part of the Donmar Trafalgar season, on 13 December 2012. The cast was as follows:

KURT	Daniel Lapaine
THE CAPTAIN	Kevin R. McNally
ALICE	Indira Varma

Director	Titas Halder
Designer	Richard Kent
Lighting Designer	Richard Howell
Composer and Sound Designer	Alex Baranowski
Movement Director	Laïla Diallo

Characters

THE CAPTAIN, *at a coastal artillery fortress,*
late fifties/sixties
ALICE, *his wife, forties*
KURT, *newly appointed Master of Quarantine, forties*

Setting

An island near a port in Sweden, 1900.

ACT ONE

The interior of a round fortress tower built of granite.

Upstage are a large pair of doors with glass windowpanes, through which can be seen the sky at dusk and a distant shoreline with some lights. To the side of each door is a window.

There is a dresser with some framed pictures and books; a piano; a table with some chairs; an armchair; a mounted mercurial barometer and a desk with a telegraph machine. There is also a kind of 'bar' – a high table against one wall – with glasses and bottles of liquor with a mirror above it. There are a few rugs, but the walls are bare granite and nothing can take away a feeling of foreboding – this building used to be a jailhouse. On one wall hangs a portrait of ALICE *in costume on stage in a production twenty-five years ago.*

There is a lamp suspended from the ceiling. A heavy door, stage right, leads to steps going down to the kitchen, and beside this is a large free-standing hat stand on which hang coats, pieces of military equipment: gloves, helmets and swords.

It is a mild autumn evening. The doors are open. The sea is dark and still.

ALICE, *an attractive woman in her forties, sits at the table listlessly staring into space.*

The CAPTAIN, *a well-built but tired-looking man in his sixties, is sitting in the armchair, fingering an unlit cigar. He is dressed in a worn dress uniform with riding boots and spurs. A discarded newspaper lies on his lap. In the distance they can hear snatches of a military band drifting in on the wind.*

CAPTAIN. Play something?

ALICE. Play what?

CAPTAIN. Whatever you like.

ALICE. You never like what I play.

CAPTAIN. Well, you never like what I play.

ALICE. Edgar, you can't play. Do you want the doors left open?

CAPTAIN. I don't mind.

ALICE. Well, are you going to smoke that cigar?

CAPTAIN. You know, I'm not sure strong tobacco agrees with me any more.

ALICE. You should take up a pipe.

CAPTAIN. A *pipe*?!

ALICE. Why not? Why deny yourself your 'only pleasure', as you call it.

CAPTAIN. Pleasure? Hmph, I've forgotten what that is!

ALICE. Well, don't ask me to describe it for you! Have a glass of whiskey.

CAPTAIN (*shudders at the idea*). Better not. What's for dinner?

ALICE. How would I know? Go down and ask Christine.

CAPTAIN. Isn't this the time of year for mackerel? Autumn?

ALICE. I suppose so.

CAPTAIN. Yes, it's autumn – outside and in. You see, what you do is, you take a mackerel, grill it, drizzle a little lemon on it, serve it up with a huge glass of white Zinfandel – and one doesn't feel quite like blowing one's brains out any more, does one?

ALICE. You're asking the wrong person.

CAPTAIN (*smacking his lips*). Have we any of that Zinfandel left, chilling away down there in the wine cellar?

ALICE. We don't have a wine cellar.

CAPTAIN. What happened to our wine cellar?

ALICE. You mean the laundry room?

CAPTAIN. I mean the wine cellar, where we keep the wine.

ALICE. There is no wine.

CAPTAIN. Well, this is not good enough. We have to stock up for our silver wedding celebrations.

ALICE. You really want to celebrate that?

CAPTAIN. Well, of course I do. Don't you?

ALICE. I thought we might show more decorum by keeping our long miserable mistake to ourselves.

CAPTAIN. Oh come, Alice! We've had fun. (*Beat.*) Now and then. And soon it will be all over. We'll be dead, and all that's left is your rotten carcass. And all it's good for is to fertilise the cabbages.

ALICE. So we go through all of this just for the sake of the cabbages?

CAPTAIN (*picking his paper up*). Listen, I don't make the rules.

ALICE. Well, it seems like a stupid waste if you ask me. Was there any post?

CAPTAIN (*affirmatively, while he reads*). Mm-hm.

ALICE. The butcher's bill?

CAPTAIN. Mm-hm.

ALICE. And?

CAPTAIN (*still reading, he takes the bill from his pocket and holds it out to her*). I can't read his writing.

ALICE (*coming to take it*). That's old age, you know.

CAPTAIN. What?

ALICE. Your eyes.

CAPTAIN. Rubbish!

ALICE. Well, I can read it.

CAPTAIN. Your scrawl is worse than his.

ALICE (*reading*). Oh my God! Can we pay this?

CAPTAIN. Of course we can. Just not at the moment.

ALICE. Then when? In a year's time when your miniscule pension kicks in? Which won't even be enough for the doctor's bills when you're sick.

CAPTAIN. Sick? How dare you? I've never been sick. Not one day in forty-four years of military service!

ALICE. That's not what the doctor says.

CAPTAIN (*dismissively*). 'The doctor'... What does he know?

ALICE. Well, who else would know?

CAPTAIN. Now, you listen to me. There's nothing wrong with me
and there never has been. Real soldiers don't get sick. They just
drop dead where they stand, in their boots. Bang! Just like that.
And I have twenty good years left in me, you know…

ALICE (*simultaneously with him*). 'Twenty good years left in me…'
Yes, well you're half-deaf already. You probably can't hear that
music is coming from the doctor's house. You do know he's
throwing a party for the entire command this evening.

CAPTAIN. Yes, I do know actually, and do you want to know why I
wasn't invited? Shall I tell you? Because I refuse to mix with that
scum – and because they all know I'm not afraid to speak my
mind, that's why.

ALICE. You think everyone is scum.

CAPTAIN. They *are* scum!

ALICE. Except you.

CAPTAIN. Hey, I have always behaved in a decent, civilised manner,
no matter what life has ever thrown in my path. You know I am
not scum! (*Beat.*) Alice.

Pause.

ALICE. Do you want a game of cards?

CAPTAIN. Not if you're going to cheat, I don't.

ALICE. I won't!

ALICE *gets the cards and starts dealing.*

Yes, well, apparently it's the first time the regimental band has
ever been given permission to perform at a private party.

CAPTAIN. Well, if I spent the bulk of *my* working life creeping
round the garrison, sucking up to the Colonel all day, I could have
the regimental band in here while I ate my bloody breakfast if I
wanted! But I don't. (*Takes up his cards.*) That doctor was always
a little dirtbag.

ALICE. There was a time I used to be quite friendly with Gerda.
Until I found out she was backbiting me.

CAPTAIN. They're all backbiters! What's trumps?

ALICE. Where are your glasses?

CAPTAIN. They don't work. They've never worked, just tell me.

ALICE. Spades.

CAPTAIN. Spades! Typical...

ALICE (*playing*). None of the new officers' wives ever speak to me.

CAPTAIN. Who cares? We're better off. I don't even like parties.

ALICE. Well, that's alright for you – and even for me, but what about the children? They have no friends.

She reaches to take a trick.

CAPTAIN. I'll take that, thank you.

He takes the trick.

ALICE. What are you doing?

CAPTAIN. Six and eight – fifteen.

ALICE. Six and eight are only fourteen.

CAPTAIN (*bluffing*). Yes, six and eight, fourteen, and two, sixteen, it's your trick. That's what I said. Take it.

ALICE. What are you talking about? You should go to bed.

CAPTAIN. No, no. Deal.

He gets up and wanders to the window, listening to music in the distance, a rousing military march with drums pounding.

Listen. That's the full band! You can hear it all the way over here! Can you imagine how loud it must be in his little house? What an idiot.

ALICE (*dealing cards*). Do you think Kurt has been invited?

CAPTAIN (*as though sick of talking about Kurt*). Kurt! Kurt, Kurt, Kurt, Kurt, Kurt, Kurt! (*Short pause.*) My spies tell me he arrived on the seven o'clock train this morning so he'll have had plenty of time to get his glad rags on. Although I notice he hasn't managed to drag himself up here to say hello!

ALICE. It's quite an honour when you think about it. My cousin being appointed the Quarantine Master.

CAPTAIN. Sharing your family name is no honour, darling.

ALICE (*with sudden anger*). Now you listen to me, if you want to start dragging families into it, I'm happy to do that all night!

CAPTAIN. Alright, alright…

ALICE. We've agreed to stop doing that!

CAPTAIN. Alright, calm down, let's not start all that nonsense all over again. It was just a joke. (*Pause*.) All the same. Quarantine Master. He'll have a lot of clout.

ALICE. Really?

CAPTAIN. Oh, yes. They'll all bow and scrape before him. You know what they're like.

ALICE. Will he be a kind of doctor?

CAPTAIN (*disparagingly*). Of course not! Can you imagine a lunatic like him knuckling down to medical studies? No. He'll just be another overpaid pen-pusher, that's all.

ALICE. Well, I'm glad things have come right for him. He's never had it easy.

CAPTAIN. He cost me a bloody fortune, Alice! Leaving his wife and children in the gutter, chasing round after some whore! He's a disgrace!

ALICE. How can we know what goes on in any marriage, Edgar? Let's give him the benefit.

CAPTAIN. Oh, please. Gallivanting about in America ever since! And it's a shame, because even though he was such a loose cannon, he always managed to be such an absorbing philosopher, debating with me, far into the night!

ALICE. You only say that because he always gave in to you.

CAPTAIN. Gave in? He was invariably crushed by the weight of my superior logic – that's all! There's no point even beginning a philosophical discussion with half the dimwits on this island. Was ever a greater horde of imbeciles crowded into so small a space? I doubt it.

ALICE. Do you think it's just a coincidence?

CAPTAIN. What?

ALICE. That Kurt should arrive just in time for our silver wedding anniversary?

CAPTAIN. Well, I hope it's a coincidence! You think he'd come all this way just to witness the dregs of his handiwork? What a terrifying idea!

ALICE. Well, he did bring us together.

CAPTAIN. He certainly did! And what a match!

ALICE *laughs*.

You may laugh. It's me that's had to live with it!

ALICE. And me!

CAPTAIN. I mean you too. I mean us both.

He laughs ruefully. For a moment they are linked by their pain.

ALICE. Oh, Edgar, just think, if I had stayed in the theatre...!

CAPTAIN. Oh, here we go!

ALICE. Everyone I started out with is a celebrated artist now!

CAPTAIN. I think I will have that drink.

He goes to pour himself a large whiskey at his 'bar'.

ALICE. They're all such big stars!

CAPTAIN. You know what we need here? A low rail along here, see? So you can lean your boot up here and perch on the bar. Pretend you're having an evening drink at the American Club in Copenhagen.

ALICE. That's a good idea! (*Joins him.*) We can stand here and pretend we're in Copenhagen when we were happy.

He pours her a drink.

CAPTAIN. Do you remember? The late-night lamb stew upstairs in Nimb's? Eh? God, my mouth is watering just thinking about it.

ALICE. The concerts at the Tivoli. And the plays.

CAPTAIN. The plays! You see, that's what it is – your taste was always just that little bit too...

ALICE. Too what?

CAPTAIN. Refined. That's what makes you so unhappy.

ALICE. You should be proud to have a wife with refined taste!

CAPTAIN. No, I mean, I am, but...

ALICE. I've heard you – on more than one occasion – bragging about how, when you first clapped eyes on me... on stage at the St John Playhouse...

CAPTAIN (*looking out of the window at the darkening sky*). Listen to that.

ALICE.... When you've had enough whiskey, of course...

CAPTAIN. It's time for dancing. They've gone into three-four time.

ALICE (*listens*). It's the Alcazar Waltz. (*Lost in thought.*) I used to believe I could dance all evening to the Alcazar waltz.

CAPTAIN. Do you think you still could?

ALICE. Of course I could. What do you mean, do I think I still could?

CAPTAIN. Well, I mean...

ALICE. I'm fifteen years younger than you!

CAPTAIN. That makes us the same age though.

ALICE. How do you deduce that?

CAPTAIN. Because the woman is supposed to be younger.

ALICE. How pathetic, Edgar. Just face it – you're an old man. And I'm still young.

CAPTAIN. Well, flirt away to your heart's content then, Alice.

ALICE. I never flirt!

CAPTAIN. Well, you should, shouldn't you?

They look at each other for a moment.

ALICE. Do you think we should light the lamp?

CAPTAIN. I suppose so.

ALICE. Will you call Christine?

She goes and gazes out at the sea.

CAPTAIN. Well, of course.

The CAPTAIN *goes to a speaking tube by the wall and blows the whistle. He listens for a moment then speaks into it.*

Oh, Christine? Hello, how are you, my dear? (*Listens, then speaks into it again.*) Oh. Oh, I see. Oh well, no, because we were just remarking it looks as though may be nearing twilight now so, if you had a spare moment, we were wondering if you might be able to make your way up to us.

ALICE *glares at him, irritated by his deference to the maid. The* CAPTAIN *listens and speaks into the tube again.*

Well, you see, because it would be very nice if we might have the lamp lit! Ha ha ha. (*Listens.*) Oh. Oh, I see, well, in that case...

ALICE. Oh, for God's sake!

ALICE *goes to the tube and pushes the* CAPTAIN *away.*

Christine, get up here and light the lamp. Straight away! (*Listens.*) What's that got to do with it? (*Listens.*) What did you say? How dare you speak to me like that when I ask you a question?

CAPTAIN. Now, Alice, just...

ALICE (*into the tube*). You are an impudent brat and you are lucky I don't come straight down there and thrash you with the Captain's belt! What's that?

CAPTAIN (*trying to get the tube*). Alice!

ALICE (*holds the* CAPTAIN *at bay, listening to the tube, then replies to Christine*). Yes, well, pack your bags then, I don't care. Go on then!

ALICE *slams the tube back in its holder.*

CAPTAIN. Oh, Alice...

ALICE. Do you think she'll go?

CAPTAIN. Well, I wouldn't be surprised after that! We'll be in a right fix then!

ALICE. It's your fault, you know!

CAPTAIN. How is it my fault?

ALICE. You always mollycoddle the servants!

CAPTAIN. Rubbish!

ALICE. You ruin them so they're no good!

CAPTAIN. What are you talking about? They're always perfectly polite with me.

ALICE. That's because for some perverse reason you always ingratiate yourself with your inferiors, and then you look down your nose at your superiors – and you wonder why you've never risen up the ranks!

CAPTAIN. Oh, you know all about the army now, do you?

ALICE. I know they can spot a bully and a coward!

CAPTAIN. Oh, shut up!

ALICE. Yes! And a tinpot tyrant when they see one!

CAPTAIN. Yes, you'd know all about that.

ALICE. Do you really think she'll go?

CAPTAIN. Just go down quickly and apologise, say you have a migraine.

ALICE. You do it.

CAPTAIN. What? And have you on at me all night for flirting with the maid? No fear.

ALICE. Look at my hands. If she leaves they'll be ruined doing the housework.

CAPTAIN. And I'll tell you one thing – we won't get another one to come out here. That new lot who work the ferry can't keep their hands off a young girl. And even if she made it here for an interview, our sentries would never stop trying to maul her.

ALICE. Yes, you really manage to keep your sentries in line, too, don't you? Every time I go down in the kitchen, they're either chasing Christine round the kitchen table or else they're helping themselves to the last of our bread and butter and you never say a word!

CAPTAIN (*involuntarily sotto*). Listen, if I spoke to them like that, they'd clear off to the mainland. Then we'd have no troop, no commission, and no function – we'd be kicked out!

ALICE. We can't afford to feed them, Edgar! We have nothing for ourselves!

CAPTAIN. That's why I'm encouraging the high command to sign my letter – petitioning the King.

Pause.

ALICE. The King?

CAPTAIN. Yes. For a special allowance.

ALICE. For us?

CAPTAIN. No, for the sentries.

ALICE. For the sentries?!

CAPTAIN. Well, of course.

ALICE (*laughs*). Have you really written to the King?

CAPTAIN. I haven't sent it yet, but…

She laughs.

Go on, have a laugh. This one's on me.

ALICE. I thought I'd forgotten how to laugh.

Silence. The CAPTAIN *gazes out of the window and* ALICE *wanders to the table. They hear snatches of music and laughter from the party.*

Do you want another game?

CAPTAIN. No, put them away.

ALICE. Well, I'm pleased for Kurt. The only thing that bothers me is that my own cousin gets a plum job – Quarantine Master – and he runs off to cavort with our enemies before he even drops in so much as a card.

CAPTAIN. Oh, who cares?

ALICE. And did you see in the paper? He's described as 'a man of independent means'. I wonder how he got rich.

CAPTAIN. I know. A rich relative. That'll be a first.

ALICE. Maybe in *your* family…

CAPTAIN. Well, I don't care. Rich people don't impress me. I mean, what's money at the end of the day? I mean, what is it?

ALICE *just looks at him incredulously. The telegraph machine starts tapping.*

ALICE. Who is it?

CAPTAIN. Sh!

ALICE. What does it say?

CAPTAIN. I'm trying to listen!

He goes to the machine, holding his hand up for ALICE *to remain quiet, while a ribbon of white paper emerges.*

It's Sergeant Alfredsen, the children are with him over at the guardhouse in the harbour. They can see our light.

ALICE. Well, where else would we be?

CAPTAIN. He says Judith is sick.

ALICE. Ask him what's wrong with her?

CAPTAIN. She's not going to classes this week.

ALICE. Of course!

The CAPTAIN *starts tapping a reply.*

What are you saying? (*Pause.*) What are you saying?

CAPTAIN. He says she needs money for books.

ALICE. More books?!

CAPTAIN. He says she's going to fail her exam if she doesn't get them.

ALICE. Tell him to tell her she'll just have to take the exam next year.

CAPTAIN. Yes, you try telling her that!

ALICE. You're her father!

CAPTAIN (*angrily*). Do you think I haven't tried telling her what to do? I'm blue in the face trying to tell both of them what to do! I'm sick of it!

ALICE. That's how you've raised them!

The CAPTAIN *turns in exasperation and walks away from* ALICE. *He raises his head to the sky and lets out a long groan.*

Is that all you have to say?

CAPTAIN. Alice. There's plenty I could say, like, 'Yes, well, they're your children too,' or 'Why don't you just shut your stupid face,' or 'Let's just get a divorce,' or any of the other regulars from the old bag of crap. I could say any or all of them if you like, but you know what? Just take your pick, because I'm too tired.

ALICE. What's got you in such a bad mood all of a sudden?

CAPTAIN. Oh, I don't know. You think Christine will bring up some dinner?

ALICE. I doubt it. (*Short pause*.) The doctor has ordered supper from the Grand Hotel.

CAPTAIN. The Grand Hotel? (*Whistles, impressed*.) They'll all be having grouse then. There is no finer bird than a grouse that's just been blasted out of the sky – freshly delivered to its master from the salivating jaws of a hungry dog.

ALICE. Edgar! You'll make me sick.

CAPTAIN. But whatever you do – you must never ever *ever* stuff a grouse with pickled peanuts. It's utter insanity!

ALICE. Well, I'm sure most people would agree.

CAPTAIN. You'd be surprised! Those ignoramuses over there won't even know what wine to drink with it. You know, one almost feels sorry for them really.

ALICE *has wandered to the piano without much enthusiasm*.

ALICE. What'll I play?

CAPTAIN. You can play whatever you like as long as it's major keys only please. As soon as you drift into the minor I hear all your true feelings seeping out: 'I wish I was dead.' 'I wish my husband was dead.' 'I wonder if we're actually dead.'

ALICE *gently plays a few sad notes*.

I'll tell you what. Sod the lot of them. Let's break out that bottle of champagne!

ALICE. No, it's mine. I'm saving it for a special occasion.

CAPTAIN. Oh, don't be such a miser!

ALICE. Look who's talking!

CAPTAIN. I'll dance for you.

ALICE. No thanks. I wouldn't want you to do yourself an injury.

CAPTAIN (*with circumspection*). You know, I *was* going to suggest... that perhaps, some evening, we might, eh... well, invite a female companion up for a... for an evening. You know.

ALICE *stops playing. Pause*.

ALICE. I'd prefer we invited a male friend.

CAPTAIN. Right. Well… I'm not sure that worked out too well the last time. I mean, it is a while ago and it was certainly interesting. I'm not saying no, but, my God…

ALICE. Yes I know, afterwards was…

CAPTAIN. Yes, the aftermath was…

There is a sharp knock at the door, which makes them both jump.

ALICE. Who is it?

There is no answer.

Who can that be? Christine never knocks.

CAPTAIN. I don't know.

ALICE. Well, open it!

The CAPTAIN *approaches the door and opens it with apprehension. There is nobody there. He sees two cards on the floor outside the door and picks them up.*

CAPTAIN. Two cards.

ALICE. Who from?

CAPTAIN (*reading the first card*). Christine. She's gone.

ALICE. Oh no!

CAPTAIN. Well, you've done it now, haven't you?

ALICE. You'll just have to use your authority and march down there and tell one of your men you're assigning him to our kitchen and that's all about it.

CAPTAIN. Are you mad?!

ALICE. Can't you give an order?

CAPTAIN. Well, yes, but not without… not without…

ALICE. Without what?!

CAPTAIN. I mean, it's a chain of command…

ALICE. Oh, for God's sake! Who sent the other card?

CAPTAIN. What?

ALICE. The other card?!

CAPTAIN. Oh. (*Peers at the second card.*) I can't read it.

ALICE. Oh, give it to me. (*Takes it and reads.*) It's Kurt!

CAPTAIN. What?

ALICE. It's Kurt! It's Kurt! Go down to him!

CAPTAIN. Why didn't Christine bring him up?

> *The* CAPTAIN *hurries out.* ALICE *immediately goes to the mirror, fixes her hair and smoothes her eyebrows. She quickly does a circuit of the room, tidying up and lighting candles, then faces the door, expectantly, almost a new person. The* CAPTAIN *returns with* KURT, *a haunted-looking man in his forties.*

> Here he is, the old rogue! Well, come in, come in, we don't stand on ceremony round here!

ALICE. Kurt. You are welcome.

KURT. Thank you. It's been too long.

CAPTAIN. What are we talking about, fifteen, sixteen years? Look how old we've all gotten! Ha ha ha!

ALICE. Kurt hasn't changed at all.

> *A beat while* KURT *and* ALICE *take each other in.*

CAPTAIN. Right, well, don't just stand there, give me your coat, that's right. Sit down. Now, tell me, what are your plans for the evening?

KURT. Well, I've been asked to drop up to the doctor's big bash...

ALICE. Oh, no, no, no. You'll dine with us, Kurt, you're here now, so...

KURT. I'd like to, of course, but the doctor is my superior, so I better at least... I mean...

CAPTAIN. What are you talking about? He's an idiot! Drop by on Monday, it's time enough!

KURT. He knows I'm here...

CAPTAIN. Now you listen to me. This island is a snake pit! Don't get off on the wrong foot – show him who's boss, and Alice will tell you – when I've got your back you are invincible. Alice?

ALICE. Oh, shush, Edgar! The doctor will understand you had to see your relatives, Kurt. Stay here with us. Anything else would be improper.

KURT. Of course. You are right, Alice. You make me feel so welcome!

CAPTAIN. Why wouldn't you be welcome? There's no problem. I mean, I don't have a problem, and you don't have a problem…

KURT. No!

CAPTAIN. There's no problem! Alright, there was a time you were a bit all over the place. But you were just extremely immature and now you're older. And I've forgotten all about it. I don't bear grudges, Kurt. Alice?

ALICE (*ignoring the* CAPTAIN). I want to hear all about your travels, Kurt.

KURT. My wanderings more like!

CAPTAIN. Yes, your wanderings which have led you straight back to the man and woman you stitched together twenty-five years ago.

KURT. Oh, I can't take credit for that! But it's certainly gratifying to see you both still so happy after all that time.

CAPTAIN. I won't lie, Kurt. We've had our ups and downs! Ha ha ha… But yes, as you see. Here we are. Still together. The money that flowed in from my writing has certainly helped.

KURT. Your writing?

CAPTAIN. Oh yes, you'll hear my name quite a lot in the military tactical sphere.

KURT. Oh, of course! I remember – they asked you to write that manual for their new rifle!

CAPTAIN. Absolutely, yes, and it's still very sought after. Those particular rifles have been decommissioned now, of course. But my manual is still… you know… it's still right there. On the shelf. In the library. At the old academy.

Pause.

KURT. Well, that's… and you've been abroad, I believe?

CAPTAIN. Yes. Five times!

KURT. Five times?

CAPTAIN. Yes. And each time – to Copenhagen!

KURT. Each time?

CAPTAIN. Each and every time, to Copenhagen. You see, Kurt, when I rescued Alice from the theatre…

ALICE. Rescued me?

CAPTAIN. Yes, dear, rescued.

ALICE. Well, now…

CAPTAIN. I mean the *types* who hung around that laneway leading down to the stage door, Kurt. You could smell the cheap schnapps on their breath from up on the street! But, of course, what thanks do I get? Why, the endless drill of reiteration about how I ruined her career. Her *career*, no less! So five times, I've had to take her back to make amends. I ask you! You know Copenhagen?

KURT. Not very well. I've been in America all these years.

CAPTAIN. How can anyone live in America? No tradition, no honour?

KURT. Well, it's… it presents great opportunity.

CAPTAIN. Great what?

ALICE. Did you ever get to see your children in all that time, Kurt?

KURT. No.

ALICE. I don't know how anyone could bear to stay away from their children for so long – if you don't mind me saying.

KURT. I had no choice. The court took away my rights.

CAPTAIN. Oh, let's not get into the whys and the wherefores. Alice. The past is gone!

Pause.

KURT. Yes. Well. And your children are doing well?

ALICE. Oh yes. Fifteen and sixteen now.

KURT. My word!

ALICE. Oh yes. They attend the school in town. They board there.

CAPTAIN. Both like me. Very bright. The boy is brilliant. Officer class – already a dazzling strategist.

ALICE. If the academy takes him.

CAPTAIN (*with sudden fury*). What are you talking about? 'If the academy takes him'?! Of course they'll take him! They'll be lucky to have him! (*Pause.*) Ha, ha, ha…

An awkward pause.

KURT. So! I've been ordered to set up a quarantine station for cholera. I'll have to report to the doctor mainly. Is he a nice man?

CAPTAIN. He's neither nice, nor a man.

KURT. Well, that doesn't sound so good!

ALICE. Well, he's not the worst, but he's somewhat…

KURT. Yes?

ALICE. Well, sort of calculating.

CAPTAIN. He's just another career scumbag is what he is. Him and all his cronies; the postmaster, the excise officer, the chief of police, and the biggest crook of the lot, what's the new name they made up for him?

ALICE. The Alderman.

CAPTAIN. Oh yes, 'the Alderman' if you don't mind. Who wears a silver *chain*, if you please, like this, all down to here.

KURT. Don't you get on with any of them?

CAPTAIN. No.

ALICE. They're really not nice people, Kurt, I'm sorry to say.

CAPTAIN. You see, what they did was, they rounded up every power-mad jobsworth in the country and posted them all them right here.

ALICE. Yes, all of them!

CAPTAIN. Oh, you're referring to me? Listen, I've never been a dictator. Not in here at any rate!

ALICE. No, well, I'd like to see you try!

CAPTAIN. Yes! Ha, ha, ha… Don't listen to her, Kurt. We joke back and forth like this all the time. You won't find a more united husband or wife. Now, please, have a whiskey.

KURT. Oh, not for the moment, thanks.

CAPTAIN. Oh God, don't tell me you've become a... a...

KURT. I haven't become anything. I just don't drink.

CAPTAIN. What is that? An American thing?

KURT. Perhaps.

CAPTAIN. Well, I find that incomprehensible. A man should be able to hold his liquor. At all times.

The CAPTAIN *gets himself a drink.*

KURT. I may have to, if our neighbours are all as bad as you make out!

ALICE. Just do your best, dear, you'll always have us to return to.

KURT. You must find it hard going!

ALICE. Well, it's not a lot of laughs, let's put it that way.

CAPTAIN. It's not hard going at all! Your enemies give you something to push against! They make you stronger and develop your guile. And on the day I die, I'll be able to stand up and say I never got something for nothing in this life, my friend! I earned all my achievements.

ALICE. Yes, I think it's safe to say Edgar's particular path hasn't been strewn with rose petals.

CAPTAIN. No, in fact, it's the opposite. You wouldn't believe the obstacles I've had to surmount. But one man's strength can bulldoze a fortress.

KURT. Mm, I wonder.

CAPTAIN. Yes, and that's why you're so pathetic.

The wind has started to make one of the upstage doors bang open and closed. The CAPTAIN *goes to close it.*

ALICE. Edgar!

CAPTAIN. We used to have a name for people like you in our regiment, Kurt. You are a nincompoop.

KURT. A nincompoop?

CAPTAIN. Yes, a man who can neither fight nor shite!

KURT *bursts out laughing*.

You think it's funny now, but you should heed my philosophy before it's too late, I mean it. There it is – that wind has come right up. I knew it would, I said so earlier.

ALICE. Kurt, say you'll stay for supper.

KURT. Well, only if I'm not imposing.

ALICE. Oh no. It may only be a cold plate. We're between maids, I'm afraid.

KURT. A cold plate is just what I'd like.

ALICE. Oh, Kurt. Always so accommodating!

She takes KURT*'s hand with affection. The* CAPTAIN *taps the barometer and looks at his watch.*

CAPTAIN. Storm's coming.

ALICE (*aside to* KURT). You make him so nervous!

CAPTAIN. Oughtn't you be making us something to eat, dear?

ALICE. Yes, I'm going! You can philosophise to your heart's content. Only, whatever you do, Kurt, don't contradict Socrates here or he'll have a convulsion. And he wonders why they never made him a major.

She starts to leave, looking at the CAPTAIN *who glares at her.*

CAPTAIN. You just make sure you bring us a decent meal, woman.

ALICE. You give me the money and you can have whatever you like!

She leaves.

CAPTAIN (*calling after her*). I've given you everything I have! (*To* KURT.) Money. It's all she ever bangs on about. You've been there…

KURT. Well…

CAPTAIN. I know you have. Your wife was unbelievable!

KURT. Well, that's all over now.

CAPTAIN. She was a right tulip! In fairness to Alice – she was never a dunce.

KURT. No.

CAPTAIN. In fact, you know, on the whole, she's actually not a bad wife.

KURT. Well, of course not!

CAPTAIN. She's certainly not the worst. If she could just...

KURT. What?

CAPTAIN. Well, keep that damned temper of hers under control, she'd actually be quite a pleasant person. Although there were times, I have to admit, I cursed your guts for tricking me into marrying her.

KURT. Well now, hold on there, my friend...

CAPTAIN. Yah, yah, yah, yah, yah, you always talk gobbledegook when you know you're in the wrong. I'm a commander of men. I know a man's mettle, so don't take it personally, it's just my job...

KURT. But just a minute, Edgar, as I remember, it was you who begged me to introduce you...

CAPTAIN (*ignoring* KURT, *loudly*). Life! It's a funny old thing though all the same, isn't it?

KURT. It certainly is!

CAPTAIN. And growing old – it's horrible. But it is interesting – I'd imagine. I mean, I'm obviously very far from being old, but it's just... when you start to notice that all your friends have died, I mean, you start to feel dreadfully alone.

KURT. Well, any man who has a nice wife to grow old with is very lucky. Take it from me.

CAPTAIN. Yes, you have to cling on to the wife because even the children piss off. And to think you abandoned yours!

KURT (*angrily*). My children were taken away from me, Edgar!

CAPTAIN. Well, don't get angry with me about it!

KURT. Well, it wasn't like that! Alright?

CAPTAIN. Alright! Take it easy! Jesus Christ! Who cares what it was like? The upshot is you are completely alone!

KURT. Yes, well. There are worse things.

CAPTAIN. Really? You really think that?

KURT. Yes, I do.

Pause. The CAPTAIN *goes to fill his glass.*

CAPTAIN. Anyway, good to see you, Kurt. Tell me, what have you been doing with yourself – these past fifteen years?

KURT. God, what a question! So many things have happened. Let me see… When I left here, my plan was to spend a year in Paris, but then…

CAPTAIN. Kurt, I'll come straight to the point. I hear you've gotten rich.

KURT. Well, not rich exactly.

CAPTAIN. It's alright, I'm not going to ask you for a loan.

KURT. If you were, I'd be more than happy to. I mean it.

CAPTAIN. Take it easy. The truth is I have too much money.

KURT. How so?

CAPTAIN. The bank tell me I have too much in my account. They're on at me all the time to become an investor. But I've no time for that. You see, I'm a soldier! But thank God I do have a massive bank account, because – (*Sotto.*) the day I don't? (*Indicates the door.*) She'll be gone. Like that. (*Snaps his fingers.*)

KURT. Oh, come now…

CAPTAIN. I'm serious. Nothing gives that woman more pleasure than watching me squirm when we can't pay a bill.

KURT. I thought you just said you had a massive bank account.

CAPTAIN. I know. I do.

KURT. But if you can't pay your bills, it can't be that massive, I mean, as the term is commonly defined.

CAPTAIN. Oh no, it is, it is. It's just…

KURT. What?

CAPTAIN. Well, it's just, it's never *enough*, is it?

KURT. I'm sorry, but I don't…

CAPTAIN (*with sudden volume*). Life! My God, life is a strange thing, don't you think? You see? Oh, how I've missed our philosophical conversations!

The CAPTAIN *drains his glass and stands looking at* KURT. *The telegraph machine starts tapping.*

KURT. Good Lord, what is that?

CAPTAIN. It's our telegraph – the guardhouse at the harbour sending me the evening report. Storm's coming up.

KURT. Don't you have a phone?

CAPTAIN. No. (*Getting himself another whiskey.*) We got rid of it because the girls at the exchange were listening in and reporting all my business to the postmaster who passed it to the Colonel.

KURT. That's terrible!

CAPTAIN. That's life, Kurt. Life is terrible. I could never understand people like you. People who actually want more life, some in eternal hereafter. More life! Why?

KURT. Well, I'm not so naive as to think it will be all plain sailing, but the older I get the more convinced I am that one day we will meet our Creator, and we will all have to account for…

CAPTAIN. What balls! When I die – just annihilate me. Body and soul!

KURT. How can you be sure such annihilation would be painless?

CAPTAIN. Listen, when I drop dead, I'll just go – bang – without any pain.

KURT. Oh, and you know that, do you?

CAPTAIN. Yes, I do know that, as a matter of fact. Bang. There you go. You're gone.

Pause.

KURT. Right… You don't seem very happy with your lot, Edgar.

CAPTAIN. Happy? I'll be happy the day I drop dead, Kurt, and that's all.

KURT (*gets up*). It's this house, isn't it? What is it? Is it even a house?

CAPTAIN. Well, it was the old jail, before they built the new one. They used to hang prisoners downstairs.

KURT. I knew it! Can't you see what it must be doing to you? One can almost feel the suffering and the hatred – the corpses screaming in the walls. (*Pause.*) I'm sorry. I shouldn't have said that. I'm just so tired. It's been a very long journey and I... (*Pause.*) Edgar?

The CAPTAIN *stares into space.*

Edgar? Edgar? Are you alright? (*Shakes the* CAPTAIN*'s shoulder.*) Edgar?

The CAPTAIN *stirs as though coming out of a deep sleep. He looks around him trying to figure out where he is.*

CAPTAIN. Alice? (*Looks at* KURT.) Oh. I thought you were Alice. (*Sinks into a chair and stares into space again.*)

KURT. Edgar.

KURT goes to the door and calls out.

Alice! Alice! Quickly! Come at once!

ALICE (*off*). What is it?

KURT. It's Edgar!

ALICE *comes in wearing an apron, holding a limp old cabbage.*

ALICE. What's wrong?

KURT. I don't know. Look!

ALICE (*calmly*). Oh. Yes, he goes off like that sometimes. If I play, he'll come round. Hold on.

She goes to the piano and plays.

KURT. Can he see us?

ALICE. No.

KURT. It doesn't bother you?

ALICE. Hm?

ALICE *plays while* KURT *stands looking at the bizarre scene.*

KURT. Alice. What's happening in this house?

ALICE. Don't ask me – ask that.

KURT. 'That'? He's your husband.

ALICE. That man is a stranger to me, Kurt. He's as much a stranger now as he was when I married him twenty-five years ago. I know nothing about him, and I don't care to either.

KURT. Alice! He'll hear you.

ALICE. He has no idea what's happening at the moment.

Outside, a trumpet sounds the changing of the guard. ALICE *stops playing. The* CAPTAIN *suddenly gets to his feet and automatically takes his helmet and his sword.*

CAPTAIN. Gentlemen, you will excuse me, I must inspect the sentries.

He exits through the double doors at back.

KURT. Has he lost his reason?

ALICE. With Edgar, how could one tell?

KURT. I notice he's drinking.

ALICE. He was never able to drink.

She goes and looks out at the purple sky.

KURT. Should I go after him?

ALICE. What good would that do? It's too late. I've allowed myself to be locked in this tower for a whole generation with a man I hate so much that I fear – on the day he dies – I will probably just burst out laughing at the news.

KURT. Why haven't you separated?

ALICE. We were separated – for five years!

KURT. And you reunited?!

ALICE. The mistake we made was that, while we were separated, we both continued to live here.

KURT. Well, that's hardly separated!

ALICE. I know! Finally we had to recognise that we are bound by some evil force. Something only death may dissolve. So we wait for death.

KURT. What are you talking about? Surely your friends or your family – or someone – might have advised you before now?

ALICE. If only! No, Edgar isolated me, you see. You don't even see it happening! First he cut my siblings away. And then he set about my friends, one by one, until he had poisoned them all against me.

KURT. So I assume you did the same to him.

ALICE. I had to!

KURT. Right. And then what's worse is that I walk in and he blames me! Do you know that the first time he ever saw you he came to me and begged me to help him? I actually said no, because I knew only too well how cruel you could be to… to men.

ALICE. Well, thank you very much!

KURT. Oh, you know I'm right, Alice. You played one against the other so often, men were driven insane!

ALICE (*laughs*). Kurt!

KURT. I warned him. But he wouldn't leave me be until I finally wrote him a glowing letter of introduction! Well. Let him blame me then. But I'll tell you one thing – I won't have him or anyone else telling me I abandoned my children. I swear to God I'll punch him in the face if he says that again.

ALICE. Kurt, I know. It's despicable, and the thing is he actually likes you! He always has. But please don't turn your back on us now. You were meant to come to us…

ALICE*'s face crumples.* KURT *goes to comfort her.*

KURT. Oh, Alice. Listen, I know! I thought my marriage was rotten, but this is mind-boggling!

ALICE. You can see it's not my fault.

KURT. You know, I don't care whose fault it is. It's just sad. Whatever way you look at it.

ALICE. But will I tell you what he fears most in the world? That if he dies – I'll remarry.

KURT. Well, then he must love you.

ALICE. Oh, perhaps, who knows? But that doesn't stop him hating me.

KURT. Yes, I know that particular emotion – hate and love forged together in the foundry of Hell. You probably still love him too, you know.

ALICE. Oh, I don't know.

She laughs.

KURT. What?

ALICE. No, it's just, sometimes he asks me to play a mindless tune called 'The Entry of the Boyars' on the piano. He insists on dancing to it.

KURT. Oh no, don't tell me he still dances!

ALICE. Oh yes! He dances up and down. And he's so proud of himself and it's so funny that I can never help laughing. And at times I like that, I sort of marvel at him, and I pity him. But can you call that love? I don't think so! (*Beat.*) You know that two of our infants died, Kurt. You know that, don't you?

KURT *nods silently.*

And our other two. I couldn't let them stay here because he turned them against me!

KURT. So you turned them against him.

ALICE. I had to! You see, being in this family is like a curse.

KURT. Oh, we're all cursed. Since our first sin.

ALICE. Do you think it was a sin?

KURT. I mean our original sin – the fall of man.

ALICE. Oh. I thought you were referring to… when you and I…

KURT. No.

An awkward pause.

ALICE. Oh, Kurt, I was always so terribly mean to you. Can you forgive the time I invited you to come and see me, just after you had gotten engaged? I was a beast.

KURT. Let's not speak of it now.

ALICE. I suppose it must give you such pleasure to see me getting my just desserts.

KURT. No. I could never feel that way, Alice.

Pause. They look at each other. Something undeniable passes between them. ALICE breaks the moment.

ALICE. You have no idea the mood he'll be in now when he comes back. It's the humiliation, you see. Inviting you to dine with us and he has nothing to give you!

KURT. Oh, look, I'll run out and get us something.

ALICE. Kurt, don't you know where you are? You'll find nothing open.

KURT. But isn't there a café or a…

ALICE. No. This island is a fortress. They drink, they don't care about food.

KURT. Well, look, no matter. I'm not hungry. I'll pour him a moderate drink and you can play for us and we'll keep the mood light and gay and we'll…

ALICE. I can't play – my hands are wrecked from all the housework.

KURT. Where are your servants?

ALICE. We can't get anyone decent to come and live on this rock so the truth is we are always without! Oh, Edgar is going to go berserk when he gets back.

KURT. Has he ever hit you, Alice?

ALICE. Well, no, not… I mean he…

They hear the CAPTAIN *calling.*

CAPTAIN (*off*). At ease, men, at ease! You know I don't go in for all that bollocks-ology!

ALICE (*with sudden fury and despair*). Oh, I just wish this house would burn down!

KURT. Is that him?

ALICE. Yes. Look, if you want to leave, Kurt, I understand.

KURT. I won't leave you.

The CAPTAIN *comes in the doors at back and stands looking at* KURT *and* ALICE *without speaking for a few moments.*

You're back!

CAPTAIN. Yes, old Bluebeard is back. I suppose she's been spilling her guts about what a bastard I am.

KURT. Well, of course! What do you expect? Ha ha ha! Actually we were talking about music we like. Alice tells me you enjoy 'The Entry of the Boyars'.

Short pause.

CAPTAIN. You know it?

KURT. Know it? I love it!

CAPTAIN. Well, you're in for a treat. Watch this!

He prepares to dance.

Alice, what in God's name are you doing with that apron on? Play!

ALICE *gets her sheet music while the* CAPTAIN *limbers up.* KURT *goes to the piano to turn the pages for* ALICE. *The* CAPTAIN *stands with his hands on his hips, ready to go.* ALICE *starts playing and the* CAPTAIN *begins to perform a Hungarian folk dance very seriously with vigorous clapping and stamping, enjoying how his spurs ring out.* KURT *watches, dumbfounded, then turns to concentrate on the music with* ALICE. *While she continues to play, the* CAPTAIN *suddenly collapses out of sight behind some furniture. Neither* KURT *nor* ALICE *notices he is gone for some moments.* KURT *looks up and wonders where the* CAPTAIN *is before realising he is lying on the floor.*

KURT. Oh my God!

KURT *rushes to the* CAPTAIN. ALICE *turns round.*

Edgar. Edgar. What happened?

ALICE. Is he dead?

KURT. I don't know. (*Pause.*) No, he's alive.

ALICE (*disappointed*). Oh!

KURT. Come on. That's it, me old sausage.

KURT *helps the* CAPTAIN *to his feet and gets him to a chair. The* CAPTAIN *pushes* KURT *away.*

CAPTAIN. What in God's name are you doing?

KURT. You fell!

CAPTAIN. What are you talking about?

KURT. You collapsed!

CAPTAIN. When?

KURT. Just now! Sit down, Edgar, please.

The CAPTAIN *suddenly scrunches up his face and puts his hand to his head, sinking into the chair.*

CAPTAIN. Jesus… *Christ!*

ALICE. You're sick! Don't you see that, you stupid old fool!

CAPTAIN. Well, shouting at me won't help! (*Winces, putting his hand to his head again.*) Ah!

KURT. Where's the nearest phone?

ALICE. In the sentry box at the bottom of the steps.

KURT. I'll call the doctor.

KURT *goes out.*

CAPTAIN. I don't want that damn doctor! If he comes near me, I'll stab him. (*Winces again.*) Ah!

ALICE *takes off her apron. The* CAPTAIN *watches her.*

Get me some water, will you?

ALICE (*with unconcealed contempt as she pours some water from a jug*). Oh!

CAPTAIN. Well, forgive me for being sick!

ALICE. *Are* you sick?

CAPTAIN. What – do you think a person can fake this kind of pain?!

ALICE. It was you who said real soldiers don't get sick, Edgar. (*Short pause.*) Well, that's it. You're going to have to take great care, aren't you?

CAPTAIN. Well, you're not going to look after me!

ALICE. You've got that right!

CAPTAIN. It's the moment you have longed for all these years.

ALICE (*matter of factly*). And the moment you dreaded.

CAPTAIN. Alice.

ALICE. What.

CAPTAIN. Please don't be cross with me.

Pause. She looks at him. KURT *enters.*

KURT (*breathless*). Well, this is unbelievable!

ALICE. What happened?

KURT. He hung up! As soon as I mentioned your name.

ALICE. Well, this is it – this is what you get, isn't it? You stupid old twit!

CAPTAIN. Oh God, I can't feel my hands!

KURT. Isn't there another doctor?

ALICE. Only in town.

KURT. Can we phone the mainland?

ALICE. No. We have to send a telegraph.

CAPTAIN. And I can't move my arms!

ALICE. Oh, I'll do it.

She goes to the telegraph machine and starts sending a message.

CAPTAIN (*rising*). Now you just hold on one damned second! You mean to tell me you can, in fact, telegraph after all these years?

ALICE. Yes. And I always could.

CAPTAIN. Yes, of course. (*To* KURT.) You see? This is what we're dealing with!

ALICE. Oh, shut up.

She continues to send a telegraph.

CAPTAIN. Kurt. Will you hold my hand?

KURT *goes to him.*

It's like I'm rising up and falling all at once. It's absolutely horrible.

KURT. Has anything like this ever happened before?

CAPTAIN. Never.

ALICE (*in utter disbelief*). What?!

CAPTAIN. She doesn't know what she's talking about.

KURT. Look, we can't wait for someone to come all the way out here on a boat. This is madness! I'll phone the doctor again and I'll... I'll just tell him – this is not good enough. Has he ever treated you before?

CAPTAIN. Well, if you can call it 'treating' me.

KURT (*going*). I mean, for Christ's sake, wouldn't you think the Hippocratic oath might drag him away from his canapés?

CAPTAIN (*calling after him*). Not on this island! (*Short pause.*) Isn't Kurt a good man? It would do you good to see how a man can change.

ALICE. I know. He has assumed a new... I don't know... attractiveness. And now we've dragged him down – straight into our slurry.

CAPTAIN. He'll be a fine ally for us here. It may tip the balance. Although I notice he's reluctant to give us any real detail about what he's been up to.

ALICE. In fairness, I don't remember anyone really asking him.

CAPTAIN. Oh God, Alice, what do you think is wrong with me?

ALICE. You tell me.

CAPTAIN. Well, it's either my heart. Or my head. Or maybe it's my soul. Maybe I should just... let it out.

ALICE. Do you think you could eat something?

CAPTAIN. Well, of course I could! I'm bloody ravenous – as usual! Nothing can change that! And here we are with not a sausage in the larder, and Kurt walks back in the door. It's just so humiliating!

The telegraph starts clicking. They listen.

You hear that? An accident at the shipyard. No one can be spared. Absolutely bloody typical. And aren't you the one? How much of my life have I wasted decoding that blasted machine for you, and you bloody well knew what it was saying all along!

They laugh.

ALICE. And all the times you lied to me about what it said.

The CAPTAIN *stops laughing.*

Well, you've certainly got your comeuppance now, haven't you? You were always such a stingy old squirrel. 'Send me your bill, my good man!' 'Send it to the Quartermaster's office!' Well, they're all on to you now.

CAPTAIN. Oh, shut up, Alice.

ALICE. And I'll tell you another thing. Kurt won't be back either. Phoning the doctor was his ruse – so he could – (*Cocks her thumb and gives a short whistle – meaning 'depart'.*) 'The Hippocratic oath...' Did you ever hear such codswallop?

CAPTAIN. I know! He was always a cowardly little bastard. I spotted it the day I first laid eyes on him. He's on his way up to the doctor's now in search of a good feed, the wretched little shit.

KURT *enters.*

KURT. I got him. I told him I'd report him. He wasn't one bit happy!

CAPTAIN. What did he say?

KURT. He said it's your old complaint – calcification of the heart.

CAPTAIN. Calcifi–what–tion?

KURT. Calcification.

ALICE. A stone heart, dear.

KURT. Yes. You can't smoke any more cigars – it's absolutely lethal – and whiskey will kill you, so you have to stop that immediately.

CAPTAIN (*with panic*). This is terrible!

KURT. And he says you have to get straight into bed.

CAPTAIN. Well then, that's it! It's all over! You see, once they tell you to get into bed, that's the end. You never get up! No, no, no – I just need to eat something, that's all.

KURT. He said you can't eat anything for three days, just a glass of milk.

CAPTAIN. I can't drink milk! I hate milk!

KURT. Well, you'll have to learn.

CAPTAIN. I can't learn! What are you talking about? I'm too old to learn!! (*Winces, placing his hand to his head.*) Oh Jesus *Christ*.

The CAPTAIN *lapses into a state of catatonia once more, staring into space.*

ALICE. He's gone.

KURT. The doctor said he could die, Alice.

ALICE. Thank God!

KURT. Alice…

ALICE. What.

KURT. Perhaps you should get him a blanket and a pillow.

ALICE. Oh, so now I'm going to take my orders from you?

KURT. I don't care what you do. I'll get it.

ALICE. I'll get it!

She goes. KURT *takes the water carafe to get a drink for the* CAPTAIN.

KURT. I'll get you some warm water. (*Exhaustedly to himself as he goes out.*) Oh God…

The wind whips up and the doors at back creak open once more. The CAPTAIN *looks round and sees someone come to the door. He is terrified. The audience see nothing.*

CAPTAIN. Who are you? (*Pause.*) Well, that's impossible. (*Pause.*) Well, because… because I'm… Well, I'm just not ready. (*Pause.*) But, my dear lady, that's no concern of mine. (*Pause.*) I don't care what it's like! I told you – I'm not ready!

The CAPTAIN *is distracted by* ALICE *coming back with some blankets. She starts making a bed for the* CAPTAIN. *The* CAPTAIN *goes to the doors and looks out into the night.*

Alice, did you see anyone in here just now?

ALICE. No.

CAPTAIN. You didn't see an old woman?

ALICE. I saw old Maja coming up the steps from the workhouse, but she couldn't have gotten in.

She sees the CAPTAIN *looking at the doors. She goes to close them.*

Why, did you get a fright?

CAPTAIN. A fright? Me? That's a good one!

ALICE. Right. Lie down here.

The CAPTAIN *goes to the bed she has made. He tries to take* ALICE*'s hand.*

Oh, get off me!

KURT *enters with the water carafe.*

CAPTAIN. Kurt, stay with me tonight, won't you?

KURT (*to* ALICE). I'll sit with him.

ALICE *looks at* KURT.

CAPTAIN. Thank you. Well, goodnight, Alice. That will be all.

ALICE (*shoots the* CAPTAIN *a withering look*). Goodnight, Kurt.

She goes.

KURT. Right. (*Pulls a chair over to the sofa.*) Aren't you going to take off your boots, Edgar?

CAPTAIN. No.

KURT. Wouldn't you be more comfortable?

CAPTAIN. No. I never take them off.

KURT. Why?

CAPTAIN. Just in case.

KURT. In case what?

CAPTAIN. You know, you can be quite stupid at times, Kurt.

KURT. Alright.

CAPTAIN. I'm going to say something completely startling, Kurt, are you ready?

KURT. I think so.

CAPTAIN. I've realised, just this evening, you're the only person I really can talk to, isn't that something?

KURT. Well, it's not so unusual for men to have only a few confidants.

CAPTAIN. Hm. If I die, tonight, I mean. I want you to do something for me. I want you to take care of my children. Will you do that for me?

KURT. Well… it's not really my place, is it? I mean, it's a big…

CAPTAIN. Thank you, Kurt. You see, it's nothing personal but the reason you and I could never be friends is simply because I have never believed in the concept.

KURT. The concept?

CAPTAIN. The concept of friendship. I mean, what is it? At the end of the day? 'Friendship', I mean, come on.

KURT. Well... I suppose the question is simply – do you trust me?

Long pause.

CAPTAIN. Kurt?

KURT. Yes?

CAPTAIN. Do you think I'm going to die?

KURT. Yes.

CAPTAIN. Oh God.

KURT. In the sense that we are all going to die.

CAPTAIN. Oh, don't give me a smart-alecky answer at a time like this! What's wrong with you, man?!

KURT. Why? Are you afraid of dying, Edgar?

CAPTAIN. Well, it's just, what if it isn't the end?

KURT. That's why one must be prepared for anything, Edgar.

CAPTAIN. Even Hell?

KURT. Yes. Surely you must believe in Hell, Edgar. You are smack in the middle of it, it seems to me.

CAPTAIN. Oh, that's just a saying, a metaphor – (*Disparagingly.*) 'I'm in Hell...' I'm talking about what if there really *is* a Hell? That's what I'm talking about. Come on, keep up with me.

KURT. Well, maybe this *is* Hell, and part of the agony is that we don't even realise it?

CAPTAIN. Yes! I *am* in agony, Kurt.

KURT. Physical?

CAPTAIN. No.

KURT. Well, then you are in spiritual pain, Edgar, there's no other alternative.

CAPTAIN (*takes* KURT'*s hand*). You see the thing is – when you get down to it – I don't want to die!

KURT. But a few moments ago you were talking about how you would relish annihilation!

CAPTAIN. Only if it's absolutely painless, Kurt!

KURT. But it can't be.

CAPTAIN. Is this it?

KURT. It's the beginning of it, yes.

CAPTAIN. Oh God!

The CAPTAIN *sinks back in despair. Pause.*

KURT. Well, goodnight, Edgar.

The CAPTAIN *just looks at* KURT, *then turns away, wrapping himself in the blanket, curling up like a child. Music and lights take us to morning. A pale dawn rises behind the windows and the sea breaks evenly on the shore. Some birds chirp while the* CAPTAIN *lies in the same position and* KURT *sits with him, looking absolutely exhausted.* ALICE *comes to the door. She is munching a piece of fruit.*

ALICE. Is he still asleep?

KURT. I dosed him with morphine.

ALICE. Morphine?

KURT. I had to. He wouldn't stop talking.

ALICE. Do you have morphine?

KURT. Strictly for moments of extreme anxiety.

ALICE. Well, absolutely.

KURT knows she will badger him till he gives her some. He takes out his bottle and puts a few drops on her tongue.

Huh. Look at him. The first time I met him he had no coat, just two shirts against the snow. I thought he was noble! I actually thought he was so brave bearing that ugly face with such resignation.

KURT. Yes, his ugliness was always frightening. Whenever he got angry with me, I used to have nightmares for days.

ALICE. And I married him!

KURT. You saw his good qualities.

ALICE. Well, of course. He can be kind and sensitive. You should hear him talk about Judith, but by God is he a horrible enemy to have. He's so sneaky.

The CAPTAIN *turns round and looks at them.*

CAPTAIN. Thank God! It's the morning.

KURT. How are you feeling?

CAPTAIN. Awful.

KURT. Shall I phone the doctor?

CAPTAIN. No! I want to see my little girl. I want to see Judith.

ALICE. Well, she's not here, is she?

KURT. You know, talking of your children, Edgar, I was thinking it may not be a bad idea to set your affairs in order before too long.

CAPTAIN. Why?

KURT. Well, in case something were to happen.

CAPTAIN. What could happen?

KURT. Only what could happen to anyone.

CAPTAIN. Listen, I'm not going to die just yet, my friend, and not for a long time either, so don't go making plans, Alice.

KURT. I know, and I hope that's the case, but anything can happen to any of us at any time. Imagine if Alice were to be cast out in the street for no better reason than that you wouldn't call a lawyer to pop in for half an hour to just...

The CAPTAIN *winces, putting his hand to his head.*

CAPTAIN. Oh, here it is! Here it is! It's back!

ALICE. Oh, for Christ's sake!

She goes. The CAPTAIN *recovers.*

CAPTAIN. So, Kurt, tell me. This 'quarantine station' of yours, how are you going to set about getting it up and running?

KURT. I'm sure I'll manage.

CAPTAIN (*laughs*). Oh really? You do understand that to all intents and purposes I'm in charge on this island. I mean, nothing can really happen without my acquiescence.

KURT. Alright. And you've seen a quarantine station in operation, have you?

CAPTAIN. Seen one? Listen, mate, I've been seeing quarantine stations in operation all up and down the continent since before you were born! Don't you worry about that, and I'll tell you one thing, never ever *ever* put a quarantine station next nor near the water.

KURT. But we're going to build it right on the shore!

CAPTAIN. Well, there you go! You see how much you know about it? Bacteria thrive in the water!

KURT. Not in saltwater! In fact – we're building a bathing facility!

CAPTAIN. Kurt, you are an idiot. Now, listen to me, you should bring your children here.

KURT. It's not up to me to bring them anywhere.

CAPTAIN. Well, you'll just have to persuade them. It doesn't look good, Kurt. Coming here on your own. Dumping your children…

KURT. Now, hold on a minute, I've already told you…

CAPTAIN. Because people will ask how any man can just abandon vulnerable little children…

KURT. Edgar!

CAPTAIN. Just so he can traipse off like a ninny, prancing around the place…

KURT. I told you I was ordered by the court to have nothing to do with my children!

CAPTAIN. It looks just awful…

KURT. I was stripped of my custodial rights! My wife forbade me from seeing them! You have no idea what it's done to me! I fought and I fought to get them back! You have no idea what you're talking about!

CAPTAIN. Alright, calm down… there's no need to raise your voice, Kurt, I know how this island works and I'm simply trying to give you some friendly advice. No need to leap off the handle like some bloody madman.

Pause. KURT *composes himself.*

And I'm not very well at the moment.

KURT. Yes. I know. Can I get you anything?

CAPTAIN. Well, yes, if you don't mind. I'd like a fillet steak, please.

KURT. Don't be ridiculous, Edgar, that'll finish you off!

CAPTAIN. Oh, come on. Is it not enough that I'm ill? You all want me to starve as well?

KURT. You know it's not like that.

CAPTAIN. Do I? I suppose you're all having a good laugh – no drink, no tobacco, 'Let's watch him suffer'…

KURT. Not at all. Death demands sacrifices, otherwise he comes at once.

CAPTAIN. That's supposed to sound clever, is it?

ALICE *enters with several bunches of flowers, telegrams and letters. She throws the flowers on the desk.*

ALICE. These are for you, apparently.

CAPTAIN. For me? From who?

ALICE. From the non-commissioned officers and the sentries.

CAPTAIN (*to* KURT). You see? (*Sorts through the letters, handing them one by one to* KURT.) Aha – this one is from the Colonel's office, if I'm not mistaken. You'll find the Colonel is a gentleman, Kurt, even if he is a duplicitous little shit. And, look, from Judith! I can't read these tiny telegrams, can you read that please? And look at this, that's from Staff Sergeant Alfredsen, the old dog, you'll be getting to know him, Kurt, that's for sure! Look at all of these…

ALICE. I don't understand what's happening. Is everyone writing to congratulate you on becoming ill?

CAPTAIN. You see, Alice, an unfortunate hyena like you that hasn't a friend on the face of the Earth *couldn't* understand an outpouring of warmth such as this, so I won't bother explaining.

KURT (*reading*). Judith says she won't be able to come and see you this weekend because she's promised to help her tutor pick a veil for the harvest parade.

CAPTAIN. Is that it?

KURT. No, she... she...

CAPTAIN. What, what is it?

KURT. She also says... well...

CAPTAIN. What, damn you?

KURT. She begs you to please stop drinking.

Pause.

CAPTAIN. Well, that's... (*Gives a pathetic little laugh.*) That's...

Pause.

And the Colonel? What does the Colonel say?

KURT. You have been relieved of your command.

CAPTAIN. What?! That's impossible! I haven't requested to be relieved of my...

ALICE. I asked him for it.

CAPTAIN. Why?!

ALICE. Because you are unwell.

CAPTAIN. What did you do that for, you stupid woman?! Don't you see what you've done!?

ALICE. Yes, I do.

CAPTAIN. Well, I... I refuse to accept the order. I didn't hear it. You didn't see it.

ALICE. But it has been issued.

CAPTAIN. He's obviously been misled! I'll just have to speak with him. Have a friendly word.

ALICE (*handing the* CAPTAIN *his bunches of flowers*). You see, Kurt? No laws, be they natural, physical or legal may proscribe this man. The universe bends to his every whim.

ALICE *is on her way out of the door.*

CAPTAIN. I suppose you have invited Kurt to breakfast with us?

ALICE. No.

CAPTAIN. Well, I'm inviting him. Two fillet steaks, straight away, please.

ALICE. Two?

CAPTAIN. Yes, I'm also having one.

ALICE. There are in fact three of us.

CAPTAIN. Well, three fillet steaks then, straight away, thank you. That will be all.

ALICE. And where am I supposed to magic three fillet bloody steaks from? Out of my backside?!

CAPTAIN (*to* KURT). You see?

ALICE. You invite Kurt to dinner *and* breakfast and we can't even give him a cup of coffee!

CAPTAIN (*an indulgent laugh*). She's just angry because I didn't die last night.

ALICE (*with fury*). No, I'm angry because you didn't die twenty-five years ago and spare me the degradation of watching you ruin my life before my very eyes!

She weeps into her hands.

CAPTAIN (*a little laugh*). You see, Kurt, this is what happens when you set about matchmaking two people who are simply not of the same class. Now, you will excuse me.

He goes and takes a large artillery helmet with a long plume of feathers on top.

KURT. Where are you going?

The CAPTAIN *takes his sword and cloak and goes to the doors at back.*

CAPTAIN. To attend to my duties. If anyone needs me, tell them I've gone to inspect the battery.

KURT tries to stop the *CAPTAIN.*

KURT. You are not well, Edgar.

The CAPTAIN *pushes* KURT *roughly back into the room.*

CAPTAIN (*with sudden ferocity*). Stay out of my way, you impudent pup!

The CAPTAIN *leaves.* ALICE *rushes to the door and shouts after him.*

ALICE. Yes, that's it! Go on! Walk away! Do what you always do when the fighting gets hot! Run away! Run away, you cowardly drunken liar!

KURT *gapes at* ALICE, *trying to recover his breath.*

This is nothing.

KURT. God, it's all so *awful*!

ALICE (*tone of 'this is what I live with'*). Well…

KURT. Where will he go?

ALICE. Oh, he'll go down and start drinking with the conscripts. He'll put his feet up on the table in the guardroom, malign the officer command for a few hours and then stagger home looking for something to eat.

KURT. You know, the reason I came here was I thought how peaceful it would be!

ALICE. Oh, Kurt, let me get you something to eat, I'll scrounge us up something if you can wait here for an hour.

KURT. No, don't do that. I'll go up to the doctor's house and introduce myself. Maybe he'll give me some breakfast I can bring us down.

ALICE. I'm so ashamed!

KURT. The time for shame has long gone.

KURT *is on his way towards the door.*

Alice, did Edgar have anything to do with me losing custody of my children?

ALICE. Oh, Kurt, it's all so long ago.

KURT. No. Tell me.

Pause.

ALICE. When you sent him to mediate with Martha on your behalf he... well, he began an affair with her. (*Pause.*) And then he... he introduced her to a lawyer to help her gain full custody.

Pause.

KURT. Last night he asked me if I would provide for *his* children should anything ever happen to him.!

ALICE. Please don't avenge yourself on my children.

KURT (*putting on his coat*). No, my vengeance would be to show him I am not like him. That I am capable of keeping my promises.

ALICE. Then you are a better class of person than us, Kurt.

KURT. No, I've just been along a different road. Alright, well, I'll go and see if I can find us some warm bread and some coffee. Will you be alright?

ALICE. Yes. Thank you, Kurt.

KURT. What will you do now?

ALICE. Why, I'll wait for you.

Pause. She goes and kisses him on the mouth. She pulls away and they stand looking at each other. Then KURT *leaves.*

Lights down.

ACT TWO

Early morning. ALICE *sits in a shaft of sunlight looking out of the window.* KURT *enters.*

KURT. Alice?

    ALICE *turns to look at him.*

ALICE. Oh, it's you.

KURT. Yes. Your front door was wide open. I hope you don't mind.

    They hear a blast from a ship's horn.

There's the ferry.

ALICE. Yes, he'll be home soon.

KURT. I could see him from my little window in the hostel, standing at the prow in his full dress uniform. The sun was glinting on his helmet.

ALICE. Yes, he went to town to see the Colonel – to ensure his continued dominance.

KURT. Over whom?

ALICE. Good question.

    She gazes out of the window.

KURT. Alice, what's in your hand?

    She looks down at a handful of her hair.

ALICE. Oh, just my hair. It comes out in clumps! My two babies who perished in here died for lack of light. (*Turns and puts a handkerchief away.*)

    KURT *realises she has been crying.*

We must steel ourselves now, Kurt.

KURT. Why?

ALICE. Because the Captain's campaign has started in earnest. Against me – and against you.

KURT. Against me?

ALICE. Kurt, as soon as you read that telegram from Judith, I saw it. A darkness I know all too well fell across his brow. You see, he could never harm Judith, so I saw him decide to destroy you.

KURT. Just like that?

ALICE. Oh yes, exactly like that! Why else do you think he was he hanging about, down at your quarantine site, all day yesterday?

KURT. He was offering us his advice.

ALICE. Huh! He was surveying the terrain. What he really wants is to ruin your reputation.

KURT. Yes, well, it's a bit too late to worry about my reputation, I'm afraid.

ALICE. Well, you should worry – because his main goal is to wreck the future for your children.

KURT. My children?!

ALICE. Yes! You see, our boy has inherited Edgar's frenzy for whiskey whilst our daughter, no matter what Edgar thinks, was always just a greedy little tart. To see your children flourish while his own... (*Makes a dismissive gesture.*) well, that's the final dagger in his guts.

KURT. But he couldn't do anything to my chil...!

They hear a door slam and the heavy tread of the CAPTAIN *on the stairs.*

ALICE. Now listen, just be polite, pretend everything is perfect. (*With poise, as though they are above arguing with people.*) When he lies, just humour him. Never rise to his taunts. Our advantage is that we are sober and we can think straight. So just...

ALICE *breaks off while the* CAPTAIN *appears in the doorway stage right, wearing a helmet, a long cloak and white gloves. He looks tired but resolute as he stands there – attempting to conceal that he has been on a night-long bender. He removes his sword and scabbard from his belt and crosses unsteadily to a chair where he sits, holding his sword on his lap. He speaks with a slight drunken slur he labours to correct.*

CAPTAIN. Kurt. There's a pleasant surprise. You will excuse me for being seated in your company, but I'm afraid it's been a very long night over in town.

KURT. Of course!

ALICE. Good morning, Edgar.

CAPTAIN. Good morning, Alice.

KURT. How are you feeling?

CAPTAIN. Good! Feeling no pain! Just very tired!

ALICE. Any news in town?

CAPTAIN. Yes. I visited the doctor over there. And he says – I have another good twenty years in me!

ALICE *shoots* KURT *an incredulous look.*

ALICE. Well, that is good news.

CAPTAIN. Yes. It is!

A silence descends which KURT *instinctively goes to break, but* ALICE *signals to him to say nothing.*

Now, Kurt…

ALICE (*aside*). Here he goes.

CAPTAIN. I beg your pardon?

ALICE. No. Nothing.

CAPTAIN. Did you want to say something?

ALICE. No, I didn't say anything.

CAPTAIN. Right, well, you see, Kurt. I was in town. As you know. And I was in the company of some fine men from my old regiment and we visited this place, and that place, and whose acquaintance did I make? Only a fine young man, a cadet from the academy, a fine young chap, and as we are always short of cadets over here, I arranged it with the Colonel that he be posted over here with us. And I thought I'd tell you, because this news should give you particular pleasure, Kurt.

KURT. Why me?

CAPTAIN. Because he is your eldest son!

ALICE (*to* KURT). I told you.

CAPTAIN. What?

ALICE. I didn't say anything.

CAPTAIN. Well, stop mumbling then! Myself and Kurt are trying to have a conversation here, what's wrong with you?

ALICE. There's nothing wrong with me. You need to get the wax flushed out of your ears.

CAPTAIN. Oh, be quiet! (*To* KURT.) Hm? What do you make of that? He's grown into a fine, fine young chap, you'll be pleased to hear.

KURT. Yes, well, while any father would be thrilled to see his little boy again, under these particular circumstances I have to say I'm rather displeased, Edgar.

CAPTAIN. I don't understand.

KURT. You don't have to. I don't want him coming here so that's… I forbid it.

CAPTAIN (*laughs*). Oh, you forbid it, do you? Then allow me to inform you that he is already under my command as of this morning! My command!

KURT. Well, then I will make him transfer to another regiment.

CAPTAIN. But, you see, you can't do that because the courts have taken away your rights over your son and you have no legal standing!

KURT. Well, I shall go to his mother.

CAPTAIN. But there's no point in that. (*Beat*.) Kurt.

KURT. Why?

CAPTAIN. Because I have already spoken to her! Yes!

ALICE (*to* KURT). You see?

CAPTAIN. Yes, my dear?

ALICE. I didn't say anything! You're an old man and you're going deaf.

CAPTAIN. Yes, I must be! So come here closer to me till I tell you something just for your ears.

ALICE. No, I prefer a witness for anything you have to say to me.

CAPTAIN. Very well – a witness may be advantageous for us both. First of all, has my will been notarised?

ALICE (*hands him a document*). The regimental lawyer did it yesterday evening.

CAPTAIN (*peers at it*). Everything goes to you. Alright. Fine. (*Tears it up in front of her.*)

ALICE (*to* KURT). Have you ever seen such behaviour?

KURT *shrugs and turns away, sitting down.*

CAPTAIN. Now, I have this to say to you, Alice…

ALICE. Yes?

CAPTAIN. Yes, I'm saying it! Now, in light of your long-expressed desire to bring our unhappy arrangement to an end, and on account of your cruel and uncharitable treatment of your children and your husband and your cavalier attitude regarding the household finances, I have filed a petition for divorce at the town court.

ALICE. I see. On what grounds may I ask?

CAPTAIN. On the grounds I have just… on the aforementioned grounds!

ALICE. Yes, well, good luck with that!

CAPTAIN. And…! And! I have… other grounds of a more personal nature. As ascertained aforthwith, now that it has been appraised of me that I will definitely live for another twenty years or more, I am therefore am obliged to terminate this unhappy union in order to commence one with someone who can show me the requisite devotion, who might bring some longed-for youthfulness into my home, and some yearned-for attractiveness!

ALICE *rips her wedding ring from her hand and throws it at the* CAPTAIN.

ALICE. You conceited prick! You think you can just toss me into the street and shack up with some young… girl in here under my own roof?

CAPTAIN. Yes. Will the witness please take note: the spouse rescinds her wedding ring.

The CAPTAIN *retrieves the ring and puts it in his pocket.*

ALICE. Alright, let's play it that way then! Kurt, you are a witness. This man has attempted to murder me.

KURT. Murder you?

ALICE. Yes, the summer before last, he pushed me into the sea.

CAPTAIN. There are no witnesses.

ALICE. That's a lie – Judith saw what happened.

CAPTAIN. No she didn't.

ALICE. She did, and she can testify!

CAPTAIN. No, she can't, because she's already told me, she didn't see anything of the sort.

ALICE. When did she tell you?

CAPTAIN. Last night. We had a nice supper and we discussed that self-same stormy afternoon; how slippery the pier wall was, and how anyone could have lost their balance, and how, if anything, I *saved* you.

ALICE. Is that how she described it?

CAPTAIN. Yup. In precisely those terms.

ALICE. That little bitch.

CAPTAIN. Yes! Because I thought you might try and pull that old sausage out of the sack! Now! I take it the fortress surrenders. Here is my watch. The time is twenty minutes past eight. I give you, the enemy, ten minutes to withdraw from the field. Ten minutes starting from… oh!

He clutches his heart. ALICE *goes to him.*

ALICE. What's wrong?

CAPTAIN. I… I don't know.

ALICE. Kurt, quick, bring some brandy.

CAPTAIN. No brandy! I don't drink any more! What are you trying to do? Kill me? You saw that, Kurt. Now, ten minutes, you hear me? No quarter will be given. (*Draws his sword.*) Ten minutes.

The CAPTAIN *goes out.*

KURT. Who is this man?

ALICE. He's not a man. He's a devil.

KURT. What does he want with my son?

ALICE. He wants to hold him hostage in order to control you and isolate you, and make you look so bad that you might never hold your head up again. (*Pause.*) Kurt, I haven't been entirely honest with you.

KURT. How so?

ALICE. I lied when I said that Edgar never hit me. He's been beating me, on and off, for nearly twenty years.

Pause.

KURT. You know, when I came here, I had no anger, no grudge. Any slander or humiliation I had suffered in the past – well, I... I forgave him. Because, to be perfectly honest with you, there were times in my past that I... Well, I took things a bit too far when people made me angry so I... Well, I... But now I ... I mean... I...

ALICE. Yes, that's right.

KURT. I hate him.

ALICE. Yes.

KURT. This animal who has separated me from my family...

ALICE. Yes.

KURT. Who beats up his own wife...

ALICE. Yes.

KURT. And holds my son like a ransom demand. My own son who I have not seen for sixteen years!

ALICE. Yes!

KURT. I mean, I... I want to kill him!

ALICE. Yes!

KURT. To think he even went and tracked down my wife to lay his groundwork! Why couldn't that pair have met thirty years ago and spared us all?

ALICE. I know. They're soulmates! But just as he has his allies, so must we exploit his enemies.

KURT. Yes, you're right! Who is his biggest enemy on the island?

ALICE. The Alderman. He hates Edgar. And he has long suspected something I know to be true. Something about Edgar and Staff Sergeant Alfredsen.

KURT. What?

ALICE. Well, a few years back, everyone thought they were heroes because they made a big show of setting up the first ever fund for officers' widows. No one could refuse putting money in, and before long they had a massive bank account. Has he told you about it?

KURT. Yes, I think he...

ALICE. Yes, well, Sergeant Alfredsen has invented two extra 'widows'. He forged papers for them! And guess who they are! Yes! Edgar and Sergeant Alfredsen get all their drink money paid directly into their own pockets every month!

KURT. Oh, that's...! Look, I don't know if I want to do it that way. It's so tawdry! Does anybody even care!?

ALICE. You need the killer blow, Kurt. You must be prepared to strike directly at your enemy's weakest point.

KURT. No, no! (*As though restraining his darker nature, trying to remain calm.*) Life will do it to them.

ALICE. Do what?

KURT (*with restraint*). I just discovered over time, in cases like this, that... life... administers its own justice sooner or later – you'll see.

ALICE. What will I see?

KURT. That justice usually gets done in the end. A kind of... natural... justice.

ALICE. 'Justice'? What are you talking about? There's no such thing as justice! If you want to wait around for justice to come knocking on your door, you're welcome to it, 'cause I won't! Your son is being taken away from you right before your eyes and you wait for someone else to do the dirty work before you lift a finger?! No wonder you lost everything, Kurt. Well, I'm going to dance on his bloody head. I'll do the 'Entry of the Boyars' all over his stupid face for him with my boots on.

KURT *watches her, his eyes blazing.*

KURT. You are a devil too, aren't you, Alice?

ALICE. Yes. I am!

KURT. Yes, you are.

ALICE. You always called me that, remember? When we were younger?

KURT. Yes.

ALICE *lets down her hair.*

ALICE. You see, I'm not old, Kurt. Not like him.

KURT. No.

ALICE. I'm young and I have desires. I'm going to change into something more becoming, pop up to see the Alderman and in two hours I'll be free of that old fart. (*Goes to the mirror and fixes herself a little, opening a few buttons on her blouse.*) I know that shy men often like crude women, Kurt.

KURT. Yes, that's true.

ALICE. And crude women often like shy men.

KURT. Do they?

ALICE. Yes, always. And I know you always liked me, Kurt. (*Pause.*) Now, turn away while I change.

Pause. KURT *does not turn away.*

(*Coyly.*) Kurt. I'm changing my blouse.

KURT *does not turn away.* ALICE *continues to unbutton her blouse revealing her bosom and her bodice.* KURT *is unable to contain himself. He rushes at her and grabs her, lifting her high into the air. Then he bites her throat. She screams.* KURT *throws her on the chaise longue, looking down at her in horror. She holds her hand to a bleeding wound while blood drips down* KURT*'s chin from his lips.*

KURT (*breathlessly*). Alice, I... I...

He rushes out of the door stage right. Music plays and the lights gradually change through dusk to evening. ALICE *holds a napkin to her wound and leaves. The* CAPTAIN *enters through the double doors at back, closing them after him. A wind has come up.*

He wears old, worn-looking fatigues. He is hollowed-eyed and exhausted. He lights a half-dozen candles and sits at the table in the semi-darkness, absent-mindedly turning playing cards over. The doors rattle behind him in the wind. He turns and stares at them. There is no one there. He goes to the 'bar' and takes out a whiskey bottle and a glass. He looks at the whiskey for a moment, then takes two more bottles of whiskey out and carries them all to the window. He opens the window. Wind whips into the room. He throws all the bottles out. Then he takes his box of cigars and sniffs them. He brings them to the window and throws them out.

He closes the window, comes into the room and stands there wondering what to do with himself. He sees the painting of ALICE. *He takes it from the wall, puts his fist through her face and rips it apart, before tossing the pieces out of the window. He goes to his bureau, takes a bundle of letters wrapped in a black ribbon, brings them to the stove and burns them. He puts his face in his hands and weeps.*

The windows rattle. The CAPTAIN *is startled. He turns and looks out but sees nothing. He steps out of the double doors and closes them after him, walking off into the evening. The music ends and the door stage right opens.* KURT *peeps in. He leaves and returns with* ALICE *who is dressed in a black outfit.*

Well?

ALICE *raises her hand for* KURT *to kiss.*

ALICE. Thank me.

KURT. What happened?

ALICE *keeps her hand raised.*

ALICE. I asked you to thank me.

KURT *takes her hand and kisses it.*

I have made my deposition and named three witnesses. Two of whom I count as unassailable in a court of law. The prosecutor shall convey his answer here – right into the heart of the fortress – by means of that telegraph.

KURT. So it's done.

ALICE. You bet it's done.

KURT. What's happened to the room?

ALICE. Looks like he's preparing to move me out. I'll say one thing, he better have stored my pictures nicely, because he's the one who's moving. Into a six-by-three cell.

KURT. I'm glad you're finally separating, but surely one must feel pity for an old man who's going to jail. It will be tremendously frightening for him.

ALICE. Pity? Where's the pity for me – who never did anything wrong in my life and gave up my career for that monster?

KURT. I remember your career, Alice. It wasn't all that glorious.

ALICE. How dare you?! Everybody knew who I was and what I was capable of!

KURT. Really?

ALICE. Yes, really! Another year or two and I'd have been the leading actress in Copenhagen.

KURT. If you say so.

ALICE (*aghast*). Don't *you* start in on me now as well!

KURT. I'm not starting in on you. I'm merely pointing out that your career, as you call it, was hardly…

ALICE *suddenly flings herself around* KURT*'s neck and kisses him. He pins her arms by her sides and starts nuzzling her throat.*

ALICE. Oh Kurt! Oh…

KURT (*rapidly, passionately*). Oh, Alice, my God, I want to bite your throat and rip all your blood out like a wolf.

ALICE. No, don't! You'll hurt me!

KURT. You have awakened a part of myself I've tried for years to suppress with deprivation and torture. But now I know – I am the worst of all of us! When I saw you in your ravishing nakedness, passion clouded my vision and everything shone in the full glare of evil all over again. And now, well, I want to cover your mouth and suffocate you with my teeth.

ALICE. Oh, Kurt! Look at my hand! You see the mark of the ring that was there? The mark of my shackles? I suspected only a wild beast could ever break them!

KURT. Yes, I am a beast. And I'm going to bind you down and have you until you are no more.

ALICE (*laughs*). And to think I thought you had found religion!

KURT. Religion?!

ALICE. Yes! When you were banging on about the fall of man!

KURT. That wasn't me.

ALICE. I thought you had come to start preaching to us!

KURT. You listen to me. We're going to go down and get on that ferry and in one hour we'll be in town and we'll lock the door and then you'll see what I am.

ALICE (*pulls away with the energy of a bright idea*). Kurt! Let's go to the theatre tonight!

KURT. The theatre?!

ALICE. Yes! Let's walk in arm in arm and show everybody what a dismal little creature my husband really is.

KURT. Isn't it enough that he's going to prison? You want to rub his face in the dirt?

ALICE. No, it isn't enough!

KURT. Then you will be the prisoner because you'll let hatred rule your life – all the while believing you are free! You see, the difference between you and me comes down to this: while you dream of parading around some stupid theatre house like a giant child – (*With great passion.*) I am thinking about my son!

As KURT says 'son', ALICE slaps him across the face.

ALICE. Edgar's right. You're pathetic.

KURT raises his fist to bash her, but manages to restrain himself.

Pause.

KURT. I'm sorry.

ALICE. Very nice!

KURT. I'm sorry!

ALICE. Oh no, no no.

KURT. You won't accept my apology?

ALICE. Not like that. On your knees.

Pause. KURT kneels.

KURT. I'm sorry.

ALICE. On your face.

KURT. Excuse me?

ALICE. Get down on your face.

KURT. My face?

ALICE. Get down on your face.

> KURT *lowers his face to the floor before her.*

> Kiss my boot.

> KURT *moves toward her boot about to kiss it.*

> Lick it.

> *As* KURT *goes to do so:*

> (*With disgust.*) Don't lick it! And never, ever, do that again. Now get up.

> KURT *gets up and stands there.*

KURT. I don't know who I am any more!

ALICE. Oh, don't give me that. You know.

> KURT *is startled by the sudden appearance of the* CAPTAIN *in the doorway stage right carrying a stick.*

CAPTAIN. Kurt. May I speak with you alone, please?

ALICE. Is it about safe passage for your poor defeated enemy?

CAPTAIN. I just want a moment's peace to speak with Kurt if I may.

ALICE. Oh! Talk of peace! Well, Kurt, you are honoured! Be seated! And bask in the glory and wisdom such as only ripe old age may impart! But please, gentlemen, should a telegram come through, please be so kind as to inform me. I am awaiting some news. Au revoir.

> *She goes out. The* CAPTAIN *sits with his walking stick and considers* KURT.

CAPTAIN. Can you explain how I got here? In my life I mean.

KURT. No more than I can explain mine.

CAPTAIN. Isn't there any meaning?

KURT. I used to think that *was* precisely the meaning. We cannot know, and so we must bow to the mystery.

CAPTAIN. But how can I bow to something I don't know exists?

KURT. You studied mathematics. You find an unknown fixed point by using the ones you do know.

CAPTAIN. I failed mathematics! They only let me graduate because I was so good at throwing.

KURT. You just have to find it.

CAPTAIN. How have you achieved such resolution, Kurt?

KURT. You overestimate me.

CAPTAIN. Well, I'll tell you the art of living – the real trick of life – are you ready?

KURT *shrugs*.

Elimination! You wipe the slate clean and you move on. You take a bag, and you stick all your humiliations in it and you chuck it in the sea and you walk away. It's that simple.

The CAPTAIN *clutches his heart*.

KURT. Are you alright?

CAPTAIN. The doctor in town says I won't live much longer.

KURT. When did he say that?

CAPTAIN. The day before yesterday.

KURT. So it wasn't true?

CAPTAIN. What wasn't true?

KURT. That he said you were going to live for another twenty years?

CAPTAIN. No, that wasn't true, I'm afraid. I just said that to…
(*Signals: 'Annoy Alice.'*)

Pause.

KURT. And the rest of it?

CAPTAIN. Of what?

KURT. About my son.

CAPTAIN. What about him?

KURT. About my son joining your regiment.

CAPTAIN. Does your son want to join our regiment?

KURT. You said he already had!

CAPTAIN. That's the first I've heard of it, old chap, I didn't even know he was in the army!

KURT. Yes, your ability to disown your past misdeeds is quite effective. Isn't it?

CAPTAIN. I'm not with you.

KURT. And your divorce?

CAPTAIN. What divorce?

KURT. You just made that all up too?

CAPTAIN (*dismissively*). Oh, we always talk about getting a divorce! We could never get a divorce!

KURT. And your dinner with Judith? When she agreed to say that Alice slipped and fell in the water?

CAPTAIN. Judith? Judith barely speaks to me. She would never invite me to dinner!

KURT. So you're just... what? You're just a casual... liar!

CAPTAIN. I'm not a liar! Liar is such a strong word. Can't you indulge a little...

KURT. What...

CAPTAIN. ...Banter? I can't even remember what I said! We all need a little forbearance, Kurt. Even the best and even the worst of us.

KURT. Oh, you've come to see that, have you?

CAPTAIN. Yes, I have. I have come to see that. Please forgive me, won't you, Kurt? Forgive me for everything. If you ever can.

KURT (*gets up*). I'm not sure I am entitled to forgive anyone.

CAPTAIN. Life! Life is so *strange*, don't you find? You see when one is *surrounded* by evil, it's very, very difficult to...

He notices that KURT *is on his feet, looking anxiously at the telegraph machine.*

What's the matter?

KURT. Can this machine be switched off?

CAPTAIN. Not very easily – it's wired directly to the station.

KURT *goes to the window and looks out.*

Is something coming through?

KURT. No, not yet.

CAPTAIN. Anyway, I was just going to say – life! It's just so awfully...

KURT (*interrupting the* CAPTAIN). There are some men with a lantern down at the pier – climbing out of a boat. Do they normally run boats this late?

CAPTAIN. What colour is the lantern?

KURT. Red.

CAPTAIN. It's what we call a 'welcoming committee'.

KURT. What's that?

CAPTAIN. Some poor wretch is about to be arrested.

KURT. Oh.

CAPTAIN. Mm. A night in irons. And up before a court martial at dawn. Now, tell me, now you've had a bit of time with Alice, what do you make of her? Be honest with me.

KURT. I have no idea! I understand less and less the older I get. Edgar, did you really push her into the sea?

CAPTAIN. I did.

KURT. Why?

CAPTAIN. I don't know. It just seemed so natural! There she was. And there was the fifteen-foot drop to the water. And the angle was just absolutely perfect.

KURT. You didn't regret it?

CAPTAIN. No. Not for a second. It was delicious.

KURT. Didn't you know she'd come for revenge one day?!

CAPTAIN. I fully expected her to! And she's been exacting revenge every day since!

KURT. You're very philosophical about it!

CAPTAIN. Staring death in the face changes you, Kurt. Will you give me your hand, and let us part on good terms?

The CAPTAIN *stands and offers* KURT *his hand.* KURT *considers him and comes to make up. They shake hands. Then the* CAPTAIN *throws an arm around* KURT. KURT *steps into the embrace, burying his head in the* CAPTAIN*'s shoulder, weeping.*

There now, my good man, that's alright.

ALICE *appears in the doorway.* KURT *steps away, composing himself.*

ALICE. Well now, look at this! Sorry to interrupt, but has my telegram come?

KURT. No.

ALICE. My great failing was always my impatience. But then again, perhaps it's a great strength. (*Lifts her parasol like a rifle and aims it at the* CAPTAIN.) So let's get this over with. Now, how do I fire this thing? Oh yes, I remember now – I read that manual you wrote. Myself and three others – the lucky few. FIRE! (*Makes an explosive sound.*) So how's the new wife? The beautiful young one? I haven't seen her around lately. Oh, you don't know? Oh dear. Well, I know how my lover is!

ALICE *puts her arms around* KURT*'s neck.* KURT *pushes her away.*

He's well, he's well. He's a little shy, but he's very well. And he's not the first. You see, your problem was that you were always too big-headed to be jealous, so you never saw all the other times I led you by the nose! Yes! Many times!

The CAPTAIN *draws his sword in a cold fury and advances on* ALICE. *She realises he is serious and she darts away from him.*

Kurt! Help me!

KURT *moves to shield her. The* CAPTAIN *advances on them, hitting the furniture, knocking tables and chairs over. Suddenly he stops, clutching his heart.* ALICE *and* KURT *watch as he sinks to his knees.*

CAPTAIN. Judith...!

The CAPTAIN*'s head comes to rest on the seat of a chair and he falls still.*

ALICE. Hooray! He's dead!

The CAPTAIN *sits up.*

Oh...

CAPTAIN. No, not yet. (*Stumbles towards a chair and sits, exhausted.*) Oh, Judith...

ALICE (*to* KURT). Right, let's go.

KURT *does not move.* ALICE *goes to him and grabs him by the arm.*

I said, let's go!

KURT *pushes her to the floor. He goes to the door.*

KURT. Go back to Hell.

ALICE. No, no! Wait! I'm sorry! Wait!

CAPTAIN (*simultaneously*). She'll kill me, Kurt. Don't go! Kurt!

KURT *is gone. Pause.*

ALICE (*with a sudden change in attitude*). Well, that's friends for you! (*She gets up.*) There are no real men any more. At least a woman knows where she is with someone like you.

CAPTAIN. Alice. Come here to me.

ALICE *goes to the* CAPTAIN.

I'm dying.

ALICE. What?

CAPTAIN. The doctor told me.

ALICE. But you said...

CAPTAIN. I was lying! I was drunk! I was lying!

ALICE. What about the rest of what you said?

The CAPTAIN *shakes his head.*

Oh my God! What have I done?

CAPTAIN. We can fix things up. Don't worry.

ALICE. No, you don't understand. This can't be fixed.

CAPTAIN. Of course it can – you just forget and you move on.

ALICE. No, I've blown us to smithereens, Edgar.

CAPTAIN. No you haven't.

ALICE. Why did you have to tell so many lies!?

CAPTAIN. Oh, can't we just forgive each other?

ALICE. Oh God, this is like a horrible dream and I can't wake up! I'd do anything to change it. If we could just get out of this, I'd... I'd... I'd...

The telegraph machine starts clicking. ALICE *looks up at the heavens.*

Just let us out of this!

CAPTAIN. Out of what?

ALICE (*shouts*). Don't listen!

CAPTAIN. Alright, calm down.

ALICE *runs to the window and looks out. She runs back to the* CAPTAIN *and puts her hands over his ears.*

ALICE. Don't listen! Don't listen!

CAPTAIN. I won't. I won't, it's alright... Lisa...

A ribbon of paper comes out of the machine and the clicking stops. ALICE *stands there, breathlessly with her hands over the* CAPTAIN'*s ears. Then she goes to the machine and takes the paper.*

What is it?

ALICE (*reading the message, she laughs with relief*). Oh thank God! It's the evening report. It's raining over on the mainland and all is well. (*Goes to the* CAPTAIN *and kisses him on the forehead.*) It's nothing.

ALICE *goes and sits on a chair, taking out a large handkerchief.*
She covers her face and cries into it.

CAPTAIN. What dreadful secret are you expecting?

ALICE. Please don't ask me.

Pause.

CAPTAIN. You know, when I collapsed that first time, I stepped a
little way over the far side of the grave. And I saw something
there.

ALICE. What was it?

CAPTAIN. Hope – for something better.

ALICE. For us?

CAPTAIN. Yes. It's hard to describe but I... I realised that this might
be our life. I had never thought so before. I always believed we
must be dead, playing out some dreadful penance.

ALICE. With each as the other's tormentor.

CAPTAIN. Yes.

ALICE. Do you think we have tormented each other enough?

CAPTAIN. Yes. And then some!

They laugh mordantly.

Shall we tidy up?

ALICE. If we can.

CAPTAIN. Well, it may take more than this evening.

ALICE. Oh, who cares any more?

CAPTAIN. So. You didn't get away this time.

ALICE. No.

CAPTAIN. But I wasn't taken away to jail either.

ALICE *looks at him.*

Yes, I heard all about your little plan, but the only snag is that
none of the regiment ever put any money into the widow's fund.
They're all too mean! Even if I had wanted to, there was never any
money to embezzle, so your deposition was pointless. (*Pause.*) So!

You have your wish. The angels have heard your prayer and they have whisked you out of your predicament.

ALICE. So I'm supposed to be your nurse now?

Pause.

CAPTAIN. Only if you want to.

Pause.

ALICE. Well, what else would I do?

CAPTAIN. I don't know. (*Pause.*) You know, Alice, I'm not sure if it's the light this evening, but you... you really are a particularly attractive woman.

ALICE. Really?

CAPTAIN. Yes, I mean it. You look, well, positively seductive!

ALICE. Oh, Edgar, please.

CAPTAIN. I mean it.

She looks at him openly. He extends his hand to her. She takes it.

ALICE. And you are still handsome.

CAPTAIN. I was never handsome.

ALICE. To me you were.

They regard each other.

Our eternal torment will return, you know.

CAPTAIN. Yes, but if we can be patient, death will come, and then, perhaps, life begins.

ALICE. If only.

CAPTAIN. You think we're bad? I read in the paper the other day about some old codger who's been married seven times, and then at the age of ninety-eight he goes back and marries the first wife again! Now that's what I call torment! (*Pause.*) Don't be angry with Kurt, Alice. He was always weak. And in three months' time we will celebrate our silver wedding anniversary, and you just watch: Kurt will be our guest of honour. Christine will come back and cook for us, the Alderman will make a speech. The Colonel will lead the toast and even the good doctor himself will come and gatecrash it, knowing him!

ALICE. Mm.

CAPTAIN. What. Tell me.

ALICE. I'm just thinking about the Alfredsens' silver wedding.

CAPTAIN. Oh God...

ALICE. You remember? Evelina had to wear the ring on her right hand because Sergeant Alfredsen had chopped off all the fingers on her left – with a cleaver!

CAPTAIN. I know. I can still see the look on the minister's face! It was awful, I mean, it was sort of hilarious, but... I don't know.

ALICE. Perhaps... we laugh and we cry in equal measure. Perhaps that's just the way life has to be. None of us can say if it's all terribly serious or just some pointless joke. And sometimes the joke is so painful that being serious – gloomy even – brings its own kind of relief.

CAPTAIN. Celebrate our silver wedding with me. (*Pause.*) Oh, say yes. Let them laugh at us. We'll laugh too. Or maybe we'll be terribly serious about it – whichever way it turns out. Who cares?

Pause.

ALICE. Alright.

CAPTAIN (*tenderly, simply.*) Our silver wedding. (*Raises himself up.*) You forget and you keep going. I mean, what can we do? You keep going!

They look at each other.

Lights fade.

**Other collections by Conor McPherson,
published by Nick Hern Books**

PLAYS: ONE
Rum and Vodka
The Good Thief
This Lime Tree Bower
St Nicholas

PLAYS: TWO
The Weir
Dublin Carol
Port Authority
Come on Over

www.nickhernbooks.co.uk

facebook.com/nickhernbooks

twitter.com/nickhernbooks